SPORT$BIZ

An Irreverent Look at Big Business in Pro Sports

Dale Hofmann
Martin J. Greenberg

Leisure Press
Champaign, Illinois

Library of Congress Cataloging-in-Publication Data

Hofmann, Dale, 1942-
    Sport$biz : an irreverent look at big business in pro sports /
Dale Hofmann, Martin J. Greenberg.
        p.   cm.
    Includes index.
    ISBN 0-88011-333-2
    1. Professional sports--United States. 2. Professional sports-
-Economic aspects--United States. I. Greenberg, Martin J., 1945-
. II. Title.
    GV583.H63   1989   66701
    338.4'7796'0973—dc19   88-33312
                                                             CIP

ISBN: 0-88011-333-2

Developmental Editor: Peggy Rupert
Copy Editor: Laurie McGee
Proofreaders: Phaedra Hise, Karin Leszczynski
Assistant Editors: Holly Gilly, Robert King, Valerie Hall
Production Director: Ernie Noa
Typesetter: Sandra Meier
Text Design: Keith Blomberg
Text Layout: Jayne Clampitt, Denise Mueller
Cover Design: Jack Davis
Cover Photo: Wilmer Zehr
Tables By: Kathy Fuoss
Printed By: Braun-Brumfield

Printed in the United States of America

10 9 8 7 6 5 4 3 2 1

Leisure Press
A Division of Human Kinetics Publishers, Inc.
Box 5076, Champaign, IL 61825
1-800-342-5457
1-800-334-3665 (in Illinois)

Contents

Acknowledgments

There are no unassisted goals in the writing game. When we reached the last word of the last sentence and looked back to see all the people who had helped us get where we were going, there was quite a crowd. Here's our chance to say thanks.

To Beverly, Kari, and Steven Greenberg and to Sandy, Tara, Dana, Kyle, and Maren Hofmann—the patient literary widows and orphans who more or less lost track of us while this project was in progress.

To Wendy Selig and Judd Schemmel for their diligent research, to attorneys Sam Recht and Ralph Cindrich for their technical assistance on contract clauses, and to Dr. Paul Goldstein and Jo Schmidt for their constructive criticism and suggestions.

To Dean Frank DeGuire and Charles Mentkowski of the Marquette University Law School for their understanding and support, to Eugenie Maynard for help from beginning to end, and to Juanita Sisson and her wondrous word processor.

To the experts who took the time and trouble to answer our questions and to provide us with insights we never would have found on our own. They include Leigh Steinberg, Dick Berthelsen, Art Wilkinson, Richard Woods, Bob Harlan, Robin Murez, Ed Garvey, Jack Manton, Dick Kolhauser, Robert Dowling, Dick Hackett, Greg Lustig, Len Miller, Bud Selig, Michael Megna, and Bill Hanrahan.

And finally to Jim Hass, who got this train back on track one day in South Bend, Indiana, and didn't even know it.

Sources

Various interviews and magazine and newspaper articles served as resources for this book. The authors wish to acknowledge the contributions of the following sources:

p. 9, Leigh Steinberg, personal interview; p. 26, Barry Rona, Associated Press (AP), 1/12/88; p. 43, Ricky Hunley, AP, 10/15/87; p. 45, Jim Kelly, AP, 10/16/87; p. 48, Dick Berthelsen, personal interview; p. 50, Peter Ueberroth, AP, 1/24/88; p. 54, Art Modell, *USA Today*, 10/13/87; pp. 59-60, Dick Berthelsen, personal interview; p. 60, Art Wilkinson, personal interview; pp. 67-68, Richard Woods, personal interview; pp. 68-69, Bob Harlan, personal interview; p. 71, Ted Steinberg, *Milwaukee Journal*; p. 73, Leigh Steinberg, *Sporting News*, 11/16/87; p. 73, Ed Garvey, personal interview; p. 75, Ed Garvey, personal interview; pp. 76-77, Jack Manton, personal interview; p. 80, Norby Walters, AP, 5/15/87; p. 80, Judge Charles Brieant, AP, 12/18/87; p. 83, Jim Abernethy, *Atlanta Constitution*, quoted in AP, 12/15/87; p. 83, Jack Manton, personal interview; p. 84, Sylvester Gray, AP, 4/26/88; pp. 89-90, Robert Dowling, personal interview; p. 91, Greg Lustig, personal interview; p. 95, Tom Brunansky, AP, 2/7/87; pp. 103-104, Lute Olson, *USA Today*, 12/11/86; p. 106, Donald Dell, *Sports Marketing News*, 4/13/87; pp. 107-108, Lenny Del Genio, AP, 11/20/87; pp. 108-109, Len Miller, personal interview; p. 117, Rankin Smith, *Atlanta Falcons '88 Fact Book*, p. 13; p. 126, Jack Kent Cooke, *Time*, 6/11/79; p. 126, Joe Gibbs, *USA Today*, 1/28/88; p. 127, John J. McMullen, *New York Times* Biographical Service, 5/29/82; pp. 127-128, Al Rosen, *New York Times* Biographical Service, 5/29/82; pp. 131-132, Ted Turner, *Sports Illustrated*, 6/23/86; p. 132, Edward Bennett Williams, *Sport*, 7/11/82; p. 138, Joan Kroc, *MacLeans*, 9/30/85; pp. 138-139, Marge Schott, *Milwaukee Journal*; p. 141, Graig Nettles, AP, 1/2/88; p. 143, Vincent Piscopo, AP, 12/31/87; p. 144, Stephen Halas, AP, 1/21/88; p. 145, Bud Selig, personal interview; p. 154, Michael Megna, personal interview; p. 154, John Christison, *Sports Marketing News*, Jan. 1987; p. 157, Vincent Schoemehl, AP, 3/16/88; p. 158, E.J. Junior, AP, 10/30/87; p. 161, Judge Ralph Cappy, AP, 2/17/88; p. 162, A. Ray Smith, AP, 3/2/88; p. 166, Don Fehr, AP, 5/18/88; p. 182, Bum Bright, AP, 12/10/88.

Foreword

Are we all crazy? Did the last 25 years really happen or have I been dreaming, like Rip Van Winkle?

It seems like only yesterday that I was playing with the New York Knickerbockers and making $6,200 a year, a figure that today would not buy you six good seats to the Super Bowl, the World Series, or the NBA or NCAA championship games. Sure, I know the price on the ticket may say $30, $40, or $100, but the actual monies paid, either under the table or through connections, more than add up to my yearly salary as a sub player on the Knicks' bench.

Am I jealous? I'm not sure. In the early '70s I was involved in discussions with a team owner of the American Basketball Association regarding my star center, Jim Chones, and his pro contract for $1.6 million for five years. I was in my early forties, and I remember standing in front of the mirror repeating "one-point-six million, one-point-six million" to give myself confidence for the informal conference. Midway through the next season, Jimmy went hardship and signed. The ABA was looking for aircraft carriers to help them create a national TV contract and had earlier signed Artis Gilmore of Jacksonville and Jim McDaniels of Western Kentucky.

At the time, Jimmy's salary was the largest for a pro contract ever signed in any sport. And I kept saying to myself, "This ballplayer, this team, this program at Marquette University has been developed by a lot of people, but I was the one getting either the pat on the back or the kick in the pants. So why did I have to put on boxing gloves to go into the rectory and negotiate my salary of $27,000 a year? What was the reason?"

The reason was, simply, television. There were no Mr. Watsons of IBM or Henry Fords among the owners, agents, commissioner, or players. This financial escalation was all made possible by the one-eyed cyclops that controls not only sports in these great 50 states but also whom we put in the White House, what we eat, what diseases we cure first, and when we decide to have someone skip across Mars.

If you think the situation is out of hand now, I regret to tell you that the numbers you're looking at today are only fly droppings compared to those to come in the next 15 years. The networks will be bumped back to the rumble seats and cabooses of the sports entertainment world as the independent superstations start paying—listen up—billions, literally billions, for the World Series or the NFL playoffs. These events will be broadcast worldwide, and the superstars, together with the owners (because by that time they'll be partners), will become the Mellons, Carnegies, and Rockefellers of the 21st century. All because of TV.

The only thing that could stop this whirlwind momentum would be federally regulated TV sports coverage. This would insure that those who could not afford pay TV could still watch sports spectaculars, both team and nonteam events, such as Wimbledon and the Kentucky Derby. But there's about as much chance of that happening as of an inner city kid's going to a World Series or Super Bowl game.

Television aside, the past 25 years have hardened the face of sports as it has grown into a business. When I played pro ball, most owners made their living from the clubs they owned, and even though players made good salaries, there was no thought that they could retire on them. There was a world and a job after sports. Today, athletes not yet graduated from college are negotiating salaries that will allow them to retire by age 33.

Although modern-day coaches and managers have more knowledge than ever before, they are also the most expendable figures in sports. Owners have taken over the identities once earned by coaches, and the Steinbrenners, Katzes, and Davises have replaced the Stengels, Auerbachs, and Lombardis of yesteryear. While the coach is caught in limboland between having to please the owner and trying to avoid making adversaries of the superstars, the owner (who has probably never played the sport as a pro or an amateur) enjoys the identity, the ambience, the personal publicity, and the front row seats.

This book is a keeper, whether you follow TV sports or cheer your own local team. It will give you insight into the factors that have gradually transformed sports into a business and will describe how this change will affect you, the sports fan.

What do I see in my crystal ball? I see our children of the 21st century going to the library to look up the word "amateur." They'll find it in the same area as "dinosaur" and "trolley car." Our high school athletes will attend special schools where they will be trained, nurtured, massaged, and worked to a level of efficient performance that is only imaginable through high technology and ever-advancing computerization.

There will be no more neighborhood sandlot baseball or football, no more blacktop basketball. Instead, 9- or 10-year-old student-athletes will be competing in tournaments around the world, in places like Hong Kong and Auckland. They will bring entourages that would make Madonna and Michael Jackson look like lounge acts. You may think this is off the wall, but there will be that much color (money) available.

Imagine Dr. James Naismith's surprise if he could have foreseen that by hanging up that peach basket in Springfield, Massachusetts, he was opening a trapdoor to King Solomon's Mines.

Al McGuire

Preface

It's your money

Tom Roberts would like his friends and neighbors to know he's not responsible for the price of beer at Dodger Stadium.

Sure, Tom.

In case you have forgotten Thomas Roberts, he is the Los Angeles attorney who served as arbitrator in the first great major-league baseball collusion case of 1987. He's also the guy who awarded Fernando Valenzuela a $1-million contract in the star left-hander's salary dispute with the Dodgers.

That very same season, the Dodgers bumped the price of beer by a quarter, and Roberts says his neighbors have blamed him ever since. It just doesn't pay to do your job anymore.

Of course, we all know life is much more complicated than that. No doubt when the management of the Los Angeles National League Baseball Club made the wrenching decision to reevaluate its marketing of bleacher brew, it took into consideration a variety of related factors.

Player depreciation, collective bargaining agreements, lease agreements, licensing agreements, legal precedents, air time, overtime, hang time, free agency, free speech, everything but free beer. And when they were all through . . . surprise! It cost more to be at the old ballpark.

That is a fact of modern American life: It costs more to be at the old ballpark. Another fact of American life is we're willing to pay whatever it costs. And not just at the ballpark either. We'll do it at the golf course, the sporting goods store, the race track, the tennis courts, and right in our own homes watching our own TVs.

Sports has become a modern, merchandising monster. And it eats money.

Incredible amounts of money. Mind-boggling mounds of money. *Sports inc.* magazine conducted a study in 1987 to try to find out just how much money, and the results were right out of a Pentagon budget session. The magazine pegged the gross national sports product at $50.2 billion.

That's more than we spend in this country on oil and coal and even automobiles. It's about 1% of the gross national product. In other words, for every hundred dollars that changes hands in the United States, a buck finds its way to one kind of game or another.

Not only that, but the creature's getting fatter every year. Most of us play or watch something. If we don't, we buy products or services from companies with big investments in athletes or athletics. Even little old ladies in tennis shoes get the shoes with Boris Becker's autograph on them.

Sociologists and psychologists offer a million sophisticated theories on why people are willing to part with all that bread for fun and games, and we'll let them argue about that. The name of the game here is just to show how wild the whole thing has become, how it got that way, and what the zany and occasionally scary results can be.

For just a taste, we need look no further than the 1988 Super Bowl in San Diego. Question: How much does a $100 Super Bowl ticket cost? Answer: There is no such thing.

The price on the face of 73,000 or so tickets that were printed for the game in San Diego was $100, but the chances of the average fan actually buying one for that amount of money were roughly the same as that fan's chances of playing in the game. Corporations get tickets; players and club officials get tickets; movie stars get tickets; networks get tickets; but fans?

The National Football League holds a national lottery every year, and the 2,000 winners earn the right to buy a pair of Super Bowl tickets at face value. That's 2,000 out of how many millions? For the rest of the football fanatics in the country, there are ticket brokers and prices that range from $750 for an end zone seat to $1,900 for something between the 20-yard lines where you can actually see the game.

OK, so you stayed home and watched it on television instead, right? And put up with the commercials. How much do you suppose a 30-second network commercial cost during the 1988 Super Bowl? $100,000? $200,000? Half a million? Piker.

The going rate was $650,000. While you went out to the kitchen for a minute to pop open a beer, a couple of corporations were spending maybe more than you'll make in a lifetime showing something you went out of your way not to see. With the networks paying each NFL team $17.7 million a year, they can't be turning the Super Bowl over to public service messages.

Besides, somebody has to pay the players. The guys on the winning team at the '88 Super Bowl received $36,000 apiece for that one game. That just happens to be three times the minimum salary players were getting 20 years ago for an entire season.

Top ticket prices in 1968 were about $6 for an NFL game, which, when compared to the $1,900 Super Bowl ticket, comes to . . . oh, never mind.

You say you went looking for a little action on that game? Of course you did. Doesn't everybody? The '88 Super Bowl attracted somewhere between $35 million to $40 million in wagers to the legal books in Nevada, and Lord only knows how much in bets nobody can count. It was a down year, too. The average is around $50 million.

The good people of San Diego didn't much care who won, just as long as lots of folks came and brought their credit cards with them. The town spent an estimated $2.1 million to put on this party and figured its efforts were rewarded to the tune of $141 million pumped into the local economy. Hotels, motels, bars, taxis, stores . . . it all adds up.

And when the game was over and the Redskins won, what's the first thing quarterback Doug Williams said? He smiled at the cameras and declared, "I'm going to Disneyland." Now why do you suppose that popped into his head?

It may be years before we know what the endorsement take was for the players and coaches.

Claiming a significant share of that will be a relatively new breed of sporting personality known as the agent. An old breed of sporting personality known as the owner doesn't care very much at all for the new breed.

Owners think agents are at least partially responsible for putting athletes in tax brackets formerly reserved for sheiks, oil barons, real estate tycoons, and . . . owners. They don't like unions either for the same reasons, and they're correct on both counts.

Owners do like to quote numbers that show professional basketball players' salaries averaging more than $500,000 a year, baseball players' salaries averaging more than $400,000, and football players' salaries averaging more than $200,000, because those figures put fans on their side.

They aren't crazy about numbers that show only six or seven NFL clubs making money in 1987, the year of the Awful Strike, but they don't go to a lot of trouble to conceal them either.

It would be easier to feel sorry for these fellows if the value of their investment weren't growing like bread dough in a Turkish bath. Somebody bought a very ordinary Phoenix Suns franchise for $44.5 million in 1987 and turned down a $60-million offer a couple of months later.

If owning a team is a bad investment, how come entrepreneurs are falling all over each other for the chance to waste their money? And how come cities and states have done everything short of calling out the militia to either steal or keep pro teams?

Why would somebody like Robert Irsay feel he had to sneak the Colts out of Baltimore in the middle of the night? How come everybody's suing everybody all the time? Do the Washington Redskins really need a $770-million stadium complex, complete with luxury hotel, shopping mall, and 500 condos?

Is there no sanity in sport? The answer is: Probably not. Hey, there's even a $730,000 fishing tournament held in Florida every year. And amateurs? What's that?

The '84 Olympics in Los Angeles made a $233-million profit. The Cotton Bowl guaranteed each of its participating teams $2.3 million in 1988, and that figure was expected to hit $3 million before long. The schools love it.

When Oklahoma won the national title in 1985, donations to the university rose $2.4 million.

So what are the kids who play the games supposed to make of all that? Does it shed a little light on why many of them are snagging as much under-the-table money as they can wrap their fists around and why they go on to treat their pro contracts like so much confetti? Everybody wants a piece of the action, and the action gets more god-awful and out of sight each year.

You ought to know. You're paying for it. How much is the tab, and how did it get that way? Sit back, and we'll try to figure it out together.

Chapter

1

Clause for Concern

All about contracts, and what good are they anyway?

Lou Gehrig's ghost gazed down at the proceedings in disbelief as the New York Yankees' newest first baseman signed on the dotted line. This was 60 years after Gehrig's fabled '27 Yankees, and Don Mattingly had just scored a clear victory for capitalism and .352 hitters everywhere.

An arbitrator had seen things Mattingly's way, brushing off owner George Steinbrenner's low ball offer of $1.7 million and awarding the all-star infielder a $1.975-million salary.

From Gehrig's lofty viewpoint, that seemed pretty reasonable, prices being what they were, and figuring Mattingly still had five or six years to play. "Yep," said the old Iron Horse, "that ought to get him through the rest of his career and leave him some change when it's over."

But then he heard some guy in a suit, who seemed to be on Mattingly's side, say, "Thank you, gentlemen. Now does anybody want to talk about next year?"

Poor old Lou almost fell off his cloud. "What the hell's an arbitrator anyway?" he grumbled as he stalked away.

Fair question. And while we're at it, what's an option year? Or a guaranteed contract? Or an incentive bonus or a right of first refusal? All of those things are found in professional athletes' contracts now, and none of them were around for the '27 Yankees. Or for the '57 Yankees for that matter.

It isn't true that nobody was paid the kind of money in Gehrig's day that Mattingly gets now. It's just that the people who did make that much owned the teams instead of playing for them.

You could buy a franchise in 1927 for less than what a starting infield costs now and have enough left over for a couple of hot dogs and a beer. No peanuts. That's what the players got.

Then America discovered television, the players discovered guys in suits, and the world of sports in general and sports contracts in particular became murky and tricky, just like any other area of high finance. And very, very lucrative.

Too lucrative? That's the burning issue the major games in America have to face. The players as well as the team owners in every sport had better be smart enough to know when they have priced themselves right out of the American entertainment business.

If it gets too expensive to pack up the kids and go to the stadium or arena, then there might not be much need for the stadium or arena anymore. Or for the players or owners.

Attendance figures show sports haven't reached that point yet. But they have come a long way down the road leading in that direction. And salaries have certainly hastened the trip.

How high are salaries and how did they get that way? Let's take a look.

Mattingly's 1987 award broke a record, but not a very old one. A week before, another arbitrator had agreed with Jack Morris, who thought $1.85 million would be reasonable compensation for another year of pitching for the Detroit Tigers.

Although those decisions put Mattingly and Morris close to the top of their profession, there were still half a dozen baseball players earning more than they were. A year later, so was Mattingly.

In the winter, he signed a new three-year deal that paid him $6.7 million. Evidently Steinbrenner was growing tired of annual appearances before the arbitrator.

The new $2-million-plus salary didn't make Mattingly the best paid player in baseball either. That honor went to Ozzie Smith, a Golden Glove shortstop who could also afford to wear gold shoes, socks, and underwear if he chose.

Smith was earning a reported $2.34 million a year, making him 1 of 11 major-league players with annual incomes of $2 million or more. That's in a sport where annual salaries actually declined in 1986 and 1987 before bouncing back up by about 10% in 1988.

The other $2-million baseball players were Mattingly, Dan Quisenberry, Jim Rice, Gary Carter, Eddie Murray, Mike Schmidt, Rick Sutcliffe, Dale Murphy, Fernando Valenzuela, and Andre Dawson.

Dawson is the most daring of the group. He played out his contract in Montreal in 1986 and wanted so desperately to leave the Expos that he signed what amounted to a blank contract with the Cubs.

He told them to fill in the figures, and the general manager, Dallas Green, came up with the number $600,000. Dawson reacted to this relatively modest figure the way teams and fans would like superstars to react. He parlayed Wrigley Field's short fences and daylight schedule into the 1987 Most Valuable Player award.

SPORT$BIZ STATS

TOP DOLLAR: Basketball (1987-88)

1. **Kareem Abdul-Jabbar**
   center, Los Angeles Lakers
   $2,500,000

2. **Magic Johnson**
   guard, Los Angeles Lakers
   $2,500,000

3. **Patrick Ewing**
   center, New York Knicks
   $2,250,000

4. **Moses Malone**
   center, Washington Bullets
   $2,145,000

5. **Robert Parish**
   center, Boston Celtics
   $2,038,333

6. **Larry Bird**
   forward, Boston Celtics
   $1,800,000

7. **Ralph Sampson**
   center, Golden State Warriors
   $1,736,333

8. **Jack Sikma**
   center, Milwaukee Bucks
   $1,600,000

9. **Alex English**
   forward, Denver Nuggets
   $1,500,000

10. **Dominique Wilkins**
    forward, Atlanta Hawks
    $1,445,000

Note. From "The Sport 100 Salary Survey," edited by D. Levine, *Sport*, June 1988, pp. 23-37. Adapted by permission.

Now, he said, pay me what I'm *really* worth, and he became a $2-million man.

A $2-million salary has become the late 1980s standard for team superstars. Curiously, nobody seems to mind very much when athletes in individual sports make many times that much money.

Sport Magazine does an annual survey of what athletes make, and according to the 1988 edition, the best paid jock of all was prizefighter Marvelous Marvin Hagler, who collected $15 million in purses. Right after him was Sugar Ray Leonard, the man who took Hagler's title from him. Leonard made $10.8 million, and behind him was heavyweight champion Mike Tyson at $6.6 million.

It could be that most fans don't object to outlandish boxing purses because they don't go to championship bouts anyway. Those are for beautiful people and high rollers. Baseball, basketball, and football are different; they are the sports where fans feel they're being priced out.

Michael Jordan will become basketball's newest double millionaire. He has never said exactly what he makes, but he was widely reported to have been offered an eight-year contract in April of 1988 that would pay him $28 million.

Is any performer worth $9,589 a day? The Chicago Bulls would probably say Jordan is. When he came to the team, the Bulls were the best kept secret in Chicago since the Republican Party. They were averaging 6,365 fans a game, and the play-offs had become a disappearing memory.

Now they are considered to be one of the league's most promising young teams, and their 1988-89 season tickets were sold out five months before the first game. A May 6, 1988 *Sports Industry News* report put Jordan's contribution to the Bulls at $7.2 million in new revenues every year.

The San Antonio Spurs are hoping David Robinson will have the same effect on their badly fading franchise. When they signed Robinson to a 10-year, $26-million deal, he was an ensign in the U.S. Navy and two years away from his first pro game.

He was to get $1.5 million for each of the seasons he *didn't* play and then $2 million for each of the first three after he came out of the Navy. It kept going up after that until the average for his eight playing years came to $3.25 million.

Too much? It depends on what he does for the Spurs. Look at the Los Angeles Lakers. They're paying the equivalent of two David Robinsons, and they have no complaints.

Magic Johnson and Kareem Abdul-Jabbar are each making almost $3 million a year. Magic had a 25-year, $25-million contract once, and it wasn't enough. His agent changed a "whereas" here and "therefore" there, and before you knew it, Magic was making as much as Kareem.

Lakers customers can afford the prices created by payrolls like that, and most of them wouldn't have it any other way. Imagine the wailing in Lotus Land if the team's followers thought management had become too cheap to keep the Lakers on top of the National Basketball Association heap.

Of course that's the Planet California. Some other NBA cities take a more down-to-earth view of team sports, and they, too, have their $2-million players. Besides Jordan, Robinson, Abdul-Jabbar, and Johnson, they include Akeem Olajuwon of Houston, Ralph Sampson of Golden State, Patrick Ewing of New York, Moses Malone of Washington, and Robert Parish of Boston.

Notice that all but two members of that group are centers. You hear it all the time. "You can't win a championship without a dominant big man." The owners know that, and they pay accordingly.

Salaries do have some relationship to reality. Owners want to win. So do fans. Many fans don't object to paying large amounts to large people if those people produce victories. Pay the superstars, they say, but don't make millionaires out of average small forwards.

That may be the biggest rap on the NBA salary structure. Although basketball has fewer $2-million players than baseball, its average salary is about $100,000 higher.

From that standpoint, the fan favorite ought to be football, where the average salary is less than half of basketball, and a player's position on the field has almost as much to do with his salary as his performance. Quarterbacks and running backs, the key to excitement if not success in pro football, are the athletes most likely to get rich.

The NFL doesn't have any $2-million players—at least not in base salary. Add the bonuses, and a few guys could be approaching that mark.

John Elway would be the closest at a reported $1.95 million, followed by Eric Dickerson at $1.74 million, Dan Marino at $1.64 million, Jim Kelly at $1.6 million, Herschel Walker at $1.5 million, and Bo Jackson at $1.39 million.

All quarterbacks and running backs, plus one outfielder with an off-season job. Jackson, whose job is baseball and who says his "hobby" is football, makes $533,000 at his vocation, or less than half of what he makes at his avocation.

Seven of the 11 highest paid players in the NFL in 1987 were quarterbacks, and 24 of the top 34 were quarterbacks, running backs, or wide receivers. Really successful quarterbacks tend to hang on for a long time in the NFL, which is another reason why so many of them are at the top of the salary pile.

It takes time to develop a good quarterback, and once a team has done that, it handles him with tender loving care. They used to say it takes five years to make a pro quarterback, but most clubs aren't that patient anymore. Most quarterbacks aren't either.

A 1987 *Sporting News* survey showed that the average quarterback in the NFL was making more than $333,000 a year in salary, which means he could become an average millionaire in just about the same period of time that it takes you to pay off your used car.

On the other end of the scale, punters were getting about $106,000 a year. According to that same study, running backs were second to quarterbacks with an average salary of $229,000, and then the numbers dropped off in this order: defensive linemen, linebackers, wide receivers, offensive linemen, defensive backs, placekickers, and punters.

So parents, if you raise your sons to be football players, teach them first to throw the ball and second to carry it. If all they can do is kick it, maybe they want to look into soccer.

One more thing, mom and dad. If your kid talks back to you all the time, maybe you're raising a coach.

There's another curious fact about fans and the salary structure in big-time sports. The two classes of employees that get the most heat in any sport are coaches and referees or umpires. But people don't seem to care very much what those guys make.

When Bill Parcells signed a five-year $3.75-million contract to coach the New York Giants, it served as something of a landmark for mentors. He was not in a class by himself. Larry Brown got $3.5 million over five years to coach the San Antonio Spurs, and Pete Rose earns $700,000 annually from the Cincinnati Reds. Coaches mostly live in the six-figure neighborhoods, and nobody minds that as long as they win.

If anybody's underpaid in big-time sports, it might be the umpires and referees. Paying a college ref $450 to work a National Collegiate Athletic

SPORT$BIZ STATS

TOP DOLLAR: Baseball (1988)

1. **Ozzie Smith**
   shortstop, St. Louis Cardinals
   $2,340,000

2. **Dan Quisenberry**
   reliever, Kansas City Royals
   $2,298,843

3. **Jim Rice**
   designated hitter/outfielder,
   Boston Red Sox
   $2,286,636

4. **Eddie Murray**
   first baseman, Baltimore Orioles
   $2,281,530

5. **Gary Carter**
   catcher, New York Mets
   $2,198,572

6. **Mike Schmidt**
   third baseman, Philadelphia
   Phillies
   $2,150,000

7. **Rick Sutcliffe**
   pitcher, Chicago Cubs
   $2,070,000

8. **Fernando Valenzuela**
   pitcher, Los Angeles Dodgers
   $2,050,000

9. **Don Mattingly**
   first baseman, New York
   Yankees
   $2,000,000

10. **Dale Murphy**
    outfielder, Atlanta Braves
    $2,000,000

Note. From "The Sport 100 Salary Survey," edited by D. Levine, *Sport*, June 1988, pp. 23-37. Adapted by permission.

Association Final Four game between two teams playing for more than $1 million apiece isn't just ridiculous, it's dangerous. But that's what the refs were making in 1988.

Pro officials are doing much better than that. The NFL has always gotten by with part-time zebras, who in real life might be doctors, lawyers, or chief executive officers. They don't work strictly for the love of the game.

NFL officials negotiated a deal that gave them a 33% raise in 1987. A rookie ref gets $600 a game, and that increases by $50 for each year he's in the league. At the top of the scale is the 20-year man making $1,800 per game. Playoff games pay $5,000, and the Super Bowl is worth $7,500.

Major-league umpires, who are full-time help, cut a new four-year deal in 1987. A first-year ump makes $40,000 a season, and a 20-year veteran tops out at $100,000. The range will be $41,000 to $105,000 in the last year of the contract.

The NBA has just gone to three-man officiating crews in a move that will cost the league $1 million. Pro basketball officials get a minimum of $32,000, while the top guys make as much as $130,000.

To earn that kind of money, officials must spend years developing an exhaustive knowledge of their games, an ability to make split-second decisions, and the skin of a Sherman tank. Those are pretty much the attributes of a successful coach as well.

Now what have athletes done to earn their keep? And why should they pull in the kind of bucks that ought to be associated with curing dread diseases and ensuring world peace?

To make the case for their defense, we're going to call in a lawyer. His name is Leigh Steinberg, and he is one of the most respected player agents in the world. Some owners would say that's like being called one of the mildest forms of the flu, but even most of them will admit that Steinberg is a fair and ethical professional.

And he doesn't deny for a minute that many athletes make a great deal of money. But then again, so do movie stars, and whose lives have they saved lately?

Steinberg emphasizes that professional athletes are entertainers, and we're willing to pay a lot to be entertained.

We'll stop paying only if the performers drive ticket prices out of the customers' reach. Everything is relative.

"There is an inherent feeling in this society that when people who are working in a wide array of professions look at their own salary levels compared to athletes', the athletes' salaries seem totally outrageous," Steinberg said. "The problem with that is definition of worth.

"Athletes in general are not overpaid if they are part of a business that in paying those salaries is keeping ticket prices at a reasonable level and is still making a profit.

"There is a relationship between three components. The athletes' interest is reflected in salary. The owners' interest is reflected in profit margin and franchise value. The fans' interest is reflected in ticket prices. If each part of that triangle could be kept in balance, then athletes are not overpaid.

"Athletes are overpaid if ticket prices are so high that the sport becomes inaccessible—if the prices threaten to kill the financial vitality of the sport by knocking out sports fans for the future because they have never seen it played live. They can't afford the ticket, and their only experience is television."

OK, but isn't that where we're headed? Put the price of tickets, parking, a few beers, and hot dogs together, and the idea of just sitting home and watching the game on TV gets more attractive all the time.

Steinberg is concerned about that, too. After all, when we stop paying athletes, athletes stop paying agents. But he seems to think that players get more than their share of the blame for the exploding prices in sport. How about looking in the owners' direction?

"Who takes the risks for professional football?" asked Steinberg. "The average career for a player is 3.1 years. It's not a field someone can practice well into their 70's.

"I just finished a contract for a news anchor in San Francisco who is

60 years old. It's going to cover five years, and he's at his most productive earning time. At that point in their lives, most athletes would be retired for years.

"So we have short playing lives here. That's the first thing to say. The second thing to say is that the athlete is the attraction. Not too many people would pay to see the owner. Nobody gets angry when Sylvester Stallone makes $16 million from a motion picture or when Michael Jackson or Bruce Springsteen makes $100 million from a nationwide rock tour. They get angry at athletes' salaries."

So what's the difference between Michael Jackson and Reggie Jackson as far as the public is concerned? Steinberg can tell you in a minute, and he makes a point most of us may not have thought about much. The point is, Reggie's just playing a game.

"Most men played the sport growing up and still think of it as a game," Steinberg explained. "They would love to play the game for free.

"But it's not a game anymore for the athletes, when the injury rate is so debilitating. Athletes will suffer injuries that stay with them far beyond their playing years. Some of my retired clients cannot bend over to pick up their kids. They can't carry groceries to the car.

"They've got physical injuries that came out of a five- or six-year playing career that will be with them for their whole life."

What about the players who never get seriously hurt, the ones who have careers that cover a couple of decades? They're lucky, that's what.

But none of them knows if he'll be one of the fortunate ones when he agrees to his first contract. And the smart athlete recognizes that before he signs anything more detailed than an autograph.

Here's where we get into the nitty-gritty of pro sports contracts. If you can understand how contracts work, you can at least get an idea of how players wind up getting paid what they do. And admittedly, sometimes their pay seems to make as much sense as a quarterback sneak on third-and-20.

Why, for instance, does a backup quarterback who might take a dozen snaps in a season pull in $800,000 while an all-pro tight end gets a fifth of that while getting his helmet caved in blocking linebackers? And why is your favorite slugger of 20 years ago driving a truck somewhere, while a .250 lifetime hitter today may be playing the stock market with hundreds of thousands of dollars tomorrow?

You don't have to be an expert in fine print to figure out the basics. What you do have to do is keep one thing in mind that's unique in pro sports.

Here it is: Every player is governed by not one, but two contracts. There's the one the athlete and agent negotiate with the team. And there's the one the athlete's union negotiates with the owners.

The players' unions do what unions do in other businesses. They hammer out working conditions, grievance procedures, benefit packages, travel expenses, and a host of other things that most of us don't want to hear about and that rarely cause strikes.

SPORT$BIZ STATS

TOP DOLLAR: Football (1987)

1. **Bo Jackson**
   running back, Los Angeles Raiders
   $1,391,750

2. **Eric Dickerson**
   running back, Indianapolis Colts
   $1,391,000

3. **Jim Kelly**
   quarterback, Buffalo Bills
   $1,225,000

4. **John Elway**
   quarterback, Denver Broncos
   $1,178,571

5. **Joe Montana**
   quarterback, San Francisco 49ers
   $933,333

6. **Boomer Esiason**
   quarterback, Cincinnati Bengals
   $900,000

7. **Bernie Kosar**
   quarterback, Cleveland Browns
   $800,000

8. **Vinny Testaverde**
   quarterback, Tampa Bay Buccaneers
   $783,667

9. **Kevin Bryant**
   running back, Washington Redskins
   $752,000

10. **Tommy Kramer**
    quarterback, Minnesota Vikings
    $750,000

Note. From "The Sport 100 Salary Survey," edited by D. Levine, *Sport*, June 1988, pp. 23-37. Adapted by permission.

They also negotiate salary minimums and player movement. We don't want to hear about those either, but we don't seem to have much choice. They *are* what players strike over.

The provisions covering them are set out in collective bargaining agreements. Remember that term. CBAs. Lately, we're reading more about them than we are RBIs or ERAs.

Once the unions are through, the agents take over. They work out salaries and bonuses for individual players with individual clubs. Just remember that in sports CBAs set minimums; individual negotiations set salaries.

There you go. Two kinds of contracts, individual and collective. Let's look at them one at a time and figure out who's doing what to whom.

Individual Contracts

There are really only two rational reasons why people own sports teams. The irrational reasons would fill a book all by themselves.

For most owners, Objective No. 1 is to win a championship. Objective No. 2 is to make some money or at least avoid going broke while pursuing Objective No. 1.

Let's give owners their due here. That is usually the order of their priorities. If their first interest were making money, they could do it in another business quicker and with less stress.

The best way for owners to realize the first objective would be to hire all of the biggest stars in the game, pay them untold millions, and sit back and watch while they beat their more poorly compensated rivals senseless. Right? Absolutely not.

It's been tried, and it doesn't work. Any more than it would work to hire the top 10 male box office stars, pair them off with the top 10 female box office stars, and put them together with the leading director in Hollywood. What would you get? Maybe a financial disaster and probably not an Oscar.

Owners have succeeded from time to time in spending their way from the bottom of the standings to a contending position, but then they seem to hit a wall. Pennants, championships, and Super Bowls aren't for sale. You can't even rent them.

According to a March 16, 1987 *Sporting News* report, the four NFL teams with the highest average salaries in 1987 were the Los Angeles Raiders, the New York Jets, the New England Patriots, and the New York Giants. They all had one thing in common: losing records. The teams that played in the Super Bowl were Washington, which ranked 9th in salary average, and Denver, which ranked 14th.

The Raiders' league-leading payroll came to $285,653 per man, compared to the world champion Redskins' $199,235.

It isn't any different in baseball and basketball. One way for owners to decide if they're getting their money's worth from their players is to figure out how much they're paying for every victory. Statisticians use a simple equation to help them arrive at that judgment. They divide a team's payroll by the number of its victories, and that gives them cost per victory.

So who won the most games in the NBA in the 1987-88 season? The Los Angeles Lakers with 62. But even with their reported $10-million payroll, the Lakers ranked only 10th in the 23-team league in cost per victory. The Boston Celtics, who were second in the league in victories, were 13th in the number of bucks they expended for each one.

The poor Los Angeles Clippers paid only $600,000 less to win 17 games than the Celtics did to win 57. And the clubs that paid the least per victory were Detroit and Dallas. Both of them won their division titles and more than 50 games.

The team with the biggest payroll in all of baseball is the New York Yankees, whose $16- million-plus figure is $2 million more than anybody else's in the major leagues. And yet the Yankees spent more than twice as

SPORT$BIZ STATS

TOP DOLLAR: Hockey (1987-88)

1. **Wayne Gretzky**
   center, Edmonton Oilers
   $948,000

2. **Mike Bossy**
   forward, New York Islanders
   $700,000

3. **Bryan Trottier**
   center, New York Islanders
   $625,000

4. **Dave Taylor**
   forward, Los Angeles Kings
   $615,000

5. **Denis Potvin**
   defenseman, New York
   Islanders
   $575,000

6. **Mike Liut**
   goaltender, Hartford Whalers
   $550,000

7. **Marcel Dionne**
   center, New York Rangers
   $500,000

8. **Mario Lemieux**
   center, Pittsburgh Penguins
   $475,000

9. **Mark Messier**
   forward,Edmonton Oilers
   $474,000

10. **Mike Gartner**
   forward, Washington
   Capitals
   $425,000

Note. From "The Sport 100 Salary Survey," edited by D. Levine, *Sport*, June 1988, pp. 23-37. Adapted by permission.

much in salaries to win two fewer games than the Milwaukee Brewers won in 1987.

The world champion Minnesota Twins had a lower payroll than eight other teams. And the club with the lowest salary costs of all was the Pittsburgh Pirates, whose players made less than a quarter of what the Yankees' players did. What's more, Pittsburgh is considered to have one of the most rapidly improving and promising teams in either league. Its cost per victory was less than a third of the Yankees'.

So what are we to gather from this? That it pays to have Syd Thrift running your baseball operation? (The Pirates thought so until they fired him in an October '88 power struggle). Maybe. That the Pirates' management is three times as smart as the Yankees' management? Probably not. That the Pirates are a very young team? Bull's-eye!

The most important thing you have to recognize about pro athletes' contracts is that players never get paid what they're worth. Or practically never. They make either too little or too much.

That's because their salary is always at least a year behind their performance.

How does a team decide how much a rookie is worth? It looks at what he did in college or the minor leagues. Then the next year when the player isn't a rookie anymore, his salary is determined by what he did the previous season.

And on and on. A player's value isn't determined by what he's doing this season, but by what he did last season. When you throw in the phenomenon of long-term contracts, the whole picture is totally out of focus.

Let's say your favorite team has signed a rookie outfielder to a two-year deal, and he plays like Babe Ruth for both those years. So your team gives him a big raise, signs him for five more years, and he starts playing like Babe the Blue Ox.

Get half a team of those guys, and an owner ends up paying World Series prices for second-division finishes.

On the other hand, a kid might take a couple of years to adjust to the pro game. The owner sees the kid's potential, signs him to a long-term contract at bargain rates based on his mediocre start, and looks like a genius. So some owners get away with murder, and some owners get murdered.

In a perfect world, it would all balance out. But it doesn't work that way on Earth. Here players *renegotiate*. Bet you hate that word.

An owner has two choices when a player is being paid much more than he's worth: (a) Try to foist him off on some other team, or (b) Swallow hard and wait for the player's contract to expire.

But if a player discovers he's underpaid, he can send his agent back to the owner and demand that the team redo the deal. If the owner balks, the player might hold out—even though he has a binding contract that says he owes the team his services for a specified period of time.

Did you ever wonder how he gets away with that and why owners don't sue players who hold out for breach of contract? One reason: It doesn't do any good.

In the normal legal world, when somebody is found to be in breach of contract, the judge makes him provide what he promised or make up the difference in money. That doesn't work in sports because no one can really say how much the loss of an athlete's services costs a team.

A judge can't determine monetary damages or make the player play. Requiring someone to provide personal services against his or her will is slavery. Even in sports, that's against the law.

What the teams can do is withhold the holdout player's salary, and sooner or later, that's usually enough. That's especially true for young players who don't want to be wasting their early years sitting in their agent's office when they could be making real money for the first time in their lives.

Most of the time if a talented young player starts out with low numbers, but he hangs in there, avoids injury, and gets with the right team, he can more than make up for it with the money he earns after he's over the hill.

From a player's perspective, that's what long-term contracts are for. Some owners like long-term contracts, too, particularly in sports where players don't need a team of lawyers and an automatic weapon in order to change teams.

We'll cover that later, but for now it's enough to say that one of the most important features of individual contracts is length. There are several features that make a big difference in how these deals work for the players and the teams. Briefly, they go like this:

Contract Length.   In baseball and basketball, there is a trend toward multi-year deals because the unions in those sports are making progress in freeing up player movement. The only way the owners can protect their investments is to sign their key players for as long as they can. They'll take their chances on renegotiation.

The NFL power structure may lose the movement battle eventually, but football owners are stubborn. It shows in the contracts they sign with their players.

When you read that running back Sylvester Slasher has signed a three-year contract with the Dallas Cowboys, don't—repeat don't—believe it. In the overwhelming majority of cases in the NFL, Sylvester has signed "a series of three one-year contracts."

What that means is he can't play for any other team for three years, but the team can cut him any time it feels like it.

It's like a wedding where only the bride is married. There are exceptions, but that is still the rule in the NFL and only the NFL.

Not only that, but most of the time if the player gets hurt during the season, the team has no responsibility to keep him the following year until he gets well enough to play again.

This brings us to the next important item in individual contracts.

Guarantees.   This is what the great majority of NFL players don't get that almost all players in the other two sports do get. Athletes with guaranteed contracts are paid even when they can't play or when their teams don't want them anymore.

You see it all the time. An aging slugger sits on the bench collecting dust and fat checks while his younger teammate drives in three times as many runs for one third the salary. The veteran's skills ran out before his contract did.

You have to remember that 10 years ago, the aging slugger might have been the underpaid young player. It's only fair.

It's also why some players are practically untradable. When a veteran player gets swapped to a different team, his contract goes with him. Whoever trades for him has to pay the salary that's in the contract.

There's one way around that. A team may just decide to cut the player and eat his contract. He goes out on waivers, and anyone in the league can sign him. If nobody does, he becomes a free agent.

Example: The Philadelphia Phillies are paying Gordon Greybeard, their knuckleball relief pitcher, a guaranteed $400,000 a year, and they have noticed that Gordon hasn't gotten anybody out since spring training. They put him on waivers, but everybody in the league has noticed Gordon's slump, too. So he passes through the waivers.

Now Gordon's agent convinces the Pittsburgh Pirates that there's a dip or two left in that knuckler after all. The Pirates figure they'll risk $75,000 to see if the agent is right.

The Pirates pay Gordon $75,000, and the Phillies have to make up the difference between that and his $400,000 guaranteed salary. Pittsburgh has a veteran relief pitcher, and Philadelphia has a $325,000 debit item on its books.

At least in that case, the team holding the guaranteed contract can get some of it off its back. With an injured player, it gets no relief. It has to pay the player his full salary for the full term of his contract whether he ever plays again or not.

Often the team and the player can't agree on just how badly the player is hurt. Then we're treated to a messy little scene that could be called "dueling doctors."

The team physician says the player is well enough to perform. The player comes back with a phalanx of medical experts who insist he's legitimately disabled. Somewhere along the way, the two parties are likely to settle on a percentage of the contract.

Isn't it interesting that the sport with the greatest risk of serious injury is football, and it's the one that provides the fewest guaranteed contracts? Great for the teams, awful for the players.

One way out of this dilemma is insurance.

If a player's agent absolutely insists upon a guaranteed contract, and the team digs in its heels all the way down to bedrock, the problem might be resolved by a call to Lloyds of London. The team could buy the player an insurance policy that pays him, let's say, $1 million if he can't play again.

One twist on that would be for the team to guarantee the contract and then buy the insurance policy for itself. If the player can't play anymore and the club has to keep paying him, it reimburses itself with the insurance benefits.

Another twist would be if the player buys his own insurance policy and names himself the beneficiary. New Jersey Nets star Buck Williams did that recently. He bought a plan that would pay him more than $3 million if he suffered a career-ending injury. And since the benefits are tax free, the payout would equal about a $6-million NBA salary. The premium was $20,000.

Signing and Reporting Bonuses.   One thing that riles football fans is to see an athlete right out of college get a couple hundred thousand dollars just to show up at training camp. Actually that arrangement isn't as bad as it sounds. Reporting bonuses are the NFL's answer to guaranteed contracts. They're just up-front money.

If a player signs a $300,000 nonguaranteed contract, but it includes a $150,000 reporting bonus, half of his salary has effectively been guaranteed. All he has to do is come to camp to get the money. Even if he gets hurt later and can't play, nobody can take the money away.

SPORT$BIZ STATS

PURSE MONEY (1987)

Boxing

1. **Marvelous Marvin Hagler**
$15,000,000

2. **Ray Leonard**
$10,800,000

3. **Mike Tyson**
$6,600,000

4. **Michael Spinks**
$4,000,000

5. **Gerry Cooney**
$1,666,667

Bowling

1. **Pete Weber**
$179,516

2. **Del Ballard, Jr.**
$163,939

3. **Pete McCordic**
$156,476

4. **Marshall Holman**
$152,563

5. **Walter Ray Williams, Jr.**
$143,873

Jockeys

1. **Jose Santos**
$1,237,543

2. **Pat Day**
$1,236,757

3. **Laffit Pincay, Jr.**
$1,195,266

4. **Angel Cordero, Jr.**
$1,166,431

5. **Chris McCarron**
$932,584

Note. From "The Sport 100 Salary Survey," edited by D. Levine, *Sport*, June 1988, pp. 23-37. Adapted by permission.

Signing bonuses are the same thing, only they're paid out as soon as a player puts his name on the contract. Brian Bosworth got a $2.5-million signing bonus after scrapping with the Seattle Seahawks for months. Dan Marino's new contract gives him an estimated $2-million signing bonus but no reporting bonus. He used to have one of those worth $850,000.

When the figures get that high for signing and reporting bonuses, players don't have to care that much about guarantees. Then it's just a matter of semantics.

Football owners know that, too, and they're getting worried. They say that from 1982 to 1987 they lost $10 million in bonus money to players they wound up waiving. Now they want to limit signing bonuses to players who make the teams' final rosters.

It's either that or put strings on the bonuses. Take Bosworth's reported 10-year, $11-million contract with Seattle. According to several accounts, he gets a $2.5-million signing bonus, with $500,000 of it paid in 1987, $500,000 in 1997, $500,000 in 1998, $500,000 in 1999, and $500,000 in the year 2,000.

That would appear to mean that Bosworth would have to have a 13-year career to collect his signing bonus. Not quite. But he would still have to be on the roster in 1996 to get the entire bonus.

Bosworth's salary in 1987 was a modest $300,000, and it was due to climb in gradual steps until it reached $1 million in 1992. However, from 1992 until the agreement runs out in 1996, the contract isn't guaranteed. The team could cut the Boz and save a bundle of money if he isn't producing up to their expectations anymore.

Deferred Salaries.   Only accountants and actuaries really understand these. They're about playing now and being paid later.

Agents know that players will get too old and creaky to run up and down courts or fields forever. And when that happens, their clients still have to eat and support their families. Agents also know that if a player takes all of his money in the years he's playing, Uncle Sam could get almost as much of it as the player does.

Sometimes it's a good idea to let the teams hold onto some of the money until way off in the future when the player will need it more and won't be in such a lofty tax bracket.

The teams tend to like that idea, too, because it keeps them from being drowned in cash flow problems. They also like it because they know about inflation. A million dollars paid in 1998 might be worth just a fraction of what it is in 1988.

Like all brilliant ideas, this one has a downside for both the player and the team. The player with a bright agent might be able to take all that money up front and invest it wisely enough to more than compensate for the tax bite. He'll still have the cash he needs for a comfortable old age.

And the team that is really taken with the notion of deferring salaries could wind up paying more to people who used to play for it than to people who do now. That happened a lot in the NBA, where the owners finally decided to put strict limits on how much of any contract could be deferred.

Deferred money makes contracts look bigger than they really are. When you read about a quarterback getting a $10-million deal, keep reading. If a big chunk of his money is deferred, he's not costing the team nearly as much in current dollars.

There's another little land mine built into this arrangement for players. Sometimes the deferred money is only paid out if the players faithfully report for duty throughout the life of the contract. The owners were able to use that provision to great effect while busting up the 1987 NFL strike.

Incentive Clauses.   Unlike a lot of other things you find in pro contracts, these are so logical you wonder how teams and players ever thought of them.

SPORT$BIZ STATS

PURSE MONEY (1987)

Men's tennis	Women's tennis
1. **Ivan Lendl,** $2,003,656	1. **Steffi Graf,** $1,063,785
2. **Stefan Edberg,** $1,587,467	2. **Martina Navratilova,** $932,102
3. **Miroslav Mecir,** $1,205,326	3. **Chris Evert,** $769,943
4. **Mats Wilander,** $1,164,674	4. **Pam Shriver,** $703,030
5. **Pat Cash,** $565,934	5. **Helena Sukova,** $490,792

Men's golf	Women's golf
1. **Ian Woosnam,** $1,793,268	1. **Betsy King,** $504,535
2. **Curtis Strange,** $911,671	2. **Ayako Okamoto,** $478,034
3. **Paul Azinger,** $844,506	3. **Nancy Lopez,** $454,823
4. **Sandy Lyle,** $767,891	4. **Jane Geddes,** $409,241
5. **Greg Norman,** $715,838	5. **Jan Stephenson,** $262,278

Note. From "The Sport 100 Salary Survey," edited by D. Levine, *Sport*, June 1988, pp. 23-37. Adapted by permission.

There's a very simple principle involved. The better a player plays, the more he's paid.

Occasionally, an owner will give a player a long-term, guaranteed contract involving mountains of money, and the player will come down with a terminal case of apathy. There aren't as many instances of that as owners would like fans to believe, but it's not unheard of.

The owner's recourse is to offer a player a more modest base salary and then pack his contract with bonuses for doing good things on the field. Often that makes players get not just older, but better.

Let's take an old right-hander as an example. Don Sutton, 42 and headed for the Hall of Fame, signed a 1988 contract with the Los Angeles Dodgers that paid him $350,000 in salary. It's a nice figure, but he had a chance to more than double it to $775,000 by reaching certain statistical goals.

He got some of the money just by staying around. Sutton received an additional $25,000 by making it to May 1 without being cut, $25,000 more for being on the roster June 1, and another $50,000 for being there July 1. Another $75,000 was built in for August 1, and $75,000 for August 31, but the Dodgers decided to save some money. They cut Sutton in August.

The rest of the bonuses were predicated on starts, appearances, and total innings pitched—for instance, $50,000 for pitching in 20 games and $25,000 more for hurling 180 innings.

Sutton's age was probably the determining factor in making this deal. There was never any question he wanted to pitch, but there was some doubt on the club's part that his body was as willing as his spirit. In other cases, it's not so much age as previous history that makes teams load up contracts with bonuses.

Darryl Dawkins is one of the most physically gifted and unfortunate centers the NBA has ever seen. When the New Jersey Nets signed Chocolate Thunder to a new contract in 1988, he had played just 86 games in the three previous seasons, and they had serious doubts about whether he would be much healthier in the coming year.

If he was, they were more than willing to pay him. Dawkins had undergone back surgery in the off-season, and his contract said if he had recovered sufficiently to play 24 minutes a game he would get $250,000 in addition to his base salary of $300,000. Why 24 minutes? Because that's what he had averaged in his 12-year career.

Dawkins's career season high in rebounds was 696, and if he could better that to 899 he would receive another $500,000. Even if he fell short and got 500 rebounds, it would be worth $150,000.

It was a two-year contract, and if Dawkins could achieve all the bonus goals, it could be worth $1.4 million to him in the first year. It wasn't worth a dime. The Nets traded Dawkins to Utah in 1987, and he never played a minute in the regular season.

Some athletes like their bonuses to be governed not only by their own accomplishments, but by how they stack up against other players in the league.

Roger Clemens, the 1986 American League Cy Young Award winner, had that in mind when he signed a two-year contract with the Red Sox that paid him a guaranteed $500,000 in 1987 and a guaranteed $1.2 million in 1988.

Not bad, but Clemens wanted to make it better with a contract full of clauses that would do wonders for the Red Sox if he achieved all of his objectives.

If he was named to the American League all-star team in 1987, $150,000 was added to his 1988 base salary. If he was named the MVP in that game, it was worth another $25,000, and if he finished first in the balloting for the Cy Young and MVP honors, it was an extra $150,000 in his pocket.

There were also monetary awards for finishing second, third, fourth, or fifth in the balloting and for being the MVP in the League Championship Series or the World Series.

Players always say it's not the dollar figure in their contracts that they're concerned with, so much as it is how their salary compares to other salaries. They want to be considered among the very best in their business, and their badge is their paycheck.

A look at another individual contract will show you how that can work. Miami's Marino is one of the fortunate few in the NFL who does make guaranteed money. In fact, it's all guaranteed. All $9 million of it for six years.

Marino can add to the total by reaching certain statistical goals. The most important one of those says if he throws for a predetermined number of yards in a season, his contract will be automatically upgraded so that he will always be among the three highest paid quarterbacks in the league.

That healthy spirit of competition among players can get expensive for owners in another way. When a player signs a rich new contract, his teammates always know the numbers. And if they think they're worth just as much or more, they're sure to let the boss in on that fact.

Some incentive clauses have more to do with what a player accomplishes off the field than on. Several players in all three sports have been able to add to their income through the simple athletic maneuver of pushing themselves away from the dinner table. They take the term "fat contract" quite seriously.

If they come into camp at a certain weight and maintain it through the season, it's worth money to them. William Perry would have been even richer if he could have trimmed himself down from Refrigerator size to a more modest appliance. How about Air Conditioner Perry?

One last kind of incentive clause that used to be popular, but has lost favor lately, rewarded a player for attracting a crowd. It's called an attendance clause. The athlete who has one of these gets a certain amount for each ticket sold after a predetermined attendance level is met.

No one really knows exactly which players the fans are coming to see, but you can make some pretty good guesses. Reggie Jackson used to have an attendance clause, and there isn't much doubt that Mr. October packed 'em in.

No-Trade Clauses. Self-explanatory. Some guys are just homebodies. They find a city they like, and they don't want to be calling the movers all the time. Maybe they have endorsement deals. Maybe they have kids, and they like the schools.

If they negotiate a no-trade clause, they can't be traded without their permission. Or they can only be traded to certain designated teams.

It's nice to think that professional athletes have some loyalty to their cities, even if teams have no particular loyalty to their athletes. Cynics will say, however, that these clauses can be and have been negotiable. Players waive them for cash at times.

Baseball is the only sport that has no-trade clauses built into its CBA. A player with 10 years in the league and 5 with the same club can veto a trade.

Miscellaneous and Oddball Clauses. This is a totally unscientific and in no way official title for a variety of provisions that pop up in contracts, thanks to imaginative general managers, agents, and promoters.

One you have to like belongs to Jordan. It's been labeled a "love of the game" clause, and it states that Jordan can play basketball any time he wants anyplace he wants. If he gets hurt playing the game during the off-season, he still has to be paid.

Another heart-warmer is found in Dave Winfield's deal with Yankees owner, George Steinbrenner. Steinbrenner is required to make certain payments to Winfield's charitable organization, the Dave Winfield Foundation. Winfield has sued Steinbrenner claiming he isn't keeping up with his charitable payments. You gotta love the Yankees.

The Philadelphia Phillies turned the tables and insisted on an incentive clause from a player. They said they wouldn't sign free agent catcher Lance Parrish unless he promised not to sue them. Parrish was considering a suit claiming that collusion among the owners had cut his earning power. The Phils didn't want to take any chances.

The Los Angeles Forum is not exactly "the house that Kareem built," but it is the one he uses. Kareem Abdul-Jabbar's contract has a provision that says he can use the Lakers' home building once a year for free.

Call this one a "fear of flying clause." Dan Mayer's deal with the Oakland A's promised he never had to stay in a hotel room above the fifth floor.

Cars are big in athletes' contracts. Gus Williams, for instance, signed a five-year pact with Seattle that guaranteed him a $172,000 white Rolls Royce. That was pretty selfish when you compare it to the request the Milwaukee Brewers got from a hot prospect from Puerto Rico.

Ramser Correa, a 16-year-old pitcher, reportedly issued a list of seven demands that included a 1987 black Corvette for himself and a Cutlass Supreme for his father. He also wanted four airplane tickets a year for five years so his family could see him play.

Coaches' Contracts.   Signing a top-flight coach isn't nearly as hard as signing a top-flight player. But keeping him is.

Colleges really worry about this, because some college coaches change jobs as often as they change defenses. Their schools and booster organizations try to make the successful ones happy with incentives like camps, broadcasting deals, and rolling horizon contracts.

No, a rolling horizon is not what a coach experiences the morning after he's celebrated a big victory. It's an arrangement whereby he gets a three- or maybe a four-year deal that automatically renews itself at the end of every season. So the coach is always on a three-year contract.

Even with deals like that, college coaches pick up and move. Pro coaches, on the other hand, usually wait until they get fired before they change jobs. Teams are fussy about that kind of thing, and if one club starts negotiating with another club's coach, it's wide open to a charge of tampering.

One of the most celebrated cases of two teams squabbling over a coach involved the Milwaukee Bucks and the Golden State Warriors in 1988.

Don Nelson, a two-time NBA Coach of the Year, was both the head coach and the director of player personnel for the Bucks when he and Bucks owner Herb Kohl experienced some major differences of opinion.

The differences were so major in fact that Nelson declared that he simply couldn't work for Kohl anymore, even though his contract was still in force.

Kohl said Nelson could leave, but he couldn't work for anybody else in the league as a coach or player personnel director.

The owner had Nelson's contract on his side. It included a restrictive covenant that said for a period of two years Nelson could not "accept employment as, become employed in the capacity of, or in any other way, directly or indirectly, carry out the duties of a coach or director of player personnel for any team operating as a member of the National Basketball Association."

Kohl wouldn't waive that clause for any other NBA team unless the Bucks got a player and/or a draft choice. Nelson took the contract to mean that he couldn't coach, but he could serve as a general manager for another NBA club.

A number of teams expressed a lively interest in Nelson as a coach, and some would have been happy to have him as a general manager. Eventually he landed with Golden State as a part owner and executive vice president, and the Warriors compensated the Bucks with a No. 2 draft choice. But first Nelson had to apologize to Kohl. He later became the Warriors' coach.

See, some contracts are binding.

None of that would have transpired if Nelson had been a player instead of a coach. Then he couldn't have even considered moving, no matter how mad he was at his boss. Then he would have been governed by a CBA.

Collective Bargaining Agreements

Remember, these are the contracts that apply to everybody in a particular sport. They're the ones that the unions negotiate with representatives of the league, not the ones that agents negotiate with representatives of the clubs. And when you look around one day and notice that the players are all carrying picket signs, these are usually at the root of the trouble.

The average sports fan figures young men with six- and seven-figure salaries need CBAs about as much as movie stars' cats need $10-million inheritances. That's one reason why the rank and file in ordinary unions sometimes have trouble thinking of striking players as their brothers in the great labor movement.

Another reason is they don't see many running backs carrying signs in picket lines outside of shut down breweries or meat-packing plants.

The NFL Players' Association (NFLPA) did at one time try to turn itself into a real union when it toyed with the notion of setting a wage scale for every position throughout the league. The proposal met with as much enthusiasm as a 10-yard punt. Ironically, now the owners seem to be thinking about resurrecting the idea of a wage scale for rookie players.

The NFLPA's idea was to have the league set aside a certain percentage of its gross revenues for salaries and then pay second-year quarterbacks X, third-year quarterbacks Y, first year running backs Z, and so on. The union reasoned that the superstars would always be highly paid, but the league's profits rarely trickled down to the journeymen tackles and punt returners.

You remember the great "percentage-of-gross" debate. You remember the Edsel, too. It was marketed just about as effectively and met with the same fate. The owners stomped it right into the turf.

Ironically, the owners went into the next season paying the players a bigger percentage of the take than the union had ever asked for. Ed Garvey, head of the NFLPA at the time, said the numbers came out to something like 58%, compared to the 55% the players wanted.

The NBA later adopted the percentage-of-gross idea, but not the pay scale. The NBA signed a new collective bargaining agreement with its union in April of 1988, keeping intact its record as the only one of the nation's top three pro sports not to insult its customers with a strike.

Basketball owners figure that's why they have the fastest growing team sport in the United States, and they're willing to make sacrifices to keep it that way. So are the players.

Why hasn't that occurred to personnel in the other sports? Excellent question. Perhaps sometime between now and the year 2000, somebody will come up with an answer.

The NBA's deal runs for six years, which is about the greatest commitment to labor peace that fans can ever expect to see in their lifetimes. They don't expect it in the other two sports.

Major-league baseball's deal with its union expires Dec. 1, 1989, and that could spell big trouble. There were dark rumblings about a possible work stoppage at least a year before the contract was up.

The NFL doesn't have a CBA, says the players' union. Yes it does, say the owners.

When the old one lapsed and the players went on strike in 1987, the owners insisted the previous agreement remained in force. The players insisted otherwise, maintaining that they were no longer bound by its provisions. A judge will have to decide who's right.

Collective bargaining agreements are about many things, but the main ones are minimum salaries, pensions, and free agency. A fourth item is very big with football and basketball but not much of an issue with baseball. That's the college draft.

The new NBA agreement did not immediately set minimums, except for first-round draft choices. Those fellows must be offered at least $150,000.

Both players and teams contribute to the league pension fund, which gives a player with 10 years in the league $1,170 a month beginning at age 50.

Major-league baseball's minimum salary is $62,500. Teams contribute $33 million a year to the player pension fund, and that goes up to $39 million in 1989. The players don't contribute anything.

The minimum salary structure in the NFL is more complicated than it is in the other leagues. Life is more complicated in the NFL than it is in the other leagues. As of the summer of 1988, a football rookie had to get at least $50,000, and the minimum went up $10,000 a year for each year he was in the league. But the owners seem awfully partial to a rookie salary scale.

The union and the owners have sued each other over the NFL pension plan, but they sue each other over everything. Under the old agreement, clubs contribute $12.5 million a year and the players contribute nothing. The players claimed the owners were $18 million in arrears on pension payments. A player with 10 years of service would get a maximum of $31,515 at age 62.

Free agency is the area that differs the most among the three sports, and it's the one that causes the most labor trouble. It's impossible to separate it from the leagues' salary structures, because it's been proven that when players are allowed to move from team to team they make more money.

The same would be true if players were allowed to choose their employer when they left college, and that's why the draft is so important in football and basketball. The draft doesn't count nearly as much in baseball where players are developed through a minor-league system, rather than through the nation's colleges.

To get a look at how player movement polices affect the three sports, it's best to take them one at a time. The NBA is a good place to start because it's the one league that knows how to negotiate this crucial item without driving itself to the brink of periodic hari-kari.

If everyone approached player movement the way the NBA and the National Basketball Association Players' Association (NBAPA) does, there might not ever be a sports strike.

Probably the most creative CBA ever reached is the one the NBA signed in 1983. It was just replaced by the 1987 agreement, but some of the most distinctive features have been retained.

The NBA lost a record $16 million in 1983. When the league opened its books, even the union had to admit that at least 10 clubs were drowning in red ink. Four appeared to be on the verge of either folding or being merged with other franchises.

No wonder. Player and coaching salaries plus insurance and pension costs were adding up to almost $300,000 more per year per team than gate receipts. Only four or five teams were believed to be making a profit.

Five teams couldn't very well provide the 276 jobs that the NBA had to offer in 1983. When players are worried about the prospect of using the college degree that most of them never got in the first place, it's a pretty good starting point for negotiations.

It certainly was in the NBA, and it gave birth to a remarkable little gadget called a salary cap.

The players agreed to place a cap on the amount of money that any team could pay in salaries. In return for that, they were guaranteed that payrolls could never fall below a certain percentage of the league's gross revenues. In this case, it was 53%.

That might not seem like a very good idea for the players when 18 clubs weren't making money anyway. But their union guessed correctly that the concession would help the league turn things around. The name of the game was to protect the owners from their natural enemies—each other.

Certain owners were distorting the talent market by paying marginal players much more than they were worth. Nobody objected to the idea of paying superstars as if they were matinee idols. Those were the fellows selling the tickets after all. But a few teams were turning journeymen into millionaires, and that's when the league screamed for help.

The players came to their rescue, but they had a price. Along with the salary cap came a salary floor that was also computed as a percentage of the gross revenue.

Naturally there were some gaps in the contract and some teams that were drawn to them like a tongue to a toothache.

For instance, five clubs were already paying players more than the amount specified in the cap, and they were allowed to continue doing so. The union wasn't about to negotiate salary cuts for its members.

The owners also found a free agent loophole that put many teams way over the cap. Despite all that, almost every club was in the black by 1987, and the salary cap jumped 25% to $6,164,000 per team while average salaries were settling around the $500,000 mark. In 1988 the cap went up another 17% to $7.23 million.

It was about as cozy an arrangement as could be expected in pro sports, but the players had some major changes in mind by the time it lapsed in 1987.

They knew the owners thought they needed the cap to survive, and they wanted to make them pay for it by loosening up on free agent movement and changing the college draft.

Under the old CBA, clubs had the right to match any offer another team might make for one of their free agent players. That's called the right of first refusal, and it put a huge block in the road of any player hoping to change teams after his contract ran out.

Let's say the Boston Celtics had a player whose contract expired, and the Philadelphia 76ers wanted to sign him. The Celtics would immediately let the 76ers know that they would match any offer the Sixers extended for the player. Philly would figure why bother even making an offer? It happened like that all the time.

The NBAPA went to court to change that, claiming the league was violating antitrust law. It challenged the draft and the salary cap at the same time, and we'll never know if the union would have won its case. It accepted a most generous settlement instead and dropped the suit.

The new NBA agreement of 1987 keeps the salary cap in place, with a 53% minimum, but it also guarantees that salaries will reach $11 million a team by the 1992-93 season. That means the *average* salary in the league will be $900,000.

It also limits the college draft to three rounds in the first year of the contract and two after that.

And most important, it makes players with seven years in the league total free agents when their contracts run out. No right of first refusal. In the second year, five-year veterans will be totally free, and then four-year men the season after that.

To make this thing work, the NBA will have to double its revenues by the end of the six-year deal, which is precisely what it is planning to do through TV payments and your ticket money.

Now on to the NFL.

NFL players had all the same problems in 1987 that NBA players did, and they were being paid less than half as much. If anything, their free agent woes were worse.

Not only did clubs have right of first refusal on veterans who played out their contracts, but they were also entitled to compensation in the form of draft choices if one of their players joined another club. That issue never came up, because nobody had changed teams in 10 years.

The draft system was the same in both leagues. If a rookie didn't sign with the team that drafted him, he didn't play at all.

When the NFL collective bargaining agreement expired, the players tried to wipe out these restrictions, and they met with the typical response. The owners wouldn't budge.

So the players struck. Again. And the owners broke the strike. Again.

Only this time, the players followed the NBA example and went to court claiming that the NFL rules on player movement violated federal antitrust laws. This was not a new argument. They had proved that charge in court in 1977, but they allowed the disputed practices to go on for certain concessions. They allowed it again in the 1982 CBA after another strike.

They didn't want to allow it in 1987, and so it was back to the court. While this tiresome exercise was dragging on, the owners were threatening to impose a wage scale on rookies calling for $60,000 to $70,000 maximum salaries and scaling signing bonuses from $500,000 for the No. 1 draft choice to $5,000 for the last guy picked.

As the 1988 season wound down, football didn't seem much closer to a new CBA than it was the previous fall.

OK, now baseball.

Baseball's CBA, which expires at the end of this year, has the most complex system for free agency of all three sports. Any player with six years of service is eligible for free agency when he plays out his contract. His old club is entitled to compensation if it loses him, and the compensation is based on the player's statistics.

Excellent players are Type A free agents. Good ones are Type B, and average ones are Type C. The higher the type, the more compensation.

That's not all. Any player with three years of service who isn't signed for the next season can have his salary determined by an impartial arbitrator. He submits one figure, the club submits another, and the arbitrator picks the one he thinks is most reasonable.

No compromise. One side wins, and one loses. The biggest winner of all was Mattingly in 1987 with his $1.975-million award.

Most players who file for arbitration settle with their teams before they ever get in front of an arbitrator. The majority of the cases that do get to arbitration are won by the owners. That was true in nine of the first 13 years the system was in operation, including seven in a row as of 1988.

The owners are not impressed by those statistics. They say even when they win, they lose. To illustrate their point, they cite 1988 when 108 players filed for arbitration.

Ninety-three of those settled and received an average raise of 65%. Even the players who did go to arbitration and lost their cases averaged more than $200,000 in raises.

As much as the owners dislike the arbitration system, the players hate the compensation system even more. They have felt that way since 1985 when teams' interest in veteran free agent players dived like a Bert Blyleven curve ball.

From 1985 to 1987, no free agent got an offer from a new team unless his old team declared it wasn't interested in him anymore. Coincidentally, major-league salaries took a discernible dip.

The players saw that as more than a coincidence. They called it collusion, and they filed a grievance with an arbitrator on behalf of the players who became free agents in 1985 and couldn't seem to get any offers.

Then they filed another one on behalf of the free agents in 1986. And another one for 1987.

They won the 1985 case, and six players became instant free agents, increasing their bargaining leverage substantially. In August of 1988, the union won again in *Collusion II*, and it was favored to make it a sweep in *Collusion III*.

Still to be determined as the 1988 season ended was the amount of damages the owners would be penalized for conspiring to freeze free agency. The union reportedly was asking up to $90 million.

Barry Rona, the owners' chief negotiator, thought $90 million would be too much. On the day the union filed its third collusion grievance he told reporters, ''The irony is that the same day every newspaper is carrying headlines that we are setting records with respect to player salary numbers, the association decides it's appropriate to once again claim that the clubs are engaged in price fixing.

''The charge is ludicrous. Unfortunately, this union will never stop filing charges and will never be satisfied unless everyone has a five-year guaranteed, multimillion-dollar contract.''

The day that happens is still a long way off. But it's quite a bit closer than Lou Gehrig ever would have thought.

Chapter

 2

Judgment Calls

Sports in the courts: The jury is always out

How does the old joke go? "Congratulations, you have just won an all-expense paid, one-week vacation to the Arctic Circle. Second prize is two weeks."

In the summer of 1986, the late and mostly unlamented United States Football League won third prize.

"Congratulations," said a New York jury of five women and one man whose sense of justice was exceeded only by their sense of humor. "You have proved the National Football League is a bunch of grinches who have monopolized pro football in this country.

"Nice going. Here's a buck."

Well, three bucks actually. When you win an antitrust case in this country, everything counts three times. So it took just 42 days of arguments and testimony and millions of dollars in attorneys' fees for the USFL to demonstrate what everybody's known all along. When it comes to pro football, the NFL really is the only game in town.

Judging from the results of *United States Football League v. National Football League*, that won't change anytime soon.

When the USFL owners filed a federal suit against the NFL on October 17, 1984, they weren't just trying to attract attention, something their teams were never able to do. They weren't just trying to prove a point either. They were trying to make the law of the land accomplish what the law of supply and demand couldn't. Namely, to keep their league alive.

So they asked the court to award them the modest sum of $440 million, multiplied by three, which comes out to something that has nine zeroes in it and could sustain a pro horseshoe league, let alone a pretend football league, well into the 21st century. Not only that, but they wanted the court to tell Pete Rozelle's NFL bullies to behave themselves.

The USFL accused the NFL of interfering with the younger league's chances of getting a network TV deal, increasing its rosters so the younger league wouldn't have any good players, tampering with USFL players already under contract, hogging all the referees, hogging all the coaches, insulting the USFL in public, and not letting USFL teams use any of the big stadiums in the country.

Now does that sound like the NFL? Sure it does. And maybe the league would have had to stop all that if the jury had given the USFL enough money to keep it going. Instead, it decided that all the NFL was guilty of was monopolizing football, and that was worth three bucks—which barely equaled the gate receipts at an Arizona Outlaws game.

So when USFL reality fell $1,319,999,997 short of expectations, the league disappeared like a quarterback under a four-man blitz. Of course the case was appealed. But in January of 1988 a panel of three federal judges reached the same conclusions that the jury did. They said the USFL "sought through court decree what it failed to achieve among football fans."

Even if they had won the appeal, the USFL owners knew it wouldn't revive the USFL. That would be like trying to put Humpty Dumpty back together again, and Humpty had more friends and at least as good a sense of balance as the USFL.

Still, it's useful to speculate on what would have happened if the USFL had actually won its case, because it speaks volumes about the effects courts have on the finances of big-time sports.

Start with the $1,320,000,000, which naturally the USFL never really expected to get. It might have walked away with $300 million, though. Or even $900 million.

One juror said afterward that she was pushing for $1 million in damages but would have considered as much as $300 million. Another said she was holding out for $300 million, times three.

Divide even the $300-million figure by 28 teams, and every club in the NFL winds up showing a loss for 1987. That could be absorbed a number of ways, none of which would have made season tickets cheaper.

Much more important is the effect a true USFL victory would have had on future seasons.

A high-stakes bidding war for college talent was touched off when the USFL decided it couldn't survive as a polite little summer diversion for fans who needed an excuse not to cut the lawn. Agents thought the USFL's switch from summer to fall was the greatest invention since the holdout, and player salaries in both leagues zoomed.

They would have just kept zooming if six folks hadn't buried the USFL with three token bucks.

You can bet sports advertisers were watching this whole imbroglio very closely. All this complaining about tampering with players, coaches, refs, and stadiums may have been heartfelt, but the guts of the case was television.

The USFL was planning to put together a national deal with ABC that might have given it the credibility and exposure it needed to keep bobbing along. But then ABC seemed to develop cold feet, and the USFL thought the NFL had a little something to do with that—something like a multimillion contract with all three networks.

In effect, the USFL said the NFL was telling the networks, "It's us or them." It was "us" of course. That's simple arithmetic. But if the USFL had won, it could have had some intriguing implications for the costs and placement of commercials.

Finally, there is a lingering suspicion among some NFL owners that the great minds who gave birth to the USFL didn't really want to run their own league in the first place. What they wanted was to obtain franchises in the NFL.

These are cynical people with efficient memories. They are quite capable of recalling the days of the American Football League, or the American Basketball Association for that matter.

At the time of the USFL's inception in 1983, NFL franchises were both expensive and unavailable. A new league could provide a shortcut to membership. Even a bargain. If the New York jury hadn't short-circuited that strategy, there's no telling how many leagues and how many "pro" teams might be polluting our airwaves before long.

One USFL owner who did appear to be on his way to admission into the NFL brotherhood was Donald Trump, who dumped a few million dollars into the USFL New Jersey Generals.

Shortly after the USFL settled to the bottom of the swamp, Trump demonstrated an interest in the debt-ridden New England Patriots, who were burning a wide hole into the pockets of their owners, the Sullivan family. Apparently Trump later decided the Patriots were only slightly more promising than the Generals, although he said he was willing to help the Sullivans sell the team to somebody else.

A few weeks later, he wasn't even willing to do that. It occurred to Trump that the reason the NFL establishment was encouraging his involvement with the Pats was that the USFL suit was still on appeal. Trump was a leading force behind the suit, and he thought he was being set up by the NFL.

Had Trump bought the Patriots, he would have been an NFL owner, a USFL casualty, and both a plaintiff and a defendant in the same case.

The idea of somebody suing himself is no more ridiculous than a lot of things that have gone on in sports litigation for the last six decades or so. When the claims involve games, logic often runs a post pattern, disappears into the parking lot, and never returns to the huddle.

The sports cases that have made the biggest difference in dollars and cents involve movement, and there are two kinds of those. The first kind involves players trying to move from one team to another, and the second involves teams trying to move from one city to another.

It's the player movement cases that have either settled or created the fusses that crop up in CBAs. They have the most to do with salaries and ultimately ticket prices, so we'll start there.

That means we go immediately to the famous *Federal Baseball Club of Baltimore, Inc. v. National League of Professional Baseball Clubs* case of 1922. You say you never heard of it? Sure you have. You just didn't know what it was called.

It's the one that says baseball isn't a business.

Here is where professional sports first stepped gingerly onto the thin ice of the Sherman and Clayton Antitrust Acts. Those little legislative items are at the bottom of the most important legal struggles in all of athletics.

At this point, we could provide you with a detailed history and analysis of the Sherman and Clayton Antitrust Acts, which is only slightly less exciting than watching the seventh round of the NFL draft. Or we could tell you really quickly what they mean for our purposes.

The Sherman Antitrust Act is a federal law that says it's illegal to restrain free trade or commerce. If you monopolize an area of trade or even try to, you're guilty of a misdemeanor. The Clayton Act says if you get caught violating the Sherman Act, you're liable for triple damages.

If sports is commerce, then organizations that try to monopolize a sport or restrain the people in it are guilty of antitrust violations. They can't do it legally, unless . . . And this is where the arguments start. The unlesses.

In the case of sports and antitrust, there are two.

First, you can't ignore antitrust law in sports *unless* Congress or the courts have specifically exempted you from it.

Second, you can't ignore antitrust law in sports *unless* you sign a labor contract that says it's OK to ignore it. In other words, the law gives players certain rights, but their unions can waive those rights. When the union does that, it's called a labor exemption.

It would be pretty stupid to give your boss a labor exemption, wouldn't it? But it happens all the time in pro sports.

The Federal Baseball Club of Baltimore case set baseball apart from all other pro sports, a status it maintains to this day for no logical reason on God's green earth.

The Federal League was formed in 1913 to compete with the established National and American Leagues, and it wasn't any better at it than the USFL was at battling the NFL. It tried to raid AL and NL rosters for players, and it did get some. The trouble was, once a player jumped leagues, he could never jump back. He was blacklisted.

Eventually, the Federal League owners gave up and dissolved their teams. Actually, they were paid off to get out of the American and National League owners' hair. But the Baltimore franchise in the Federal League wouldn't take the payoff, and it sued under the antitrust statutes.

It won the case in trial court, lost it on appeal, and then lost in the Supreme Court, which was the last stop.

It lost because the Supreme Court justices ruled that baseball wasn't interstate commerce. Granted, teams moved from state to state to play each other, but that was merely a by-product of baseball's main purpose, which was to put on games. And if it's not commerce, it's not covered by federal antitrust laws.

There it is: Baseball is a sport, not a business. That's what the justices said in 1913, and nobody has changed their ruling.

The courts are still saying it at a time when some teams gross more in TV revenue than their owners paid to buy them in the first place.

Congress could change all of that if it decided to pass legislation ending baseball's antitrust exemption. It even threatens to do that every once in awhile, which is one reason why the major leagues are always talking about putting a franchise back in Washington. They want to keep the members of Congress settled down.

Congress's general attitude is that the Supreme Court has made this mess, and it's up to the courts to clean it up. The Supreme Court has taken the position that the exemption must be okay, because Congress hasn't done anything to remove it. Catch 22? You ain't heard nothin' yet.

Remember Curt Flood? Good outfielder for the Cardinals? The Cards traded him after the '69 season to the Philadelphia Phillies, but Flood didn't want to go to Philly.

So he sued, challenging the reserve clause in his contract. That's the clause that says a player must stay with his team or go wherever he's traded.

Flood's lawyers mounted a triple-barreled attack. They said his contract was illegal because

1. It represented involuntary servitude. Right, slavery.

2. It violated federal antitrust law.

3. It violated state antitrust laws.

He lost on all three counts.

The court said he wasn't a slave, because he could quit baseball anytime and work at something else. That sounds fair. Nothing else does.

The court went on to say that Flood's contract didn't violate federal antitrust law because baseball was exempt from the Sherman Act. Remember, the exemption was based on the theory that baseball wasn't interstate commerce. Then it said Flood's contract didn't violate state antitrust laws because baseball *was* interstate commerce, so state laws didn't apply.

In other words, Flood couldn't win because baseball wasn't interstate commerce, and he couldn't win because it was interstate commerce. The U.S. Supreme Court affirmed the lower court decision, even though it acknowledged that the other major sports were subject to antitrust. Baseball was just . . . well, different.

The Supreme Court calls that an "anomaly," and the practical result was that baseball players could work for only one team. They could either take the money they were offered or not play at all.

So why didn't a player just serve out his contract and then make a deal with another club? The owners thought of that, too.

There was an option clause in everyone's contract that said the clubs could renew each contract for a period of one year after its term expired. And when that year was up, it could renew for another year. And then another year. And so on until the team decided it didn't want the player anymore.

This might have gone on forever if a couple of pitchers named Andy Messersmith and Dave McNally hadn't come along and filed a grievance with a federal arbitrator when their contracts expired in 1975.

Arbitration was a process created by the CBA between the players and the owners. If the owners had that one to do over again, you can be absolutely sure that they would uninvent arbitrators.

The one in the Messersmith case was named Peter Seitz. He blew baseball's reserve system right off the face of the earth, saying option clauses were effective only for one year after a player's contract was up. No more perpetual renewals. The owners went to court to get the decision overturned, but this time even the judge wasn't buying what they were selling. Seitz was upheld.

For the first time in the history of the Grand Old Game, there was free agency, and if you didn't believe it, all you had to do was watch the salaries multiply. It wasn't total free agency. It took a lot of different forms, all defined in later CBAs between the league and the union.

That's when owners like the New York Yankees' George Steinbrenner tried to buy a pennant by signing up free agents.

And then in 1985, as if by magic, free agents stopped getting offers. Not from Steinbrenner, not from Gene Autry, not from anybody. A guy would play out his contract, hang a "for sale" sign around his neck, wait for the phone to ring, and nothing would happen. He started to wonder about his deodorant.

That went on for a while before the union went looking for relief from an arbitrator again. This time his name was Thomas Roberts, the man who issued the first of the collusion rulings. And it all sprung from the Messersmith case.

About the same time that Roberts was ruling on collusion in baseball, the football and basketball unions were bringing their owners up on antitrust charges. They, too, had plenty of legal ammunition.

The football players started piling up theirs 55 years after the Supreme Court's curious ruling that baseball wasn't a business.

In 1957 a former University of Southern California football player named William Radovich sued the NFL for blacklisting him. Radovich had played three years for the Detroit Lions before jumping to the Los Angeles Dons of the All-American Football League. When he tried to get back into the NFL, the league said he had violated the reserve clause of his contract and suspended him for five years.

Radovich screamed antitrust, and he eventually got the U.S. Supreme Court to listen to him. It ruled that football was an interstate business, even though baseball wasn't. Huh?

While everybody was still scratching their heads trying to figure that one out, Joe Kapp burst onto the scene in 1974, raising hell and launching the NFL on a lengthy legal losing streak.

Kapp, a talented and well-traveled quarterback, had the audacity to challenge the language in the standard player's contract that the New England Patriots wanted him to sign. The Pats said, "OK, don't sign the contract, but you can't play for us unless you do, and you can't play for anybody else in the league."

Kapp sued. As long as he was in the neighborhood, he thought he'd take a legal whack at the college draft, option rule, tampering rule, and Rozelle Rule at the same time. Cranky Joe didn't like much of anything.

The Rozelle Rule, now relegated to labor's Hall of Shame, was the one that said NFL teams that sign other teams' players after their contracts run out must be compensated with players or draft choices. And if they can't agree on compensation, the commissioner himself decides who gets what.

The courts ruled that Kapp should get to play. Which he did. But it also said he wasn't entitled to any monetary damages.

A year after the Kapp clamor, Los Angeles Rams receiver Ron Jessie came galloping along to give Rozelle and the owners another headache. Jessie played out his contract with the Detroit Lions and signed with the Los Angeles Rams. That made the Lions angry, and they demanded heavy-duty compensation from the Rams.

When LA balked, Rozelle used his powers under the rule bearing his name to transfer the contract of Rams running back Cullen Bryant to the Lions.

Pete never stopped to inquire of Bryant how he felt about that, and if he had, he wouldn't have liked the answer. Poor Bryant was just minding his own business, carrying the ball for the Rams, not threatening to sue anybody or anything, and along comes the commissioner telling him he had to move to Detroit.

Southern Californians have never looked on Michigan as one of the world's great garden spots. Bryant went to court and won.

The judge ruled that draft choices might be treated like property, but people couldn't. And the NFL legal slump went on.

Next the league ran headlong into a Baltimore Colts tight end named John Mackey. That particular judicial collision put the Rozelle Rule right on its back.

Mackey was one of 16 players or former players who sued the league over the restrictions on player movement. Judge Earl Larson said the players were right, and the rule was wrong, and this time the decision cost the league money.

In a separate case filed by Ron Alexander in the same year, NFL owners were smacked with $16 million in damages for their antitrust indiscretions.

That had to be split up among 5,700 players, but in those days it was serious money.

Getting bumped right along with the Rozelle Rule was the college draft, compliments of a wide receiver named James McCoy (Yazoo) Smith, who was picked in the first round in 1968 by the Washington Redskins. Smith suffered a career-ending neck injury in the last game of the '68 season, and the Skins offered him nothing but sympathy.

Yazoo figured if the draft hadn't cut his signing options to one team, he could have negotiated a guaranteed contract with somebody and been paid the next season even though he was hurt. The judge figured the same way and awarded Smith $276,000.

"Yahoo, Yazoo!" shouted the NFLPA, which couldn't have been sitting prettier if somebody had given it the keys to all of the owners' vaults. In a matter of a couple of years, a covey of courts had ruled that the league's policies on tampering, standard contracts, options, free agency, and the college draft were all wrong.

The players had won everything worth winning. And how did they celebrate? By giving most of it back.

This is where the second "unless" comes in—the one that says a players' union can bargain away legal rights—the "labor exemption" thing.

In return for certain financial benefits, like increased pension payments, the players association signed a new CBA in 1977 that allowed restrictions on player movement. They were different restrictions, but restrictions nevertheless. And the union let the college draft stand.

The draft was cut to 12 rounds, but a player still had to go to the team that drafted him unless he wanted to sit out a year and get drafted again. It took two years of sitting out to make him a free agent. Two years away from the game also made him out of shape and old news.

As for free agents, only rookies had to have one-year option clauses in their contracts. Veterans could become free agents by playing out their original deals. But if they did, their teams had a right to match any contract offer they might get. And if the team didn't match and lost a player, it had to be compensated with draft choices.

The result of all that was to make NFL free agents about as mobile as waterbeds. Nobody changed teams.

Once the NFLPA figured out how badly it had been conned, its response was to keep striking all the time. And to keep losing. Finally in 1987 after getting totally shellacked in another strike, it went back to court to try to retrieve all the legal rights it had kicked away 10 years ago.

And that is how *Powell v. the National Football League* was born in Minneapolis. In addition to challenging all of the league's player restraints, the union used the suit to accuse the owners of all manner of unfair labor practices.

It said that they tried to bribe veteran players to cross the picket lines, that they threatened to trade union officials, and that their bonuses and strike option contracts for strikebreakers were illegal.

The union was hoping it could speed the judicial process by getting an injunction that would award immediate free agency to more than 300 players before the 1988 season. But that didn't happen.

Instead, Federal Judge David Doty rendered a most peculiar decision in July. He said the players would probably win the court case eventually, but that they should go back to the bargaining table anyway. In the meantime, no free agency.

In other words, the union would win if it could survive that long. Stay tuned.

Meanwhile in another court in New Jersey, pro basketball was having basically the same debate as football over the draft, player movement, and one totally separate issue—the salary cap. This one was entitled *Junior Bridgeman v. NBA*.

The basketball players filed their suit a few months before the football players, which is totally in keeping with the history of the two organizations. The NBA union has been about 50 yards ahead of its gridiron brethren in almost all areas at all times.

The cagers introduced a dramatic new wrinkle to an old argument. They began the process of dissolving their union. Poof! Now you see it, now you don't. No union.

Even the owners had to admit it was a pretty slick maneuver. The union people were saying, "Yes, we have let the owners get by with certain antitrust practices under the collective bargaining agreement. We gave them a labor exemption, but they don't have it anymore. Not only is the collective bargaining agreement up, but there is no bargaining unit for the players. How could we agree to these antitrust practices? We don't even exist."

Before the union actually broke up, a new CBA was signed.

Over the years, the NBA owners haven't spent quite as much time in court as their colleagues in the NFL, but they have covered most of the same ground. With one very prominent exception—the Spencer Haywood case.

Have you ever wondered why the top basketball players often leave the college game to go pro before they have used up their four years of eligibility, whereas football players rarely do? It's because of Spencer Haywood.

Haywood was a University of Detroit player who just about won the Olympic gold medal for the United States by himself in 1968. That was nice, but it didn't pay the rent. Haywood wanted to start making money at his game. But the NBA had a rule that said a college player couldn't go pro until his class graduated.

The rule didn't say the player himself had to graduate, only that he had to stay out of the pros until his class did. It was a four-year restriction that every team in the league observed, and Haywood's lawyers argued that it was against the law.

A federal court in Denver where Haywood was trying to get a job with the Nuggets agreed, calling the NBA's policy an illegal boycott under antitrust laws. The NBA had to let him play.

The league's failure to appeal the verdict did nothing for the cozy relationship pro hoops had always enjoyed with college hoops. For a while, the NBA said the underclassmen had to show "hardship" before they could be drafted, but everybody knew that was a sham. For some players, a four-hour physics class is a hardship.

The NFL has a four-year rule of its own, but Rozelle has already told the football owners that they had better start thinking about getting rid of it. It might not stand up in court.

Pro basketball's answer to football's Mackey case was the celebrated Robertson decision of 1975. It took five years of grinding for the courts to spew that one out, but when they did, it was a bombshell.

Oscar Robertson, the Hall of Fame guard for Cincinnati and Milwaukee, headed a group of players who sued to stop the NBA from merging with the American Basketball Association in 1970. Good move. There's kind of a separate law of gravity in sports that says when competing leagues dissolve, salaries settle back down to earth.

Not content just to meddle in the merger, Robertson also went after the NBA's college draft, option clause, and compensation rule for free agents and then sat around and waited while the American legal system went into its customary four-corners delay game. Finally Judge Robert L. Carter issued a preliminary ruling that took a dim view of all the disputed labor practices.

It wasn't a final decision, but it did result in a $4.3-million settlement for the players and some explosive ammunition for the 1976 collective bargaining sessions.

Coming out of those was an end to the clubs' right to renew players' contracts automatically and an end to compensation for teams who lose free agents.

Still standing after the '76 CBA was the college draft. The only change was that when a team drafted a player, he was tied to the club for only one year. If he sat out a year, he could go back into the draft. It remained for Leon Wood, a guard from California-Fullerton, to try to get rid of the draft completely.

The Philadelphia 76ers drafted Wood in 1982, but they didn't have any luck in signing him. So Wood sued, claiming he should be able to negotiate with any team in the league. This time the owners won.

A federal court dismissed the case, and an appeals court said as long as the draft was in the agreement, the owners had a labor exemption.

The latest NBA agreement will limit the draft to two rounds in a couple of years while freeing up player movement even more. It hardly leaves the union and the owners anything to argue about. But with six years to go before new bargaining sessions, you can bet they'll think of something.

The irony of these player movement legal wars is that they always pit owners against the Sherman and Clayton Antitrust Acts. But when owners decide to do a little moving of their own by taking the whole team to greener pastures, they take an entirely different view of the Sherman and Clayton Antitrust Acts. Then the law is on their side.

Time to see how the courts have looked at the other kind of movement in sports, teams going from city to city. This game is often played with your money, too. Tax money.

The messiest example of all comes to us compliments of vagabond owner Al Davis of the Oakland/Los Angeles/Irwindale/Lord-knows-who's-next Raiders and his former friends and frequent enemies, the Los Angeles Coliseum Commission.

In 1978, Los Angeles Rams owner Carroll Rosenbloom decided that his team was making good money in LA but it could make even better money by moving to nearby Anaheim.

The officials of the LA Coliseum were aghast, because they no longer had a major tenant. When you have been grievously wronged, there's only one thing to do. Go rip off somebody else's team.

When Rozelle told the Coliseum people they couldn't have an expansion franchise, they started looking around for a team to lure from another city. There was a problem.

The NFL had a rule in its constitution that said all 28 owners had to approve any move that put a team within 75 miles of an existing team. This is Rule 4.3, and it's made life miserable for NFL nomads.

Anaheim was less than 75 miles from Los Angeles, and Rosenbloom could have blocked a new team in LA. So the Coliseum sued, saying Rule 4.3 was a violation of federal antitrust law. The court told the Coliseum lawyers that they might be right, but they didn't have anybody moving into their place anyway. So go away.

The case worried the NFL owners enough that they changed Rule 4.3 to say that only three quarters of their membership had to approve a move into an existing team's territory. Not a bad idea, but too little, too late. Enter Al Davis.

His Raiders were playing to enthusiastic crowds in Oakland, but like Rosenbloom, he wanted more. Besides, the Oakland Coliseum where the Raiders played was looking a little run-down, and he was demanding some expensive repairs. When the city balked, Davis looked south.

The LA Coliseum people were delighted to talk with Davis about moving his club to their place. And just to make sure everything was ready, they hauled the NFL back into court over Rule 4.3.

They wanted an injunction to stop the league from preventing the Raiders' move. The federal court said yes, but the appeals court said no. Davis and the LA people kept talking anyway.

They signed an agreement outlining the terms of a Raiders move to Los Angeles. The NFL owners voted 22-0, with six of them sitting this one out, to block the Raiders. Rule 4.3 again. The LA Coliseum in conjunction with Davis went after the rule in court a third time. Three was a charm.

One trial resulted in a hung jury. But on May 7, 1982, another jury decided that the NFL's Rule 4.3 was indeed an antitrust violation, and it couldn't stop the Raiders from folding their tents and going to Los Angeles. A year later, still another jury decided how much it should cost the league for trying.

It awarded damages of $11.5 million to the Raiders and $4.86 million to the Los Angeles Coliseum. Not too bad, you say. But you're forgetting that everything gets tripled in antitrust.

Add the legal fees, and Rule 4.3 becomes one very expensive luxury. Not so expensive, though, that the stubborn NFL owners don't still have it on the books.

While the legal battle was raging in Los Angeles, the good people of Oakland weren't sitting on their hands. They wanted to keep the Raiders as much as Los Angeles wanted to steal them. So they filed a suit of their own using a most intriguing argument.

It's called eminent domain, and you probably know what that's about. Let's say the city where you live wants to build a road, and your house is in the way. All the city fathers have to do is prove the road is a proper public use for the land your house is sitting on. They can condemn your house, pay you a reasonable amount of money for it, and then knock it down and build their road.

You have to take the money and find someplace else to live.

So what's that got to do with a football team? Nothing, as it turns out, but you can't blame the City of Oakland for trying.

It filed a suit in California seeking to legally condemn the Raiders. Everybody in town was doing it every other way. The case went back and forth from trial court to appeal court three times before the city finally lost. It not only had to pay Davis $3.2 million in legal fees, but it was hit with $26 million in damages for delaying the Raiders' move. Oakland wound up paying $4 million of the $26 million.

The truly wonderful upshot of this donnybrook is that Davis has developed still another case of itchy feet, and he's trying to move his club once again. This time it's to suburban Irwindale, California. And of course he's being sued for $50 million for breach of contract by none other than . . .

The Los Angeles Coliseum. It's a great country, isn't it?

Other sports have experienced pitched battles over franchise movement. The most famous case in baseball cropped up when the State of Wisconsin tried to keep the Milwaukee Braves from moving to Atlanta. It filed a state antitrust suit, but that didn't work because the Wisconsin Supreme Court ruled that state laws didn't apply. Baseball is interstate commerce.

Of course, most courts say baseball isn't interstate commerce. We've been through that.

In basketball, the crucial franchise movement case was created by Donald Sterling, who decided to move his San Diego Clippers north to Los Angeles where he ran into NBA territorial restrictions that are similar to the NFL's. Forget 75 miles. LA's newest NBA franchise would be located a cab ride away from LA's other NBA franchise.

Sterling knew the other owners wouldn't be crazy about that, so he did what you did when you wanted a cookie and you were sure your mom would say no. He didn't ask. He just moved.

The NBA owners went directly to court, where a federal judge ruled for Sterling. So the owners went to an appeals court, where they won. There don't seem to be any single elimination tournaments in the sports of the courts. If you don't win the first one, you try again.

Sterling finally put the controversy to rest in the good old American way. He bought his way out. He paid $5.5 million to settle a suit he might very well have won, judging from the Davis example.

That was small change compared to what the Chicago Bulls were ordered to pay a Milwaukee, Wisconsin, developer named Marv Fishman when he took them to court. And Fishman didn't want to move the Bulls anywhere. He just wanted to buy them and keep them where they were.

The case is worth looking at, because it gives us an idea of what can happen to the stakes over the years while the judicial process is ambling along at its normal Sunday afternoon pace.

Fishman was one of the prime movers in landing an NBA expansion franchise in Milwaukee. Eventually he got squeezed out of that organization, but he still had the ownership itch. Chicago looked like a great place to scratch in 1972 because the Bulls were struggling. Fishman offered owner Elmer Rich $3.3 million for his club.

This was Chicago, though, the place where the smoke-filled room was either invented or greatly refined. There were other interests in the Windy City with other ideas for the future of the Bulls. Former owner William Wirtz, his son Arthur, and associate Lester Crown arrived on the scene after Fishman and came up with their own proposal to buy the team.

That shouldn't have bothered Fishman very much because he had a perfectly legal $3.3 million offer on the table. What he didn't have was an arena. The one the Bulls were using was the Chicago Stadium. And the Stadium owners just happened to be the Wirtz people. They refused to let Fishman have a lease.

Since there were no other suitable buildings in Chicago and NBA basketball is an indoor sport, Fishman couldn't buy the Bulls. Wirtz et al. could, and they did. They also got sued.

Fishman filed suit and not just for the $3 million and change he had offered for the club. He wanted $30 million in damages and ownership of the team.

The Chicago Bulls are still looking for their first NBA championship, and they may find it before this case gets settled. Ten years after Fishman made his offer, Federal Judge Stanley Roskowski awarded him $17 million. The figure was based on the Bulls' estimated worth at the time.

Naturally the Bulls appealed. An appellate panel tossed out punitive damages of $4.5 million and ordered a new trial to determine just what Fishman should get. It's not very likely to be the team, but it's almost certain to be a great deal more than $3.2 million.

And so it goes. By the time the courts and Congress decide who owns what, which players can go where, and which franchises can and can't move, all of the teams will be owned by lawyers. They're the only guys making any money off of all of this. They're making money off of a lot of other sports-related stuff, too.

Here's just a sampling of some of the other things sports needs barristers for:

- **Helmets.** In 1979 equipment companies were selling about $24 million worth of football helmets. They were being sued for $146 million. That's why helmets are so expensive now and why hardly anybody makes them anymore.

    The dam broke in 1975 when a Florida high school player filed suit against the Riddell Company after he had taken a blow to the face mask of his Riddell helmet. The player got a $5.3-million judgment when the company was ruled negligent. By 1982 Riddell was facing 30 lawsuits.

- **Fights.** Rudy Tomjanovich says he was just trying to be a peacemaker when a fight erupted on the court between his Houston Rockets team-mates and the Los Angeles Lakers. As he waded into the melee, he took a punch from the Lakers' Kermit Washington that shattered his jaw. Tomjanovich didn't sue Washington, he sued the Lakers.

    He claimed the team had put a dangerous instrumentality on the floor, namely Washington. The jury agreed, awarding $3 million to Tomjano-vich. The award was cut a little, but the Lakers paid rather than fighting it any further.

- **Numbers.** Everybody in Oklahoma and a few other people across the country who watch television know that Brian Bosworth wore Number 44 for the Sooners. He wanted to go right on wearing it, too, when he signed with the Seattle Seahawks. The NFL has a rule, however, that says line-backers can only wear numbers between 50 and 99.

    You ask, what difference does it make? Quite a bit to the Boz. He's started a company called "44-Boz" to market sunglasses and sports clothes, and that wouldn't make any sense if he were wearing another number. He's suing.

The Seahawks took a more measured approach to the problem. They asked the league to change the number rule.

- **Bats.** Cory Snyder, now of the Cleveland Indians, was in a slump that summer day in 1986 when he threw a bat into the stands in Rochester, New York. Snyder was playing for the minor-league Maine Guides at the time. Out of frustration, he said, he tossed the offending club toward the backstop, but it stuck to the pine tar on his hands and landed in the area where Dorothy Matteson, 61, was seated along with her granddaughter, Deborah Schirtz, 26.

  Matteson suffered a split lip and a broken dental plate, and Schirtz's nose was broken. They sued for $2.3 million, naming as defendants the Maine Guides, the Cleveland Indians, and Snyder, who was also charged with two counts of third-degree assault.

  The criminal charges were later dropped, and the civil suit was settled for an undisclosed amount of money.

- **In their cups.** Donald Bauer, a youth hockey coach from Hamburg, New York, was only trying to raise funds for the kids while working in a concession stand at a Buffalo Bills game. But somebody spotted him using dirty cups.

  According to his attorney, Bauer told a 16-year-old worker to clean out some of the hot chocolate cups that were left around the stand so they could be used by the workers. But a couple of them got put out front and used by the public.

  Bauer was charged with a misdemeanor under the state's public health law. His lawyer charged that the Bills were really just using him to help break their contract with the food service company. The team denied that. The important thing is the charges against Bauer were thrown out.

- **Heart attacks.** Some of his colleagues in the NFL may have suggested that Al Davis is a pain in an unmentionable area of the anatomy, but it remained for Gene Klein to go to the heart of the matter.

  The former owner of the San Diego Chargers was a defendant in Davis's antitrust suit aimed at moving the Raiders from Oakland to Los Angeles. During the proceedings, Klein suffered a heart attack, and he filed a countersuit, charging harassment by Davis.

  The jury awarded Klein $10 million, an amount that was later reduced to $5 million, plus $48,000 in medical expenses. Further review pared the award to $2 million.

So the Raiders' owner didn't get everything he wanted in the move to Los Angeles after all. Hardly anybody does when sport goes to court. But as long as there are attorneys for hire and gigantic amounts of money at stake, you can rest assured that the game plan won't change.

When in doubt, somebody's going to tell it to the judge.

Chapter

3

Let's Get Organized

Strikes, lockouts, union suits, and other unmentionables

The sky was falling on one of the more misguided work stoppages in the history of the American labor movement on this October day in 1987, and Ricky Hunley was surveying the damage. Two of Hunley's teammates had just made up their minds to cross the NFLPA picket line in Denver, a decision that both surprised and saddened the Broncos' player representative.

"The guys who are going in don't know what they're doing," said Hunley. "They're giving up any voice they ever had to effect changes in this industry. You can't put a price on that."

Sure you can. Especially if you own a football team.

The NFL owners had to figure it was worth at least $150 million to maintain the status quo, because that's the conservative estimate of what they parted with while quelling a 57-day mutiny in 1982. Some observers put the figure as high as $210 million.

The players wound up several million dollars poorer themselves in '82, although they recouped much of their loss through a $60-million one-time bonus. What they didn't get was a single inch of control, which is what the scrap was about in the first place.

Now here it was five years later, and another union attempt to storm the bridge was winding down with predictable results. The decision of Hunley's teammates would be duplicated by dozens of players before the whole strike heaved a big sigh and just collapsed.

If anything, the owners crushed this one at bargain rates.

Their costs were around $104 million, which, when you factor in inflation, amounted to a clearance sale compared to the unpleasantness of five years earlier. What's more, this strike would last only 24 days, just long enough to establish some important economic axioms in sports labor relations:

1. It's easier to conduct a kindergarten class in a candy factory than it is to keep 1,600 professional athletes focused on issues that three-quarters of them never understood in the first place. Given the choice of carrying a football for $15,000 per Sunday or carrying a picket sign for free, most players eventually will opt for the former. Players have short careers, but owners are in the game for the long run—and there are fewer of them to organize.

2. If you take the bowling team from Al's Corner Tap, dress it in NFL uniforms, and send it out on a regulation field to face Bob's Barber Shop Bombers on a Sunday afternoon, the American public will pay perfectly good money to watch what happens. If the fans don't go to the games, they'll watch them on TV. Fans never side with striking players. They see them as rich, spoiled brats. The owners are even richer, but they seem to be Teflon-coated as far as public opinion is concerned.

3. The romance between the NFL and the American television industry is the most torrid affair since Romeo and Juliet. The difference is, neither party could kill itself if it tried. If the players had experienced even limited success in interrupting the lifeblood that flows to the NFL through the networks' coaxial cable, they might have had a chance. No way. The electronic media is a mighty ally of owners, not players.

4. When two stubborn armies clash over matters of principle, the army with the most money can be the most stubborn. This is not a new axiom. It was established by the American Civil War in 1865 and reaffirmed by the NFL strike in 1987.

All of the above help explain why it is so terribly difficult for labor unions to use strikes or negotiations to gain any kind of voice in the economic system, not only of football, but of all major professional sports. The players can get more money with job actions, but not more control. Their best chance for that rests more with the courts than with collective bargaining, or at least with a combination of the two.

On the other hand, unions sure can raise a lot of hell when they put their minds to it. And very expensive hell at that.

There have been other sports strikes. Baseball had one in 1981 that made the play-off format look like something Lizzie Borden had taken an ax to. Basketball players somehow manage to avoid hurling themselves over this particular cliff, although they rush right up to the edge every few years just so athletes in other sports won't think they're wimps.

But football? Strikes have gotten to be a rite of fall in this sport, like raking leaves. And the one in 1987 gives us the best look at the impact of unions on sports finances for two reasons. It is the most recent, and it's the one in which it was easiest to tell who lost.

There is absolutely no question that the players lost. It's not easy to work up a great deal of sympathy for men in the prime of life earning five and six figures for six months of work. But if you can find it in your heart to pity rich people, consider just how thoroughly these affluent sheep were sheared by the infinitely richer people they work for.

Mike Duberstein, the director of research for the NFLPA, figures the players bled approximately $80 million of red ink in this war. He does this by very simple arithmetic, multiplying the average player salary of roughly $200,000 per year by 1,600 players and then dividing by four. That's because the players lost around 25% of their annual salaries by sitting out four games.

They sat out only three of those games on purpose. They were all set to come back halfway through the fourth week, but the owners said they caved in too late. The owners were doing just fine with their strike replacement teams anyway. The official reasoning was that the veteran players would risk injury by competing with so little practice after a long layoff.

The unofficial reasoning might have had something to do with the $450,000 to $800,000 payroll savings the clubs were realizing every week the strike went on.

Management had been arrogant through this entire fracas, but this was something special. Not only were the players getting their noses rubbed into the turf, but the paying customers were being told that they would have to accept counterfeit goods for another weekend. As usual, they bought it. But the National Labor Relations Board (NLRB) didn't.

The NLRB counsel issued a complaint a couple of months later saying the league discriminated against the striking players by setting one reporting deadline for them and another for the strikebreakers. The NLRB issues hundreds of complaints every year, and the union faced a long court struggle to make this one stick. But if it did, the players could get back about $20 million or a quarter of their losses.

That would be good news to all of the players and great news to some of them. While the average loss per player was about $15,000 a Sunday during the strike, there were a few guys who were decidedly above average. Buffalo Bills quarterback Jim Kelly, for example, was dropping $68,750 a game, and he didn't even know why.

"I'm not sure what the real reason is that we're striking," said Kelly. "I'm not sure what the issues are. When they come out and tell us what the real issues are, then I'll tell the rest of the players."

He didn't have to tell San Francisco 49ers quarterback Joe Montana, who stuck it out with his teammates but was a reluctant militant at best as he kissed away $62,500 per game. That's what it was costing quarterbacks Marc Wilson of the Los Angeles Raiders and John Elway of the Denver Broncos, too. If you put enough quarterbacks on a union executive committee, you might never have a strike.

The owners made bales and bales of public relations hay out of figures like that, neglecting to mention that the garden variety rookie linebacker or even the second- or third-year offensive tackle was not living anywhere near that fiscal neighborhood. As a matter of fact, some players were actually wondering where the rent money would come from if this thing went on very long. Nobody told them it was going to be an endurance contest.

In cases like theirs, it's best to dip into the strike fund. It's best to have a strike fund, too, but the NFLPA didn't. Duberstein said that because the average salary was so high, the players figured they didn't need one. Union executives told them they had better have one anyway because of the possibility of a strike in '87, but the players weren't interested.

You know what else? They still don't have a strike fund. And the unions in baseball and basketball don't either. That's being self-insured. Or is it self-destructive?

It might have helped, too, if all the players were in the same leaky boat. They weren't. One of the first people to jump ship was Gary Hogeboom, and for a very logical reason.

The Indianapolis Colts' quarterback wasn't losing $15,000 a game for staying home. He was risking a $1.5 million bump. Hogeboom was the nervous owner of a four-year, $7.2-million contract. The problem was that $6 million of his money was deferred. For each year of the contract, $1.5 million was set aside to fund the deferred payments. So if Hogeboom struck, he waved good-bye to a full year's deferred payment. He waved good-bye to the strike instead.

There were other players with deals like that, and the owners weren't shy about invoking the clauses that cracked the players' unity. It would have been silly to pass up the chance.

The contracts helped the owners in other ways, too. In addition to losing game checks, players were blowing their chances at earning performance bonuses while toting their signs around the stadium parking lots.

Take someone like New England halfback Craig James, who reportedly had a contract that paid him an extra $150,000 if he rushed for 1,000 yards in 1987, an additional $100,000 for 1,200 yards, and another $150,000 for 1,400 yards. That came to $400,000, which was pretty extreme as bonuses went, but it certainly made the owners' point.

One way the players might have been able to cut their losses would have been to put their own show on television. But once again the contracts got in the way. The players gave TV some serious thought, particularly after the fledgling Fox Network asked them to form teams and play games for the benefit of its cameras.

The players had lost their jerseys putting on all-star games in '82, though. And more important, most of their contracts contained provisions prohibiting them from playing football for any team outside the NFL.

At worst, the players could have voided their own contracts by going with Fox. At best, they probably would have gotten slapped with a restraining order by the NFL owners. Management had covered itself very well, and its alliance with television was in fine working order.

The union leaders should have thought about things like that before they jumped into this quagmire, but they probably would have done it anyway. Nobody could accuse those fellows of being selfish. They stood to lose more than most of their colleagues.

Player representatives reportedly were dropping an average of $16,948 a game, and union executive committee members were getting nicked an average of $27,140 every Sunday. They were putting quite a bit more than their weekly paychecks on the line, too. There was also the small matter of their careers.

That's the way the union saw it anyway, and it presented some pretty convincing evidence. One fairly well-documented owner tactic in the '82 strike was to target player representatives and union execs for destinations other than the Football Hall of Fame. They were like second lieutenants on the front line. They didn't get shot, but they were casualties in a lot of trades and roster moves.

In order to settle the '82 argument, the owners had to agree to pay all of the player reps who were still on their rosters through the season and to restore the bonuses of a couple who were sent packing. Five years later, Duberstein said player reps Curtis Weathers of Cleveland, Brian Holloway of New England, Bill Rings of San Francisco, Jerry Bell of Tampa, and Michael Jackson of Seattle were suspended, cut, or asked to retire.

Add safety Mike Davis of the Raiders, a member of the executive committee, who was also cut.

If anyone ever erects a statue to the martyrs of the 1987 NFL strike, it will have to show a player rep with empty pockets and a hole in his shoe. He would have to be standing alone, too, because when this whole job action broke down, a lot of the players were talking as if they'd been misled by their union. The poor player rep who had done the leading probably didn't want the job in the first place but took it because he believed in the cause and nobody else would volunteer.

By the summer of 1988, seven NFL player reps had resigned. One of them, Cincinnati quarterback Boomer Esiason, said the Bengals were in danger of becoming the first team in the NFL not to have a player rep because everyone on the club was afraid to succeed him. They feared reprisals for union activity.

On the other hand, Kenny Easley, the all-pro safety for Seattle, resigned because he felt he had been misled by the union.

"From the first announcement that the players were going to strike, that set the tone for an untimely, ill-fated strike," Easley said in an interview in the team tabloid, *Inside the Seahawks*. Added Easley, "A football strike is a total waste of time and money. It was a devastating thing, but this time the owners won hands down.''

Not everyone would agree that strikes are a total waste of time, but players' unions may have to start wondering whether job actions will ever be worth the cost. When Dick Berthelsen, the general counsel for the NFLPA, was asked in an interview if a strike is a viable tactic anymore, he indicated that unions have to play these games one at a time.

''I think the viability of a strike has to be determined under the circumstances at the moment,'' said Berthelsen. ''We have learned to never say never.

''Our strike in 1987 was an example of a union pursuing a strike using the labor laws and expecting there would be bargaining. It didn't happen. The NFL used its monopoly powers to replace the players and make the networks still show the games. The only way to avoid what we went through was to assume that they would violate labor laws or violate antitrust laws with impunity.

''You don't make that assumption if you are trying to pursue a good faith bargain with someone. You assume, at least at the outset, that both sides are going to want to make the process work.

''There was certainly an agreement to be made, and it should have been made last October, but they just walked away from the table. Now they face a situation where the court has to make all the rules, and the rules that the court is making subject them to treble damages under antitrust law. It's the old commercial: 'Pay me now or pay me later.' ''

It was the players who paid right away, however. One of the first things the owners did when the players walked out was suspend the payroll deduction system for union dues.

Nobody collected them during the strike, of course, and that alone amounted to a $2.5-million loss to the NFLPA treasury. Then when the players finally did get back to work, they were light 25% of their annual salaries and in no mood to hand the player rep $2,400.

If that wasn't tough enough, when the strike was over the reps found themselves trying to collect dues from the replacement players who had taken over their jobs in their absence. That's right, the scab players who stayed with the teams after the strike automatically became union members.

''That's what the law says,'' said NFLPA executive director Gene Upshaw. ''They will get the same benefits any player would get.''

The replacement players who stuck with their teams must have felt like they were tiptoeing through a mine field every time they walked into the locker room. But it was sure worth the trouble. Not only did the union have to take them, but they got to share in their teammates' play-off loot.

A clause in the 1982 CBA, which was the only CBA around after the strike, said a player who was with a team for at least three games was entitled to one-half share of any play-off earnings the club received in a conference championship game or the Super Bowl.

Wild card and divisional play-off games didn't count, but the replacement players on the eventual Super Bowl winning team could pull in an extra $27,000, which in some cases equaled a year's salary in their real jobs. "I think it's cute," said Dallas Cowboys owner Tex Schramm.

Schramm had an entirely different opinion of another little bonus arrangement that surfaced after the walkout was over. It was the only one that benefited the veteran players, and it got San Francisco 49ers owner Edward J. DeBartolo into a world of trouble with his fellow club members.

In the interest of mending fences with his employees, DeBartolo announced that he would reach into his own pocket and match his players' first-round bonuses if they made the play-offs. Other owners were miffed by DeBartolo's gesture, most likely because they didn't like the precedent it set or because they didn't think of it themselves. So they complained to Commissioner Pete Rozelle, who responded by fining DeBartolo a robust $50,000.

Still the 49ers got their bonuses—$10,000 apiece—and some of the owners wanted to have DeBartolo's team deprived of its first-round draft choice in 1988 as well.

The moral of that story was that it's OK for an owner to be a little bit gracious to his players, but let's not have any freelancing here. The biggest reason for the NFL's ability to fight off inflation, unemployment, two competing leagues, and four strikes is its affinity for doing things collectively.

These capitalists are better at collectivizing things than Karl Marx ever dreamed of being. They share everything from revenues to opinions. And if they disagree, they're smart enough to do it quietly.

The summer before the talks even began in 1982, the NFL Management Council voted to impose an owner gag rule. Anybody who said anything that could mess up the bargaining was subject to a fine of up to $100,000. An owner couldn't even talk to an NFLPA staffer without the consent of the whole Council.

The policy worked so well in '82 that the owners went right back to it in 1987, and Chuck Sullivan almost gagged on the results. The New England Patriots vice president volunteered the owners' plans for strikebreaking teams to CBS analyst John Madden three weeks before the walkout. He didn't get fined $100,000, but he did get the message. So did all of the other owners.

There were lots of messages delivered by the NFL owners in this strike, and their colleagues in other sports would have been well advised to pay attention. So would the other unions.

Rule No. 1 for either side is to be prepared by learning from your mistakes. The owners figured the biggest mistake they had made in the previous strike was shutting down the shop.

In 1982 an average NFL game was said to generate about $3 million in revenues, counting TV, tickets, parking, and concessions. So when the owners called off seven weeks of games, it was the economic equivalent of wrapping their hands around their own throats and squeezing until everybody turned blue.

The justification for that kind of self-abuse is that fans don't want to see a lot of imitation athletes sullying the Packer Green or Redskin Red and that you have to preserve the integrity of the game. After taking a $150-million bath in 1982, management decided to risk both of those consequences, and the gamble paid off handsomely.

A full five months before the strike, the owners' chief negotiator, Jack Donlan, sent a memo to his employers telling them to make plans to field strike replacement teams. When it came to foresight, management and labor were in totally different leagues.

All the clubs had to do was keep the players around whom they had cut in training camp. They did that by offering them $1,000 apiece to sign option deals under which they agreed to come back if there was a strike.

It was a simple plan, and it was devastatingly effective because it kept the stadiums open. There was one weekend without football, which nobody appeared to miss very much, and during that time rookie replacements earned $450 a week plus a $38 per diem, and veteran replacements got $500 a week and the per diem. Very few of them were making that kind of money working in park districts, prisons, and wherever else they happened to be passing the time waiting for next spring's training camps.

When the silly season actually began, the replacement players were all guaranteed at least the NFL minimum $50,000 contract, prorated on the basis of however many games they played.

Someday a sociology researcher will earn a PhD by explaining why the sporting public bought this bogus package in sufficient quantities to break the strike. In the meantime, let's just guess that it had something to do with habit and something to do with a general feeling of disenchantment toward wealthy young men going on strike to get wealthier.

That same feeling of disenchantment would probably operate if baseball and basketball ever decided to put on replacement contests, but the habit factor might not. Those games get played just about every day during their seasons, and fans expect to miss most of them. If they have to miss a few more, they'll cope. As football partisans are so fond of saying, the football schedule isn't made up of games, it's made up of events.

Whether that's true or not, baseball and basketball owners have said they would be reluctant to try to keep their seasons going with strike replacement teams even though there are more than enough players to go around. In fact, baseball Commissioner Peter Ueberroth came right out and said it three months after the strike ended. If his sport were in the same spot, he would not allow strike replacement games.

"It's obviously been discussed because it's been done in other sports," said Ueberroth in a *Hartford Courant* interview. "But be careful not to mention the other sports because they're really not comparable. This one is really an institution. I don't want to make it sound sacred, but it has a special nature among the people in the country. It's a love affair."

Whether a strike might take the bloom off that rose remains to be seen. But there were other steps taken by the football owners that can be applied nicely to job actions in baseball and basketball.

Like the $150-million line of credit the owners established to deal with any bothersome cash flow problems they might experience. For every game wiped out, the owner could draw an amount equal to what he would have made had it been played and then take years to pay the money back.

The strike didn't last long enough for anyone to have to take advantage of that, but it did tend to keep owners cool . . . and in line.

Contrast that to the players, who had no strike fund and who went into the strike thinking they would be back in a few days or at worst a couple of weeks. Maybe they were just hoping that, because the last work stoppage left them broke. When the smoke cleared in 1982, the union reportedly was $500,000 in debt.

Most important was the matter of timing. And the players should have drawn a 100-yard penalty for this infraction of the rules of clear thinking. The owners were figuring the players would strike shortly after the third game of the 1987 season, because by then they would have put in the minimum amount of time required to qualify for a year's pension.

Instead, the players walked out before the third game and long before the less prosperous ones had banked enough game checks to see them through a long strike.

If they had waited until halfway through the season or maybe even until the play-offs, the fans would have had enough emotion invested in the division races to put some pressure on the owners to get things settled. And the players wouldn't have been quite so nervous about feeding their families, to say nothing of their incentive bonuses.

Union leaderships have a common problem, however, and it's about nerves. There were plenty of players who were skeptical about a strike to begin with, and it was tough enough keeping them calm during the walkout, let alone trying to do it for five or six weeks ahead of time.

The NFLPA was also banking on the idea that the television networks wouldn't buy ersatz football. TV payments came in $115-million chunks, and one of them was due October 1. The players thought that by striking in late September they would stop that check from arriving in the owners' coffers. They thought wrong.

The networks weren't much interested in turning off all of their cameras on Sunday afternoons, and they had to put somebody in front of them. So they paid somewhat grudgingly to show the uniforms, regardless of which players the owners chose to fill them with. They knew they'd get some of that money back.

The coaches weren't all wildly enthusiastic about the situation either. Some of them happened to like their players, and others had no taste for remedial chalkboard meetings where they had to remind temporary laborers which kind of face mask to wear. Nevertheless, there were coaches who had sound economic reasons for making the best of an awkward situation.

Take Indianapolis Colts coach, Ron Meyer, whose five-year contract reportedly was guaranteed for only three. That is, unless he turned the woeful Colts into a plus-.500 team in any of those first three years. Then the rest of the pact was guaranteed as well. Meyer's fill-ins helped him satisfy that requirement in the very first year.

The coaches might have grumbled a little, but they did what their bosses were paying them for. Of course, their bosses had reason to do some grumbling of their own. The owners were the clear winners in the '87 strike all right, but nobody has ever suggested that they emerged from it without a scratch. Their final bill for 1987 may not be presented for years, after the damages in fan frustration and TV attitudes are measured.

The replacement games drew better than most people expected, but that doesn't mean there weren't a lot of embarrassing gaps in the stands. A study reported in the Nov. 16, 1987 issue of *Sports inc.* magazine estimated the owners' attendance loss at $42 million, and it tacks another $2.4 million onto the debit side in lost concessions. You can't sell people beer if you don't get them into your stadium.

The teams all gave their fans the opportunity to turn in their tickets for refunds. But they did it only one game at a time, which meant if you wanted your money back you had to go through the hassle of either mailing in your tickets or going to the ticket office every week. Some people just didn't bother.

Others applied the refunds to season tickets the following year, taking the pressure off the clubs' cash flow. Still, attendance was off about 60% during the strike, and everybody felt that.

The biggest bite by far was electronic. When good buddies like football and television get rich together, they must also expect to get soaked together if the sun goes away. It has been estimated that the 1982 NFL strike cost the networks $100 million in revenues. It also cost them and the NFL about five years in flat ratings while viewers were reacquiring the habit of spending hour after endless hour in front of the tube.

But 1987 was supposed to be the year of the comeback. Before the strike, 30-second spots during NFL telecasts were commanding $160,000 to $190,000 apiece when they were available at all. In the years immediately before that, you could hype your product during time-outs for garage sale prices. That slowed up when Commissioner Pete Rozelle sat down to negotiate a new television contract before the '87 season and had to take less for rights than he got in the old deal.

From 1977 to 1986, TV revenues had galloped from an estimated $69 million to about $493 million. Put away your calculator: That comes to more than a sevenfold increase. And now it was slowing down.

When the '87 strike came along, some of the big advertisers bailed out. From their standpoint, it was bad enough trying to peddle their wares with

SPORT$BIZ STATS

Network Payments For NFL Games (1987)
($ millions)

Network	Regular season	Playoff games	Super Bowl	Total
CBS	450	27	17	494
NBC	360	27	17	404
ABC	360	--	17	377
ESPN	153	--	--	153
Total	**$1,323**	**$54**	**$51**	**$1,428**

Note. From *QV Publishing, Inc.*, 1987. Adapted by permission.

a diluted product. It was worse if they had union contracts of their own and might be seen as supporting a strikebreaking enterprise.

The networks tried to accommodate the advertisers who wanted to take a pass, although there was nothing in their contracts to cover the situation. Most of the advertisers stuck around. Still, there were sophisticated estimates that the networks lost about $10 million in potential profits for each week of replacement games or about $30 million in all.

That's probably pretty low, because the NFL eventually agreed to pay the networks $60 million in rebates. A total of $40 million was returned from payments already made in 1987, while $20 million more came back in 1988.

According to a report in the Jan. 25, 1988 edition of the *Los Angeles Times*, the network rebate was a big factor in an all-around dismal year for NFL owners. The *Times*, citing internal reports of the NFL Management Council and the union, said all but seven teams lost money in 1987, but it wasn't just because of the strike.

There were the rebates, a $30 million tab for losing a lawsuit in the battle over the Raiders' move and $26 million in legal fees for crunching the USFL in court.

Some of the owners didn't care at all for the report, but for amusingly different reasons. The Chicago Bears, for instance, said they did lose money but nothing like the $1.7 million the *Times* reported. The Cleveland Browns, on the other hand, denied they were among the Magnificent Seven that turned a profit in '87. They said they lost money.

There's no telling what the final television costs will be to the owners until they try to make their next deal. When you can't guarantee delivery of the product, it does cut down your leverage in negotiating a new contract. The networks naturally have the same problem with potential sponsors, and they, too, must wait to see what the real costs are. Advertising revenues went down following the '82 donnybrook, and the same could happen after '87.

One intangible negative for the owners may have been that the strike took some of the fun out of owning a pro football team. As Cleveland's Art Modell put it in a *USA Today* interview, "Ninety per cent of the owners have substantial income from other sources. There are a few candy store operators like the Rooneys, the Maras, the Halas family, the Robbies, the Modells, and Al Davis. For others, it's just a hobby. And that's not to denigrate them."

Modell put himself in the candy store category and indicated six months before the picket lines formed that another strike would make him think seriously of selling the shop. "I think I would lose interest in professional sports very rapidly," he said. "I wouldn't make a prediction that the next day I would sell, but I would not be as inclined to hang around as I have for so many years."

The Browns went on to the American Football Conference championship game, and Modell changed his tune, saying he was having too much fun to think about leaving. His original sentiments sounded a tiny bit overdramatic anyway, but the sentiment did have historical roots.

In the aftermath of the '82 strike, there were ownership changes in Dallas, Denver, San Diego, Philadelphia, and New Orleans. They weren't all directly attributable to poststrike blues, but it was a contributing factor in some cases. And when the fun goes out of the business, what does it leave?

Profit of course. Hardly anybody made that either as a result of the 1987 strike. Some owners got bruised worse than others. Robbie in Miami had a new $100-million stadium to pay for. But his problems paled in comparison to those of Patriots owner Billy Sullivan, who was walking on thin ice before the negotiations broke down. When the strike came about, he almost fell right into the drink.

By the end of December, Sullivan had to admit he might not have the $3 million to $5 million he needed to make player payroll payments in January. While the rest of the league held its breath, Sullivan's attorney said later that the payroll would be met, and the Pats wouldn't lose all their players.

Any other outcome would not have set too well with proper Bostonians, who already were feeling as if they'd had their pockets picked by the strike. Like their counterparts in every other NFL city, the citizens lost more than three weekends of scintillating entertainment.

They were also short some cash. Pro football games generate big bucks for the hotels, restaurants, and watering holes in the areas in which they're played, and what those establishments make is pumped into the local economy.

The *Sports inc.* study estimated that $49 million was lost in the tourism category during the idle weekend and the three replacement game weekends. That's money that nobody was going to get back.

Only football could claim that kind of loss, and once again it was the result of the "event" status that even the regular-season games enjoyed. Baseball contributes significantly to local economies on a daily basis, but it doesn't create those kinds of special revenues for its cities until the World Series.

That's when the rich and famous people who haven't seen a game all year long gobble up the premium-priced tickets and push the regulars out of the grandstands.

Pro basketball does even less in this area because the arenas aren't big enough to pull in huge numbers of tourists.

There was one other major class of losers in the '87 NFL strike, according to the *Sports inc.* study, and that would be the folks in Las Vegas. There are people who bet on just about anything, but wagering on the strike replacement games wasn't gambling, it was stargazing.

Until the oddsmakers had a couple of weeks to figure out which of the scab players had warm blood and could hear thunder, they tended to make the home teams the favorites. Then when the bookies seemed to be getting the hang of this new game, the veterans came back.

As a result, football betting fell off about $90 million during the strike, representing roughly a $4 million profit drop for the professional gamesmen. Again, only pro football could wreak this kind of havoc, because that's the game people bet on most.

So the gamblers lost, the players lost, the owners lost, the networks lost, the fans lost, and even the cab drivers and bartenders lost in 1987. And all because a bunch of greedy millionaires let a union lead them around by their noses. Right? What do those guys need a union for anyway?

That's the way the owners would like you to look at it, and that's the way a lot of fans saw it. But a quick check of the history books shows players' associations in a different light.

If sports unions have gotten too big for their britches lately, it may be because they're trying to make up for lost time. When these organizations did arrive, they were long overdue. It started with baseball.

The first recorded instance of a professional sporting event being contested by a strike replacement team came in 1912 when the excitable Ty Cobb had been heckled half to death by an obnoxious fan at a Detroit Tigers game. Cobb climbed into the stands and coldcocked the offending customer, prompting the American League to suspend him indefinitely.

His response was to get his teammates to go out on strike the next day, whereupon the league ordered the Tigers to scare up a scab team from the sandlots.

The record shows that the replacement Tigers played exactly one game and lost it, 24-2, to the Philadelphia Athletics at grave expense to the participants. The temporary Tigers third baseman had two teeth knocked out by a ground ball, one of their outfielders was popped on the noggin by a fly ball, and the club committed seven errors in all.

Even Cobb couldn't stand that. He told his colleagues to go back to work, which they did after paying a $100 fine apiece. Cobb served a 10-day suspension and paid a $50 fine.

Sports unions were still a long way off at that point, unless you count the National Brotherhood of Baseball Players, which was created in 1885 as a secret organization dedicated to getting rid of the major league's $3,000 salary maximum and (yes, even then) its reserve system.

The first serious and sustained players' union was the Major League Baseball Players' Association (MLBPA) that came along in 1954 because everybody was mad at the way the owners were administering the players' pension fund.

At the time, the labor equation couldn't have been more lopsided in the owners' favor. The U.S. Supreme Court had just given the owners a shiny, new ruling that exempted them from antitrust regulations, and a players' contract read like an apartment lease.

All that was required of a player who wanted to work for a major-league team was talent and a blind willingness to abide by the owners' rules. If the rules changed, he had to live by the new ones, even though nobody had to give him a copy of the changes.

The formation of the MLBPA didn't do much to alter the situation, because it was one meek aggregation. It didn't even think of itself as a union. As a matter of fact, neither did the players' associations in the other sports when they started up.

Bob Feller, the MLBPA's first president, said collective bargaining had no place in baseball. And his successor, Bob Friend, took that one step further. He said unions didn't belong in sports at all. That kind of attitude went down smooth as pudding with baseball's owners, particularly since the association wasn't even pressing to get recognized.

Then along came the bad guy.

Marvin Miller had spent 16 years as the chief negotiator for the United States Steel Workers union when the players approached him about heading their organization. He said, OK, but only if some changes are made. "Uh-oh," said the owners, and they were right.

The year before Miller arrived, the minimum major-league salary was $6,000 and the average was $9,000. When you think about it, that wasn't all that long ago. Guys like Denny McLain and Bob Gibson were pitching then.

By 1969 Miller's union had the minimum raised to $10,000 and the average to $24,909, and he was just getting warmed up. In Miller's first eight years in office, the players' pension more than tripled, the minimum salary went from $6,000 to $16,000, and the average swelled to $40,956.

A few other things happened in that time, too. Baseball signed its first CBA in 1968, experienced its first training camp boycott in 1969, and, Lord help us, had its first real strike in 1972. The players were just fooling in that one, though. It lasted only 13 days.

In 1976 it was time to get grim, and there was our old friend, free agency, at the center of the storm. The players had just won a big decision from an arbitrator that allowed them to change teams, and the owners were eager to rid themselves of that annoyance. When the players wouldn't go along, the owners locked them out of training camp.

Eventually, the players gave up some of their recently won rights, but only at a price. The owners had to boost their contribution to the union pension fund from $6.85 million to $8.3 million, and they had to increase salary minimums $1,000 a year for the next three years. The minimums were only $17,000 to begin with.

Four years later that agreement was up, the two sides were still fighting free agency, and the owners gave the union something else to chew on. They wanted to create a wage scale for players with six or fewer years of experience.

Under the owners' 1980 plan, a rookie could make between $25,000 to $40,600 and no incentive bonuses would be allowed. A six-year man would get a minimum of $30,000 to a maximum of $153,600 and bonuses of no more than $20,700.

Add to that an even more restrictive free agent proposal and you can see why baseball players think they need a stubborn union. The owners said they had to have these concessions because they were losing money at a frantic clip. The players said, "Show us. Open your books."

"Never mind," said the owners. Maybe they weren't losing money so fast after all.

The parties arrived at another four-year deal only because they agreed to put off the free agency issue until the following year. Naturally, the delay didn't solve anything, and so on June 12, 1981, the players commenced a strike that would last 50 days and 713 games and culminate in a split-season play-off system that looked like it had been designed by Picasso.

The players got some things because they had the courts on their side, and the owners got some things because they had a $50-million strike insurance policy and a $15-million strike fund on their side.

But when you look at the bottom line, it showed the players averaging $185,651 a season, which is a very long shout from the $9,000 they were averaging when Marvin Miller was persuaded to leave the steel mills. What's more, the figure would balloon to $241,497 the following year.

This is not to say that Miller and his union get all the credit for hoisting baseball players out of the lower middle class, because the biggest part of those gains came after 1976 when the players first gained some right of movement. Then again, Miller had a lot to do with that, too.

That's how it always goes in the sports labor business. One guy comes in and makes waves, and the next thing you know management has battened down the hatches. In basketball, that man was Larry Fleisher.

Long before Fleisher, Bob Cousy organized the NBAPA in the early fifties. But like their baseball counterparts in those days, the players weren't very serious about it. Not until this Harvard lawyer from New York arrived in 1962. In the early sixties, Fleisher ran a low-overhead operation from his office with the smallest staff this side of a corner delicatessen. It's the only kind of operation he's ever run.

Some players are uncomfortable with the amount of power that seems to be concentrated in the hands of one man, but the NBAPA may be the most democratic of all the sports unions. At least more players have meaningful input. Come crunch time, though, Fleisher is more equal than his coequals.

He kept kind of quiet for the first couple of years with the NBAPA, but then the players made a most unseemly splash at the 1964 All-Star Game. They were locked in a dispute with the owners over pensions at the time, and they picked the occasion to threaten a boycott.

With the clock ticking down until tip-off they just stayed in their locker rooms and wouldn't come out until the owners promised to budge on pensions. The NBA union has always had pretty good timing.

It also got a huge boost in 1967 when the American Basketball Association came along and started to pick off some of the top collegiate talent before the NBA could draft it. The NBA's immediate reaction when confronted by such a well-organized and well-capitalized enemy was to try to eat it.

But until 1976, Fleisher's union led a successful fight to forestall the NBA's attempts to merge the two leagues, at which time a few teams were allowed into the older league at a considerable price.

Did the NBA players need a union? Well, as Fleisher put it, before 1967 the players had no salary minimums; no pension; no health, accident, or life insurance; and no trainer for road games. It certainly had no CBA, something the NBAPA achieved for the first time in the history of pro sports.

The union also came up with an insurance plan that would cost each club only $1,500 a year, and the owners wouldn't even go along with that. Maybe basketball didn't need a union, but it sure needed an ABA. And if the union wasn't there, the ABA wouldn't have been for very long either.

By 1976, the basketball players had pensions, insurance, trainers, a contract that said they didn't even have to carry their own bags on the road, and an average salary of $109,000. This was when baseball still had a $17,000 minimum.

NFL players wish they had it so good. Gene Upshaw's NFLPA is a 32-year-old organization with even humbler beginnings than either of its brother organizations in baseball and basketball.

In 1956 before the world had paid much attention to Vince Lombardi, a group of Green Bay Packers asked the team's management to provide them with clean, dry uniforms, socks, and jocks for each of their two-a-day practice sessions. The request was denied. Are you starting to see how the pendulum has swung?

Rashes and athlete's foot aside, the players thought maybe they needed to talk to each other, so a meeting was called in New York in December and 10 guys formed the NFLPA, changing in the process their emphasis from laundry to pensions and insurance. One year later, they had hired a lawyer from Cleveland named Creighton Miller, who threatened to do what lawyers like to do better than anything in the world—sue somebody.

Miller threatened then NFL Commissioner Bert Bell with a $4.2-million antitrust suit unless the league agreed to negotiate on minimum salaries, pay for preseason games, and provide medical expenses and salary for injured players. None of the above was available until the union was formed, but two weeks after Miller announced he was going to sue, it was all there.

What Bell didn't do was formally recognize the NFLPA, which apparently didn't bother Miller very much because he told a Senate subcommittee in 1964 that the members never did consider the association to be a union. It was more of a "loosely knit social organization."

The knit got much tighter in 1968 after Miller left and the players notified the league they planned to file with the NLRB for a union election. They didn't have to. The owners formally recognized them. It was about the last thing the two sides would agree on that year.

They battled over preseason pay, minimums, pensions, and insurance plans. The American Football League's union, which still hadn't merged with the NFL group, even though the leagues had gotten together, settled for a $12,000 minimum. The NFLPA instead voted to strike, if necessary, on June 25, and the owners responded by locking them out of training camps for 10 days. So much for the days of loosely knit social organizations.

A couple of years later, the two players' associations merged, and a year after that a young Minneapolis lawyer signed on with the NFLPA. You remember Ed Garvey.

In typical shrinking violet style, the union's new executive director filed the John Mackey suit, which challenged the Rozelle Rule limitations of free agent movement, and concluded a new four-year CBA retroactive to 1970.

Then in 1974 all hell broke loose, and the players struck for five weeks in a futile attempt to win true freedom for free agents. About all they accomplished was getting the College All-Star Game canceled forever.

The union went without a contract for three years after that, and it might have gone a lot longer if the NFLPA hadn't won a favorable decision on the Mackey case in 1976. When the players had gone back to work in '74, different owners rewarded them by cutting the union president, vice president, and three player reps on the spot.

But two years later with the Mackey victory in their pockets, the players were able to go back to the bargaining table with some leverage. They used it to get a five-year contract.

So now maybe you have an idea of why players need unions. The unions are a long way from perfect, but if they weren't doing the players any good, the owners wouldn't be so eager to break them. Ask the NFLPA's Berthelsen what his group's biggest contributions have been, and he'll tell you a lot of things.

"I think the major things are the education of the player and in turn the public," said Berthelsen in a personal interview. "In the early '70s the players were not aware of what a reserve system was, didn't even know how they were being victimized by things like waivers and so on.

"I guess secondly the impact would be on salaries and benefits. We have taken NFL economics and salary information out of the closet. It used to be that general managers would have two sets of contracts. One they would use to show players and say, 'Look, the team is now making so much money, so you shouldn't ask for anymore.'

"Now we have all the contracts, so there can't be any lying anymore about what people make."

Some critics think the NFL union has tried to do too much or that it's focused on the wrong things. The owners would qualify for that group. But so would some players and a number of agents.

The NFLPA's harshest critic is probably a former agent named Art Wilkinson, who dislikes its work so much that he has tried to replace it with a rival organization.

Berthelsen and Wilkinson differ on the number of people Wilkinson has on his side. As Berthelsen puts it, "This guy gets more ink for doing nothing than any player I have ever seen. When we go out in the field and talk to players, they say they never heard of the guy."

Wilkinson told us he has collected authorization cards from 400 players, and when he gets another 100 his group is looking to force a new election. Whether that happens or not, he does offer some interesting opinions on where the NFL union may have gone wrong.

"I think you can trace all the way back to the absolute origin of the NFLPA a goal on the part of Ed Garvey to become the czar of pro sports," said Wilkinson. "He has tried to unionize everybody from football players to rodeo riders.

"I think that kind of attitude just naturally progressed to where you could see that the NFLPA was going to get carried home on their shield over free agency every time. I think the principal failure is that they have posted as their ultimate goals things that the average player isn't really concerned about.

"If you send out a questionnaire like the NFLPA did and simply ask the players if they want free agency, what do you expect? That's like asking if you want to cure the common cold or do you want the Lord Jesus Christ to come back down from the mountaintop.

"There's never been someone to stand up in front of the players' convention and say if you want free agency, it might take a three-year strike or it might take less wages for this amount of time. Nobody has ever told them what the real cost is."

Wilkinson says one of his group's main objectives would be to find out what the players really want and what they're willing to sacrifice for it. "The only two jobs a labor organization has are to get the most money and the best benefits," he said. "There's nothing more to do."

Easier said than done of course. It takes people, money, and brains to accomplish those goals. The football grumblers seemed to think their union was using too much of the first two and not enough of the third.

They noted that baseball needed a staff of only 10 people to serve the needs of 1,000 members, and Fleisher's Ma-and-Pa NBA shop was run by three staffers for 276 players. The NFLPA, on the other hand, had 36 people on the payroll for 1,580 union members.

It's the payroll that rankled them. During the fall of '87, *Pro Football Weekly* reported that football players were paying union staffers $1.1 million a year, compared to baseball's $440,000 union payroll and basketball's $200,000. Upshaw was making a reported $150,000 annual salary during the strike, a fact that positively thrilled the more disgruntled members of the rank and file.

They weren't too keen either on the figures that showed NFL union dues almost $1,000 steeper than basketball's $1,500. Baseball dues were $1,820. Then again, it's one thing to charge dues and something else entirely to collect them. With the payroll deduction system trashed and the players feeling surly about losing a quarter of their salaries, that was no small problem. Upshaw didn't have any small problems as 1988 ended.

The Cleveland Browns' players put together a petition calling for a trimmed down NFLPA staff and a stepped-up effort to find out what the players really wanted. Fifty of them signed the petition and sent it on to the player reps of all the other teams.

Said Cleveland player rep Mike Pagel, ''The way the strike was handled was just another bit of evidence that the union's gotten too large. We do not want the legacy of a big bureaucracy. We want it under control.''

He was talking about the union, not the game. The owners had that under control, as did the owners in the NBA and major-league baseball. That can only change if the unions get a big lift from the courts. Then maybe they can take strikes out of their playbooks.

Chapter

 4

$007

Not-so-secret agents

Kareem Abdul-Jabbar's complaint totaled 100 pages and one pound, four ounces. Without the cover. That came to about $2.75 million an ounce and may have made the Los Angeles Lakers center the heavyweight champion of sports litigation.

He laid his claim to the title in California state court in 1986, naming his one-time friend and mentor Tom Collins and 30 other people and corporations in a $55-million suit charging fraud, negligence, and malpractice.

Collins served as Abdul-Jabbar's agent for six eventful years, and Abdul-Jabbar contends that Collins managed to lose $9 million of his money in that time. He says Collins got him into trouble with Uncle Sam, too.

Naturally, Collins countersued, claiming that Abdul-Jabbar owed him more than $300,000 in fees and commissions. The question of who's right should keep the legal machinery of California whirring away for years, but the debate has already proved a couple of things beyond, as attorneys say, a reasonable doubt.

It shows that sports agents have come a long way in a short time. Whether they're heading in the right direction is a different issue entirely. It also demonstrates how much their arrival has helped to make athletes major players in the big-league game of finance.

Does anybody really think Kareem Abdul-Jabbar would have taken it into his head to invest his $2-million-plus annual salary in a rib restaurant, three hotels, a sports club, a limousine service, a commodities brokerage, an exercise rope, and a cattle feed business if Collins or somebody like him wasn't looking over his shoulder? Cattle feed?

Abdul-Jabbar contends that Collins wasn't looking over his shoulder at all. It was the other way around. Abdul-Jabbar was the spectator. The athlete turned over control of his purse strings to the agent and then neglected to watch him closely enough. Several other NBA players, including Denver's Alex English, Houston's Ralph Sampson, Milwaukee's Terry Cummings, and Dallas's Brad Davis were similarly trusting, according to the suit.

Then, says the complaint, Collins got all these athletes' money stirred together in a kind of investment goulash that turned out to be not very tasty for any of them. Spicing up the mix was a separate litigation in which English sued Abdul-Jabbar, claiming that Collins had used $150,000 of English's and Davis's money to cover Abdul-Jabbar's expenses.

The papers were served to Kareem as he sat in the visitors' locker room following a Lakers game with Denver. English insisted that the lawyers wait until after the game to drop the bomb on his fellow all-star. Abdul-Jabbar didn't return the favor. When the teams met again, English was sitting on the Nuggets bench when he was served with papers including him in Abdul-Jabbar's lawsuit.

Abdul-Jabbar's lawyers said they wanted to negotiate some kind of settlement with English, but Collins's clients' money was so mixed up that it was too hard to tell who had what.

For instance, they said that one $20,000 withdrawal was recorded on Collins's books as "Cheryl's gold" without any explanation and that Collins didn't get around to filing Kareem's 1982 income tax until 1985. The lawyers said that resulted in $182,000 in interest and late fee charges. The IRS doesn't play overtime games.

Collins replied that Cheryl's gold was mined by one Cheryl Pistono, the plaintiff's former girlfriend and the mother of one of his children, and that the taxes were late because Abdul-Jabbar couldn't supply the records he needed.

Abdul-Jabbar didn't fare much better in real estate. According to the suit, Collins made him a limited partner in several ambitious ventures. He put up $780,000 for three hotels, $378,000 for a couple of restaurants, and $460,000 for the sports club, in addition to making loans and signing notes for more than $8 million.

Collins's other player-clients generally invested a little less than Abdul-Jabbar, but they were his teammates in the true capitalistic sense of the term. Coach Collins called the fiscal shots for them, although the projects themselves were run by other general partners.

Collins's defenders say he did the best job he could for Abdul-Jabbar and that it's unfortunate his new representatives prompted him to take the court route. Viewed that way, it's almost an agent versus agent dispute.

The Collins-Jabbar face-off may be the biggest of its kind, but it's hardly unique. It's not even unusual. Athletes are dealing with amounts these days that wouldn't have been thought possible even a decade ago. And one very important reason for that is the emergence of sports agents.

There's no denying that agents have caused salaries to rise and that good agents have helped players turn short careers into lifelong security.

The bad ones have been known to cost their clients small fortunes.

By the time anybody can tell the bad ones from the good ones, it's usually too late. There are literally thousands of these people ranging from first rank attorneys to back room sharks interested in a quick buck and a quick exit.

You don't have to be a lawyer to be an agent. You don't even have to be a sports fan. In most places, you don't have to be anything except a person with a client because sports and government are just now getting around to dealing with this hot topic. They're a little late.

In the old days, it took a brave athlete to risk bringing along a lawyer when he ventured into the front office to talk about a new contract. Now some players hire whole corporations to represent them in negotiating not only the amount of money they get but also how they'll spend it.

There are several national companies whose main job is to represent athletes in their deals with teams and high finance. The three biggest—International Management Group (IMG), ProServ, and Advantage International—serve hundreds of clients all over the world, generating millions of dollars in revenues every year.

IMG, which began almost 30 years ago with a handshake deal between founder Mark McCormack and golf star Arnold Palmer, now has 21 offices in 14 countries and employs more than 500 people.

IMG's biggest rival, ProServ, is the brainchild of former Davis Cup tennis player Donald Dell. It's barely 20 years old, and it has 120 people on the payroll. Advantage International is the baby of big sports agencies. It was started in 1983 by a group of former ProServ execs, and it already employs 100 people.

What kind of people? Attorneys, financial managers, tax accountants, promoters, broadcast experts . . . whatever it takes to attract clients and make it worth their while to turn over as much as 25% of their earnings to a big agency.

That's what Greg Norman reportedly pays IMG and with no complaints. The agency has arranged more than $12-million worth of investment and endorsement deals for golf's international superstar. In return, it gets a quarter of what he makes, both on and off the course.

Palmer is still the agency's showcase client, and at one time he was its only client. In 1960, before Palmer hired McCormack to represent him, he was making about $60,000 a year. Now he's making an estimated $10 million annually, only a small percentage of which comes directly from his efforts on the fairways and greens.

When Palmer first hooked up with McCormack, he insisted that McCormack give him his full attention. Nobody else allowed. Later Palmer relented when Gary Player asked if he could use McCormack's services. Then Jack Nicklaus came aboard.

This was in the '70s when that trio dominated pro golf. Nicklaus later left, but IMG now has so many of the game's top names under contract that it could probably start its own tour. Don't think the golfing establishment hasn't worried about that.

As it is, IMG not only stages its own sporting events around the world, but it also televises them. Sometimes McCormack serves as the color commentator.

Remember, this is a sports management firm we're talking about. Some people would think of it as agents run amok. Others would tell you it's just the logical extension of sports capitalism.

Golfers are still the focus of IMG, but it also has Herschel Walker, Bjorn Borg, Martina Navratilova, Chris Evert, Mary Decker Slaney, and Jackie Stewart on its client list.

Then there's ProServ. Given Dell's background, it's only natural that ProServ would be big in tennis. But it has also made a large dent in the basketball market, where it represents 30 players from 19 NBA teams.

With players like Michael Jordan, Adrian Dantley, Patrick Ewing, Sleepy Floyd, Buck Williams, and James Worthy on board, it could have a nice start on a separate basketball league.

The big agencies have enough to do without thinking about competing with the sports establishment, but there's no question they can exert tons of pressure on it.

The majority of athletes are still represented by individuals or small firms, who can also apply plenty of leverage in their own way—particularly if they happen to have a couple of key players on the same team.

That's just a matter of agents doing their job. If that's all they did, we wouldn't be hearing so much about them. But we're hearing about them all the time, and not usually in very complimentary terms.

Owners rip them, colleges rip them, coaches rip them, some players rip them. They don't even seem very fond of each other. Fans are just kind of tired of them.

Most fans might figure the best way to deal with agents is to get rid of them. That would certainly quiet things down, but would also be nearly impossible to accomplish and wouldn't be fair to the players. Besides, that was tried a long time ago before the agent business got off the ground.

Let us journey briefly to Green Bay, Wisconsin, where it's 1964 and Jim Ringo is coming off another all-pro season as the Packers' center. According to local legend, Ringo decided one summer day to stop into the Packers' offices to get his new contract settled with Vince Lombardi before training camp started.

He called first to make an appointment, but he neglected to mention that he would be bringing a guest. It turned out to be a crucial omission. The guest happened to be a financial adviser, which was a genteel term in those days for an agent.

Lombardi hadn't dealt with many agents up to that point, but the ones he had met he held in the same high regard as he did clipping penalties and Chicago Bears. So when Ringo introduced him to his negotiator, Lombardi excused himself and left the room.

When he returned, he looked at Ringo's adviser and told him, "Mister, you're talking to the wrong team. Jim Ringo has just become a Philadelphia Eagle."

Ringo himself has never confirmed that story, but plenty of people who ought to know say it happened just about that way. Whether it's apocryphal or not, it was certainly in character for both Lombardi and the times.

The Ringo trade was made at a point in time when most players were still representing themselves in contract negotiations, and their idea of a business transaction was buying a round for the house.

Three years later, things hadn't changed much. Detroit Tigers pitcher Earl Wilson had a lawyer, too, but his representative wouldn't even accompany his client into the office of Detroit General Manager Jim Campbell when it was time to discuss a new contract. The talks seemed to drag a little, because every time they hit a snag, Wilson would excuse himself and leave the room.

Campbell must have figured his pitcher had a short attention span or weak kidneys, but that wasn't the problem at all. Wilson was going only as far as the nearest telephone booth where he was calling his lawyer to get advice. The agent said later that he would have preferred being with Earl in the flesh, but it would have been impossible at that time.

At that time, according to the players' union, the minimum salary in the major leagues was \$6,000 and the average was \$19,000.

Not all players are rich today, and not all rich players have agents. Nor can you give agents all of the credit for improving the players' financial status. What we have here is a chicken and egg proposition. Did players start making big money when agents showed up to help them? Or did agents show up when players started making big money? The answer is yes.

Agents themselves don't take all the credit for rising salaries, but they don't give it all away either. Some don't even like being called agents. One of those is Richard Woods, a Mobile, Alabama, attorney whose clients included NFL stars like Bo Jackson, Cornelius Bennett, and the top choice in the 1988 draft, Aundray Bruce.

We asked Woods about the role of agents and what people think about them, and he said, "When I'm referred to in the newspapers as an agent, it has a bad connotation. I don't like it. But I recognize that that is how I'm labeled.

"But there is no way a player can go through a negotiating process on his own. No businessman would ever go through a multimillion negotiation without consulting an attorney, and a player who is a very inexperienced businessman certainly should have an attorney or an agent advising him through the process. Overall, I think the process has been beneficial.

"Attorneys and/or agents have gained much more money for players from their teams. Sharing information through the union so that you know what other players are making has dramatically changed football contracts."

The real boom in sports agency is generally conceded to be about 10 to 15 years old, although there was one pioneer about 50 years ahead of his time. Some historians believe the first athlete to hire an agent worthy of the name was Red Grange. His guy got him a $100,000 contract in 1925. The agent's name was C.C. Pyle, and the C.C. stood for "Cash and Carry."

In the decade from 1967, when Wilson was sneaking off to a pay phone to talk to his agent, to 1977 the average baseball salary grew from $19,000 to $76,066, and the minimum rose from $6,000 to $19,000. That looks pretty good at first when you figure the average grew by 400%. But let's look a little closer.

In 1977 there was still only a $57,000 difference between the average baseball salary and the minimum. Compare that to the 1977-to-1987 period when the agents got their offenses cranked up and the average zoomed to $412,454 while the minimum was only $43,500. Unions negotiate minimums, but agents negotiate salaries.

Woods acknowledges that the growth in salaries has also been promoted by a number of other developments in sports that had nothing to do with scoring touchdowns, hitting home runs, or firing coaches. And as salaries grew, so did the number of agents.

Start with television. Most things in sports do. When the networks began putting all that succulent bread on the table, everybody dug in. It's one thing for a player to sit down with Charlie in the front office and haggle over whether he's worth $5,000 more than he was last year. But when a player discovers he could be a TV star and a shoe spokesman or get paid big money to be photographed in his underwear—then it's time to call in reinforcements.

Maybe it really became time when good old red, white, and blue competition seized the professional sporting establishment by the throat and kept shaking until dollars starting falling on the ground. This is an event that can be marked by the arrival of organizations like the American Basketball Association, the World Hockey Association, the United States Football League, and its predecessor, the World Football League.

When the established leagues no longer had the only game in town, the players didn't know quite what to make of it. But agents did. Suddenly it seemed as if everybody with the price of a telephone and a briefcase became an agent.

"It was in the late '70s when it really started to go wild," recalled Green Bay Packers executive Bob Harlan, who negotiated the team's contracts between 1971 and 1985. "It used to be a few days after the draft we would call people who hadn't been drafted and bring them in just to have enough bodies in training camp. Then suddenly, those guys were telling us they'd have their agents call us back.

"Everybody had an agent. We were finding players who had two or three agents, and they had signed legal contracts with every one of them. You would get an agreement worked out with a player, and then it would take two or three months after that to straighten things out with his agents. It got to be a jungle."

If anything, the jungle is more crowded now than it was then. There are an estimated 20,000 people in America who claim to be full- or part-time sports agents. The NFLPA alone listed 1,200 registered agents working for 1,232 players in 1987.

There is a similar population problem in the NBA where 400 agents are registered with the NBAPA, and only 300 players need representing.

Why are all these people out hunting for clients? Because that's where the money is.

How much money an agent can make from an athlete depends on what he does for him and what he charges him. And both of those things can get pretty complicated.

There are four basic ways agents get paid: by the hour, by the job, by a percentage of their clients' incomes, and by a combination of the above.

Under the hourly arrangement, the agent generally makes something in the neighborhood of $75 to $200 an hour to do a variety of jobs. Whether it's preparing for contract negotiations or making an endorsement deal, all he does is keep track of his time and present the player with a bill.

In payment method No. 2, the flat fee deal, the agent agrees to an amount beforehand to perform a specific task. That could be negotiating a contract, too. No matter how long it takes or how good the contract is, the agent makes the same money. That could tend to get negotiations over in a hurry, but not necessarily to the player's benefit.

The percentage arrangements or a combination deal that involves percentages are the ones you hear the most about. The going rate is somewhere between 5% and 7%. It stands to reason that an agent who is getting a percentage of his client's income will do everything he can to maximize that income.

It makes sense to most players anyway, but this is also the kind of contract players should enter with the kind of caution mothers reserve for small children crossing busy streets.

It sounds simple enough. Power forward Crash T. Glass signs a contract calling for $1.5 million over three years. His agent, Byron Balancesheet, makes the deal and agrees that his fee will be 5% of what Crash earns over the life of the contract. So Byron walks off with $75,000, and everybody agrees to meet in three years and do lunch again.

Not so fast.

Has Byron agreed to get just 5% of Crash's basic salary, or does he also get a cut of the bonuses and incentives that he built into the contract? Maybe

Crash gets an extra $10,000 for averaging 10 rebounds a game, or making the league all-star team, or getting through an entire season without trashing a locker room or being arrested. And if Crash signs another deal to sell socks or market marmalade, does Byron get a piece of that action?

The NBAPA took an interest in those very questions a few years back when it designed a standard player-agent contract that all agents must agree to follow if they want to deal with pro basketball clients. The contract specifically defined compensation to include base salary, signing bonuses, and performance bonuses.

Those are the items that agents can collect on. Nothing else in the player's contract with a team can be taken into account when computing the agent's fee. If the agent has arranged some endorsements for a client, a television shot, or a public appearance, then a separate deal must be made to cover that.

When an athlete selects an agent in big-league team sports, he has to decide what he wants him for. Sometimes he just hires somebody to get him a good deal with whatever club happened to draft him. Then he engages somebody else to take care of the money for him. Other times, one agent does everything. And in a few instances, the athlete lets the agent do the contract, and then he handles the money all by himself.

Some agents don't want to get involved in anything besides contract negotiations, whereas others will deal with everything but that. The non-negotiators don't call themselves agents. They're representatives. And then there are the full-service, one-stop shopping types who offer a whole smorgasbord of services:

- *Money management, tax planning, and investments.* You say you recognize the Tom Collins-Kareem Abdul-Jabbar unpleasantness here, do you? Yes, but sometimes it works out agreeably for both parties. The Lakers will still be paying Magic Johnson while he's telling his grandkids Larry Bird stories, because somebody did a little tax planning. And there are some really thoughtful and energetic players in all sports who have stock portfolios thicker than their playbooks. They take the time to find out who the knowledgeable people are, and they learn enough about investments themselves to at least keep an eye on them.

- *Securing investment contracts and appearances.* There are players and coaches who make more money outside their games than they do playing and coaching.

- *Resolving disputes.* Players get into all kinds of hassles. With teams, with advertisers, with co-investors. With their wives for that matter. If an agent isn't a divorce lawyer, he probably knows one, and he'll have more than a passing interest in the property settlement.

- *Personal counseling.* This means helping young athletes keep their heads on straight and miscellaneous other services like bookkeeping, budget planning, and just about anything else either party may dream up if they have a really solid relationship. Teams have even hired agents to help keep their players out of the military. Some players don't water their lawns without calling their agents first, and others don't see them until negotiating time.

Some agents require that their player-clients grant them power of attorney, which has the overwhelming advantage to the agent of assuring that he gets paid. The athlete's check is sent directly to the agent, who deducts his fee and deposits the rest in an account for the player. Or maybe the agent takes care of the athlete's expenses, pays himself, and invests what's left over for him.

Hall of Fame guard Oscar Robertson has an interesting slant on that. He thinks the player should give the agent an allowance instead. Give him a certain amount of money and tell him his pay is based on how well he invests it. Robertson has not noticed a groundswell of support among agents for his plan.

Players' unions generally recommend that players don't grant power of attorney unless the agent is bonded and a member of an established firm. They say a one- or two-man operation is too risky. Agents counter that that risk cuts both ways.

"There is a very high no-pay factor," former agent Ted Steinberg said in a *Milwaukee Journal* interview. "A lot of times the agent takes his money right up front out of the signing bonus, because if he doesn't get it then, he may never see it.

"Often when you negotiate a contract, an athlete will look back and say, 'This guy did nothing but advise. He's not worth 5% of $1 million.' He doesn't take into consideration the time and expense involved or your expertise."

So one thing that Crash, the power forward, has to agree on right away before signing a contract with his agent, Byron, is when Byron gets his bread. Do paydays arrive simultaneously for both of them, or does the agent get his up front?

Steinberg's concerns aside, the player who pays it all out before his first kickoff or center jump has to be playing with a crystal ball—or a short deck. There are reasons for that.

There's inflation for instance. The money Crash receives in the first year of his three-year deal is worth more than it is in the third year. If you don't believe that, check on what new cars were selling for three years ago. Or basketball tickets. So if the agent gets all of his money immediately, only the player carries the inflation burden.

You're thinking right now if somebody wants to pay you $1.5 million, you don't mind a little extra inflation burden, right? Yeah, but you can't dunk. Life isn't fair.

More important is the matter of guarantees. Let's say Crash's contract is guaranteed only for the first year. If he gets hurt after that, the team doesn't have to pay him for years two and three. So Crash only got $500,000 of the $1.5 million he signed for, and he paid his agent $75,000 of that. He's down to $425,000.

Maybe less than that, particularly if he's a rookie. Baseball and basketball teams tend to pay new players less of their money in the first year of a long-term contract. The trade-off is that the first year is guaranteed. The player gets the money whether he's still playing at the end of the year or not.

So it could be Crash got only a $300,000 salary in his rookie year, and the agent picked up one quarter of that. Now he's down to $225,000 before the government comes in and claims its share. Moral of the story: Make the agent wait for some of the money.

The NCAA's standing advice to prospective pro athletes is to be suspicious of anyone who demands money up front.

The players' unions feel the same way. In fact, the NBA union prohibits payments to agents until the players themselves are paid. The unions even tell their players what agents are worth. For example, the NBAPA says an agent can get only $2,000 for contract negotiation services if the player signs for the league minimum. If he signs for more, the agent ceiling is 4%.

In the NFL, the union pegs its figures to the year of the contract. If a player is in the first year of his contract, his agent can't collect more than 10% of his salary. In the second year, it's 5%, and in the third it's 2%. The agent can do a little better if the contract is guaranteed. Then his percentage can climb to 7% in the second year and 3% in the third.

The agent should do better if the contract is guaranteed because NFL team owners pass out guaranteed contracts about as freely as they contribute money to the AFL-CIO. A "three-year contract" in the NFL is one of those colorful sporting misnomers that has been foisted on a trusting public. Other examples are "free" agent and "Super" Bowl.

Football agents also are allowed to make more than the suggested minimums in cases of exceptional achievement in negotiating a contract or in cases where an extraordinary amount of time is required to get things done. If an agent gets $1 million a year for a second-year running back who trips over hashmarks, the union reasons quite correctly that he's entitled to more than 5% and polite applause.

By now, you may be wondering where the NBAPA and NFLPA get off telling agents what they can make anyway. The answer is somebody had to do it. Nobody else was protecting players from greedy agents, and the unions appeared to be the only effective choice.

But they're only effective sometimes. Nobody's come up with a way to protect agents from dishonest athletes—it's not something fans lose a lot of sleep over.

As a matter of fact, the process of regulating sports agents is only slightly less orderly than an 0-16 football team's two-minute drill. And until that's squared away, there will be some big money flowing in the wrong directions.

By the late '70s everybody in the world who cared about those things knew that agents were raising 17 kinds of hell with the financial structure, to say nothing of the legal structure, of big time sports. But it was like the weather. Everybody just talked about it.

Discussing agents was tougher than talking about the weather because nobody knew who they were talking about. An agent could be anybody.

"In the last five years, sports representation has emerged as the hot professional field," agent Leigh Steinberg said in a Nov. 16, 1987, *Sporting News* story. "And almost anyone can play the game. If you represent the interests of another person with a third party, magically you are an agent. To be an agent in the field of sports, all you need is a client and a business card."

The client is optional as a matter of fact. Baseball requires one, but football and basketball don't. As Steinberg pointed out in a most graphic way, "The Hillside Strangler could be an agent."

Just as there were laws against the Strangler's nefarious activities, though, there is legislation covering the antisocial activities of certain agents. Just not very much of it. The federal government took a couple of stabs at monitoring agents and decided it was a bad idea. "Leave it to the states," said the Feds.

So far Oklahoma, California, Alabama, Texas, Minnesota, Mississippi, Ohio, Tennessee, Florida, Georgia, Indiana, Iowa, Kentucky, and Louisiana have some kind of law governing agents. South Carolina, Michigan, Arizona, Maryland, New Jersey, Washington, New York, South Carolina, and Pennsylvania were all considering legislation by the spring of 1988.

The laws aren't as much concerned with protecting the athletes, however, as they are with protecting the colleges where the athletes come from. They have some pretty strong collegiate football programs in those states, and lately agents' activities have had the most undesirable effects on bowl games.

The Texas law requires not only a $1,000 license fee but a $100,000 bond from representatives planning to provide financial services as well as negotiate contracts. The bond costs $2,000, but the agents say they can't get it. Bond-writing companies would prefer more predictable risks, like, say, trying to stop cattle stampedes on foot.

The Alabama law is patterned after the one in Texas, and it says that agents who operate in the state and don't get licensed can spend up to 10 years in prison and pay a $5,000 fine. If anyone ever has to face those penalties, it might make agents pay attention. But it hasn't happened yet, and many qualified observers doubt that approach will help much.

One such observer is Ed Garvey, former executive director of the NFLPA. "We got the California law passed, but it hasn't had much impact," said Garvey in a personal interview. "If you do this on a state-by-state basis, you go crazy. On a scale of 1 to 10 with all of the things state government has to worry about, how much of a priority do you think creating this kind of bureaucracy would have?"

That might depend upon how seriously the state legislature takes its football. But Garvey is right. States can't do the job all alone, and maybe they can't do it at all. By January of 1988, a not-so-grand total of 17 agents had taken the trouble to register with the state of California.

Agents themselves have formed organizations designed to keep track of ethics, but those don't work well because the crooks just don't join. So it's been left to the unions to protect the players' interest, which is to say their money, from unscrupulous agents.

Before 1987 the only thing an agent in baseball had to do to negotiate a major-league baseball contract was to bring a note from home. A little piece of paper signed by the player saying, "This guy is my agent," did the trick. Baseball has finally caught up with the rest of the world, and now agents not only must sign up with the union, but they also must fill out a 17-page form on their personal and business relationships with players and team owners.

Besides that, an agent has to be designated by a player each year even if that agent has a long-term contract with him. In other words, the player has the chance to change agents every year without getting sued. That's important, because agents and players are at each other's throats all of the time over the wandering proclivities of the modern athlete when it comes to engaging representation.

The NBAPA got around to registering agents only about a year before baseball did, but it made up for lost time by issuing a list of regulations longer than Kevin McHale's arms. To represent a player in the NBA you can't

- offer him or his family money or something else valuable. You can agree to work for less than the allowable maximum, but that's it.
- lie to him while you're trying to sign him.
- own an NBA team or even part of a team. If you own a 10% piece of the Celtics, how hard are you going to try to pay Larry Bird $3 million?
- represent an NBA coach or general manager or anybody else who could pose a conflict of interest. Or take money from an NBA club.
- charge him too much. There is a union fee scale for agents when it comes to negotiating contracts. An agent makes his own deal on endorsements, but if he rips a player off, and the player can prove it, the agent could be decertified by the NBA union.
- agree to give up anything that the player automatically has under the league's CBA. What the union giveth through hard bargaining, an agent cannot taketh away through generosity or brain lock.
- engage in unlawful conduct, dishonesty, fraud, deceit, misrepresentation, or anything else that reflects poorly on your fitness to be an agent.

Penalties for agent transgressions in the NBA range from private reprimands to loss of certification. Nobody's lost his certification yet, but then the agreement is young. If it should happen, teams simply wouldn't be allowed to talk contract with a barred agent. That agent is out of business as far as basketball is concerned.

Football was the first big-league sport to register agents, but the NFL union policy has a gaping hole in it. It doesn't cover rookies.

Only union members fall under the NFL agent program, and the league says a player isn't a member of the union until he makes a team. By then it's too late. Players need the agents to negotiate their first contract, so most of the time they sign with him before they're even drafted. Here comes the Hillside Strangler.

The NFL union tried to gain the right to represent rookies in its 1982 negotiations, but the owners fought the union off. It tried again in 1987 and was lucky to come out of that one alive. It will keep trying.

There is an immense amount of money involved in landing rookie clients, as indicated by figures the NFLPA released following the 1987 college draft. Bob Woolf represented just three of the players drafted in the first four rounds that year, but those three players signed contracts totaling $10.5 million, with an average signing bonus of $573,333.

That made Woolf the football agent champ of 1987. Second place went to Leigh Steinberg with five players in the first four rounds and five more in rounds 5 through 12. His clients' pacts totaled $7.22 million, while the eight rookies represented by third-place Marvin Demoff got $6.64 million.

Even if an agent finished 25th in this derby, he wasn't running out of the money. Mel Levine held that spot with three clients and $1.5 million in contracts.

Why wouldn't the league want the union to regulate agents who represent rookies? Garvey has a theory on that.

"I can only conclude that the NFL likes dealing with agents who are in need of a quick return on their 'investment' in the college athletes," he said. "They also like dealing with incompetent, untrained agents, who in the final analysis are no match for trained club executives."

What do you suppose Garvey meant by that crack about agents' "investment" in college players? Unfortunately, we're becoming much too familiar with that.

All agents, be they ethical, marginal, or evil, are salesmen. What they have to sell is themselves. The market for the top players is incredibly crowded, and the rules of the game are cynical and unrealistic. The rules say college athletes can't engage the services of agents until their eligibility has been used up.

The NCAA says that, and the pro unions say that. And all of the state bar associations say that attorneys can't solicit clients. Remember, most agents are lawyers.

So the polite thing for a sports agent to do is wait until all of the top athletes have been drafted by the pros and then sit attentively by the telephone

SPORT$BIZ STATS

Top Sports Agents in 1987 NFL Draft

Agent	Players per rounds 1-4	Players per rounds 5-12	Total contracts ($ millions)	Average contract	Average signing bonus
Bob Woolf	3	0	10.50	$3,500,000	$573,333
Leigh Steinberg	5	5	7.22	721,900	225,600
Marvin Demoff	5	3	6.64	830,500	243,625
Mike Blatt	2	7	6.27	696,777	164,333
Robert Fraley	4	0	5.80	1,450,000	588,750
Richard Woods	2	1	4.69	1,560,000	544,000
Ralph Cindrich	3	5	4.15	518,625	128,375
Brett Senior	4	2	4.07	677,666	218,500
Bruce Allen	4	4	3.89	486,000	97,125
Lloyd Bloom	2	3	3.62	724,800	207,600
David Ware	3	1	3.23	807,000	244,500
Tom Condon	3	1	3.11	776,500	251,750
Joe Courrege	2	5	2.88	411,429	53,286
John Maloney	2	1	2.47	822,667	287,667
Tony Agnone	2	5	2.42	346,286	59,429
Jim Steiner	2	3	2.42	483,200	99,600
Gary Kovacs	3	1	2.38	593,750	184,000
Art Wilkinson	2	2	1.92	479,750	84,750
Steve Zucker	1	0	1.78	1,780,000	725,000
Jack Mills	2	2	1.77	442,500	102,250
Peter Johnson	3	3	1.69	280,833	56,667
George Kickliter	1	1	1.65	824,500	379,500
Nick Kish	1	4	1.60	319,200	33,400
Ted Powell	1	2	1.58	527,666	99,000
Mel Levine	2	1	1.50	499,000	118,333

Note. From *Sports inc.The Sports Business Weekly*, January 18, 1988. Adapted by permission.

until some all-American quarterback or point guard calls inquiring after his services. Polite agents never ate very well, which may be why there aren't many left.

Many educated observers estimate that at least half of the players who were taken in the latest NFL draft had already signed with agents long before the selection process began. Everybody knows that if you want to make any money at this game, you get 'em when they're hot. There are those who say you take that one step further. You get 'em any way you can.

Jack Manton, an Atlanta attorney whose illustrious clients have included Herschel Walker, got out of the agent game a while ago when he got tired of pampering people. "I have a couple of players left whom I serve as an attorney, not as an agent,'' he said. "It's a tough, tough way to make a living. I was in it for 10 years, and it hasn't changed.

"It's a recruiting business, and you have to go get clients. Players are used to being recruited when they go to college, and they expect to be recruited by agents, too. Plus, a lot of coaches have their hands out. I'm not saying all of them, but there are a lot.

"The players want to know what you will do for them. It usually takes the form of a loan. They want to know, 'Will you lend me this much money or sign a note for me or get me a car?' I just got tired of it.''

Manton believes the 50% estimate on athletes already signed with agents before draft day is low.

"Basketball is cleaner than football, because there are only 25 principals,'' he said. "After the first round, a kid doesn't usually make it in the league anyway. In fact, it's more like the first 15 kids, and you have to be really sharp as an agent to know who those 15 will be.

"In football, many more players make it, and a fifth-rounder gets about as much as a third-rounder anyway. I'd say 60% to 70% of the players in football are already signed.''

You would think if the practice of signing kids early were that widespread, all of the coaches and college presidents in the world would know who the violators are. But somehow it always seems to come as a blazing surprise on campus when somebody is found out. The agents themselves know, though.

To them the signs aren't all that subtle. As Woolf explained it in a *Sporting News* story, "One guy used to give the players Rolex watches. So whenever I'd see somebody wearing one, I'd know right away who he'd gone with.''

All the athlete has to do then is hope some NCAA enforcement officer doesn't come along and ask him what time it is. The guardians of collegiate amateurism don't make much distinction between agents with an interest in a student's welfare and the hit-and-run artists who claim a big chunk of the first contract and then disappear behind a rock. The NCAA just wants them all to stay away.

That has led to a heated adversarial relationship between the NCAA and some agents, who claim the colleges' main interest is wringing that last drop of eligibility and revenue out of the athlete. "The NCAA rules are not the laws of the United States,'' pointed out Mike Trope in his book *Necessary Roughness*. "They're simply a bunch of hypocritical and unworkable rules set up by the NCAA.

"As an agent, I absolutely wasn't bound by them. NCAA rules are meaningless. The coaches themselves, the people who are supposed to be bound by them, don't abide by them either. Hell, nobody follows NCAA rules.''

Maybe that's because there are so many of them. In abridged form, the NCAA rules governing college athletes and agents go something like this:

- If an athlete wants to stay eligible he can't sign an agent while he's still playing. Don't even think about having him negotiate a contract with a team.

- He can't take any kind of gifts or expenses from the agent unless those same benefits are available to other students who aren't athletes. In other words, if an agent wants to buy cars for the entire student body, it might be OK. So far no one's had to make a ruling on that.

- He can't have his name placed on a pro draft list, because once he does that, he's not an amateur any more in the NCAA's eyes—even if he changes his mind and takes his name off the list. That's just in basketball by the way.

  The NFL has a rule that says teams can't draft underclassmen, but it keeps making exceptions so it can stay out of court. In baseball, a player goes on the major-league draft list after his junior year without even asking. The NCAA doesn't mind. Why do you suppose that is? Could it be because baseball isn't a revenue sport, so losing an underclassman to the pros doesn't cost anybody any money?

- Another thing an athlete can't do if he's an underclassman and wants to stay eligible is accept a loan with deferred payments from an agent or even from an alum. Same principle here. If those guys are offering interest-free loans to everybody on campus, that's fine, but there seem to be limits to the school spirit of even the most dedicated sugar daddy.

  When the loans are extended, athletes seem to think the payments will be deferred until their next life or until such time as giraffes sprout wings, whichever comes first.

- Finally, an athlete can't be represented by a coach with a pro team, and he can't receive professional services (say legal advice) at bargain rates.

Actually, about the only thing the NCAA allows an athlete to do with an agent is take his advice, and then only if he doesn't sign him up or take anything from him. Agents are perfectly free, however, to discuss the weather and nuclear physics with athletes.

The NCAA has done a couple of things to help protect players from nasty agents. It says colleges can form panels of lawyers and accountants and other professionals to counsel athletes on the pro job market and to acquaint them with the services of agents.

And it has begun to register agents. If an agent wants to be certified with the organization, he fills out a form listing his credentials and he agrees to notify the schools involved when he makes his first contact with a player. Only about 400 agents have even taken the trouble to do that, which is a pretty good indication of how potent the program is.

When you stop and figure how long and complicated the NCAA rules are on agents, you have to admit it was quite an athletic feat for a couple of fellows named Norby Walters and Lloyd Bloom to induce dozens of athletes to break just about every one of them in a matter of two or three years.

Walters has pointed out on several occasions that it didn't take a lot of inducement really, so maybe he deserves the benefit of the doubt on that. Either way, those two fellows have added immeasurably to the literature on sports agents while illustrating in the most graphic terms just what a big money business it is.

They joined forces in 1985 to form World Sports Entertainment Inc. and proceeded to sign more than 30 of the country's top college athletes to agent contracts. Included were 7 of the 28 players taken in the first round of the 1987 NFL draft.

That's a pretty scary accomplishment all by itself. But it was not quite the impressive exercise in free enterprise that it appeared to be. Nothing free about it. Bloom estimated that WSE spent approximately $800,000 to get all those jocks into the fold.

Some of the more noted recipients of WSE's largess were Auburn running back Brent Fullwood with a total of $8,032 in extracurricular benefits, Ohio State wide receiver Chris Carter with a $5,000 interest-free loan, Pittsburgh defensive back Teryl Austin with $2,500 in loans, Minnesota Vikings tight end Carl Hilton with $13,000 (his entire signing bonus, by the way), and the grand champion, Iowa and Buffalo Bills running back Ronnie Harmon with $54,172, most of which an arbitrator ruled he didn't have to give back.

One of the reasons these figures have been so freely available to publications like *Sports Illustrated* and the *Atlanta Journal* and *Constitution*, who have done the most thorough job of reporting this scene, is that Walters and Bloom made no particular attempt to conceal them. Yes, it's against NCAA rules, they said, but it's not against any law of the land to pay college athletes.

Besides, they pointed out that they hadn't invented the practice. It had been officially chronicled as early as 1978. They just did it better than anybody else.

They certainly did it louder than anybody else. And by the time they were through, college coaches and athletic directors all over the country were eating seven meals a day and drinking milk to coat their ulcers.

Also several athletes had been declared ineligible; most of their clients had gone to other agents; they had sued at least six former clients; the NFL held a special draft; they were saying all manner of rude things about each other; and Walters sounded as if he wished he'd never seen a football game, let alone a football player.

According to published reports attributed to Walters himself, a pretty typical arrangement would find WSE giving a client like Austin $1,500 down and $250 a month to sign a contract with the agency. The contract could be postdated until after the player's last possible game, but that was an arrangement that didn't seem to placate the NCAA very much.

When the athlete got the money would depend pretty much on how promising he was and how soon WSE got to him. Carter, for example, received a reported $5,000 interest-free loan in the spring after his sophomore year at Ohio State and a promise for $1,800 a month until his eligibility ran out. Walters noted that when he first entered the business, all of the blue chippers were already signed up.

In return for their money, Walters and Bloom got an athlete's signature on an agreement normally paying them 6% of the total value of any NFL contract they negotiated, including bonuses. They were to get that money up front (bad idea for players, remember) and it was for every year of the contract. What's more, they got 10% of all endorsement income.

And the real kicker was that they received power of attorney most times, giving them complete control of the athlete's financial affairs.

Pretty steep, huh? The players started believing that, too, particularly when other agents began whispering into their ears. As a result, they commenced to sign with some of those other agents. Trouble is they had already taken the money from Walters and Bloom, and most of them seemed to be in no raging hurry to pay it back.

So what did Walters and Bloom do? They sued the players to get their money back. Five of the first-rounders and six athletes in toto were named in the suits, shattering all kinds of precedents and setting collegiate football and eventually the pros on their collective ears.

"All they did was sign contracts with the blessing of their parents and accept support during their senior year," Walters said in press accounts. "I'm the guy who done right. They're the ones who have done wrong. That's why I'm suing every one of them."

Sounds logical, doesn't it? Not to the courts. First an arbitrator ruled that Harmon had to pay back only $5,869 of the $54,172 that he got from Walters and Bloom in cash, airplane tickets, and an automobile. He said the balance wasn't a loan at all, but an inducement to keep Harmon as a client. And that, he pointed out, is a violation of NFLPA rules.

Walters reportedly was "shocked" by the arbitrator's decision. And he hadn't seen anything yet. Shortly thereafter, a federal judge in Atlanta tossed out Walters' $500,000 suit against Fullwood. Judge Charles Brieant wasn't very polite about it either.

"We decline to serve as paymaster of the wages of crime, or referee between thieves," he said. "Both sides of the transaction knew exactly what they were doing, and they knew it was fraudulent and wrong."

Now they know it's not very profitable either. The biggest casualty of this war could be pro football's traditionally chummy relationship with the colleges. Major college football provides the NFL with what amounts to a free farm system. No beating the bushes in Boise, like baseball has to do. Films are available to pro scouts; practices are open to them; whatever it takes.

The more players Old State U contributes to the NFL, the easier it is for Old State U to recruit high school prospects with visions of pro careers dancing in their heads.

In return, the NFL has been extremely careful not to mess with the colleges' highly lucrative show. The league rules say you can't sign a player until he or his class graduates, and the rules insulate college football from spending a lot of time, money, and effort to recruit a star and then lose him in a couple of years to the pros. That happens in basketball all the time, but it's not the NBA's fault. A couple of court cases forced the NBA to take underclassmen whether it wanted them or not.

Now along come Walters and Bloom, signing everybody in sight without regard to race, color, creed, and, most of all, year in school. They caused a little stir when they publicly acknowledged in an *Atlanta Constitution* story that they were paying some NFL scouts between $500 to $1,500 for information on college prospects. You know, who's going to be drafted when. Data like that helps to choose prospective clients.

But the really big ruckus created by WSE was its signing of underclassmen Carter, Austin, and another Pittsburgh player, Charles Gladman. When all that goo splashed onto the pavement, those players were naturally declared ineligible. Since his collegiate career was over, Carter responded by threatening to sue the NFL if it didn't allow him to be drafted as an underclassman.

The NFL, which had been on something of a litigation losing streak anyway, decided it had better hold a special draft to let Carter et al. in. College coaches howled from the housetops at the prospect of the NFL rewarding miscreants with pro contracts.

And Pete Rozelle and company were firmly wedged between the proverbial rock and hard place. If they got sued and lost, underclassmen could come streaming through the gates like so many lemmings. If they accommodated Carter, they risked a Dear John letter from the college game.

So they postponed the special draft in the hopes that Carter and Austin would agree to pay WSE its money back and regain their eligibility. Gladman was another matter. He was in hot water because he wouldn't cooperate in the NCAA's own agent probe.

As it turned out, Austin did return to Pittsburgh, but Ohio State declined to try to reinstate Carter. He's playing for the Philadelphia Eagles. And the NFL and the NCAA are not so much in love as they once were. Now it's more a marriage of convenience.

The romance is gone for Walters and Bloom and their players as well. So is a pretty good chunk of cash.

Walters and Bloom didn't just mess with college football players. They also got into basketball. And when the NCAA found out they had signed a couple of Alabama players named Derrick McKey and Terry Conner, it ordered Alabama to forfeit the $233,000 the school had made from the NCAA tournament.

The university turned right around and sued Walters and Bloom for

$3 million. That's not all. The Alabama attorney general got them indicted on charges of commercial bribery, tampering with a sporting event, and violating the state's deceptive trade law.

The agents eventually settled the case by agreeing to pay the university $200,000 and promising not to deal with Southeastern Conference athletes.

Gene O'Connell, the counsel for the American Football Coaches Association in 1987, is all in favor of suits. He recommended that colleges sue all agents who sign players early, on the twin principles that it will keep agents tied up in litigation and the schools might win some of the suits. O'Connell also wants athletes who engage agents early sued for fraud.

In August of 1988, a federal grand jury in Chicago went beyond O'Connell's wildest dreams. It indicted Walters and Bloom, along with California agent Dave Lueddeke, on charges ranging from racketeering to perjury following an investigation of illegal payments and threats allegedly used to sign dozens of athletes. It also indicted Ohio State's Carter and reached pretrial agreements with 43 college athletes who had signed with Walters and Bloom, requiring the collegians to perform as many as 200 hours of community service and to testify against the defendants if called upon.

The athletes got a pretty good deal under the circumstances. They were ordered to reimburse their schools for any scholarship money they received after signing with agents, but at least they didn't have to face racketeering charges.

The Grand Jury based its case against the athletes on the NCAA-mandated statements they had signed every season saying they had not violated NCAA rules by signing with or accepting money from an agent. The statements also required the players to notify their coach if they were contacted by agents during the course of the season.

The 43 players—many of whom went on to the NFL—all admitted they had contracted with the agents without telling their schools, thereby retaining their eligibility under false pretenses. When you combine with another party to commit fraud, that's racketeering.

Walters and Bloom were charged not only with signing the players fraudulently, but in some cases using a reputed high-ranking organized crime figure named Michael Franzese to muscle athletes into signing agreements. If convicted, they faced 70 years in jail and $2 million in fines.

The Grand Jury probe seemed to bring about a nationwide spirit of confession among agents who shared Walters and Bloom's modus operandi. Atlanta agent Jim Abernethy even claimed ''a religious experience'' was one of the major factors motivating him to disclose his list of clients.

Maybe he meant everything was going to hell in a hurry. Abernethy acknowledged he had signed seven collegiate football players and two basketball players to contracts in violation of NCAA rules. His timing was awful, because the major bowl games were only a few weeks away, and his football players were supposed to participate in them. Instead, they were declared ineligible.

A former real estate tycoon who became a karate promoter before he decided to get his kicks in another sport, Abernethy designed contracts that read like NFL deals, only without so many zeroes after the numbers. They called for signing bonuses and monthly payments ranging from $300 to $1,100. There were also incentive clauses covering things like interceptions.

Providing a festive holiday touch and a deal-closer all in one was Abernethy's promise to take care of his players' families—a $750 bonus for Thanksgiving and $1,000 for Christmas. He was not much into automobiles, though. Abernethy said he gave wheels to only one athlete, and those were traced back to him because the kid failed to pay his parking tickets and the car got towed.

Like Walters and Bloom, Abernethy said he did some expensive business with the pros, paying $5,000 to "a top Dallas Cowboys personnel man" (the Cowboys denied this immediately) and $3,500 to an NBA scout for information on college prospects. He also disputed the conventional wisdom that 50% of the draftable college players in the country had signed early with agents. Abernethy thought it was more like 80%.

So in the space of a few days, he managed to implicate or infuriate nine athletes, six athletic departments, the NCAA, one NFL team, and the whole NBA. Anyone would have to agree that's a pretty potent religious experience.

Abernethy had spent $500,000 in 12 months, and of the 200 to 250 players he had talked to, all were either willing to take money or were already taking it from another agent.

"It's just time to get the whole story out," Abernethy told the *Atlanta Constitution*. "What's going on in the sports world is unbelievable: the cash, the drugs, the lifestyle." He had ample opportunity to get the story out. Abernethy was convicted on misdemeanor trade and commerce charges and sentenced to a year in jail. The conviction was overturned on appeal.

All of this judicial jockeying has certainly made an impressive mess out of what was once a very cozy, quiet, and high-stakes arrangement involving the colleges and the pros. But most knowledgeable observers figured that had to happen sooner or later anyway.

"All the stuff you're reading in the papers has been going on for years," said former agent Manton. "The problem right now is that kids are becoming ineligible. I don't think anything effective is being done. You have to understand that most of it isn't actually illegal. If an agent is giving a kid money, it's not an illegal act. College alumni used to do it all the time. They'd go down to the bank, sign the note for the kid and never get the money back.

"You could eliminate the problems just by letting the kids have agents legally. Colleges want to keep agents off campus because they want their players to stay eligible. I think they're regulating the wrong side of it. What they really want is not to have the kids leave school early. If you're a junior, you should have the right to hire an agent, be drafted and negotiate with the team that drafted you."

That might eliminate one problem anyway, although it wouldn't have helped Kareem Abdul-Jabbar. He had been out of college a long time before he hired Collins. As long as there is serious money to be made in sports, there will be agents.

From the players' standpoint, that's not all bad. It's not all good either. Nobody knows that better than Sylvester Gray, a sophomore basketball star at Memphis State who lost his last two years of eligibility when he got caught signing with an agent. Gray had one simple piece of advice for college athletes that probably won't be followed.

Said the sadder but wiser sophomore: "Don't mess with no agents at all."

SPORT$BIZ STATS

Top 25 Sport Fines (1975-1987)

Fine ($)	Team/Individual	Year	Reason
400,000	Atlanta Hawks	1975	Illegally signing Julius Erving
310,000	Vancouver Canucks	1987	Signing Pat Quinn as General Manager
250,000a	Texas Rangers	1987	Steve Howe/violating drug rules
250,000	Portland Trail Blazers	1984	Tampering with undergraduates
250,000b	George Steinbrenner	1983	Pine tar bat dispute
135,000c	Keith Hernandez	1986	Drugs
130,000	Los Angeles Kings	1987	Negotiating Quinn/Canucks deal
120,000c	Dave Parker	1986	Drugs
115,000c	Joaquin Andujar	1986	Drugs
100,000	Ray Kroc	1979	Tampering with Joe Morgan, Graig Nettles
90,000c	Jeff Leonard	1986	Drugs
80,000c	Lonnie Smith	1986	Drugs
54,000	Steve Howe	1983	Drugs
52,250c	Dale Berra	1986	Drugs
50,000	John Bassett	1985	Opposing USFL fall play
50,000	George Steinbrenner	1983	Umpire dispute
45,000c	Enos Cabell	1986	Drugs
35,000	Richard Petty	1983	Using illegal tires
35,000c	Claudell Washington	1986	Drugs
34,000c	Lee Lacy	1986	Drugs
21,000	Calgary Flames	1986	Fighting Montreal Canadiens
21,000	Montreal Canadiens	1986	Fighting Calgary Flames
20,000	Guillermo Vilas	1983	Accepting appearance money
20,000	Yannick Noah	1983	Refusing to play Nations Cup
20,000c	Al Holland	1986	Drugs

aEstimated. bPlus $50,000 in legal fees. c"Charitable contributions" ordered by Commissioner Peter Ueberroth.

Note. From *Sports Industry News*, September 18, 1987, Game Point Publishing (207) 236-8346. Adapted by permission.

Chapter 5

Sell Mates

Jocks and games for sale or rent

He is a 28-year-old, self-confessed hot dog in spiked hair and wraparound shades who butts heads with huge men when he's happy and spends almost all of his time playing kids' games. Would you buy a motorcycle from this man?

Honda hopes you would.

Or could we interest you in some house paint from a 250-pound screamer who bursts through walls and spends long days traveling short distances because he's afraid of airplanes? Ace Hardware is betting we could.

Just as Merrill Lynch is gambling that you'll allow a sailor help you decide which broker to use, and Ellesse wants you to let a tennis player pick out your next swimsuit.

There must be some reason why the nation's top commercial thinkers believe Jim McMahon, John Madden, Dennis Conner, and Chris Evert have the right stuff to pitch their products. Why else would they be paying them all that money?

And by the way, who would you rather have tell you what's good at the movies than Yogi Berra?

The old jug-eared Yankee catcher is offering 30-second film reviews on national radio and TV—paired of course with 30-second commercials.

Here's a blue-light special: For a mere $200,000 you can buy a three-year lease on Martina Navratilova's left sleeve. Computerland did it. Porsche already had the right sleeve, and somebody else had the rest of the shirt. Someday an international tennis star is going to walk onto center court at Wimbledon wearing a sandwich board.

Even better, for a tenth of what Martina's sleeve costs, Jerry Tarkanian will chew on your towels.

That's all the Nevada-Las Vegas basketball coach charged Taco Bell to put its logo on his celebrated terrycloth pacifier during the 1987 Final Four. While the national TV cameras spotlighted Tark the Shark fretting away on the bench, the folks at Taco Bell were hoping viewers would want to nip out for a nacho when the game was over.

If this is madness, there's a lot of it going around. Whatever people sell, from soup to nuts and from suds to sunglasses, they're hiring jocks to get their messages across. According to a Nov. 9, 1987, *Sports Marketing News* survey, more than 3,400 American companies spent $500 million in 1987 to get athletes to endorse their products.

Most of it is going to just a few people. People like Arnold Palmer, who hasn't won a PGA Tour event since 1973.

Do you die for Arnie as he twitches over a three-foot putt that could be worth $50,000? Relax. If he swatted the ball right into a bunker, it wouldn't make a ripple on his tax return. The acknowledged king of sports endorsers collects an estimated $8 million a year caddying for corporations like Pennzoil, Hertz, United Airlines, and Sears Roebuck. Add a couple extra million for his Japanese revenues.

Who cares if Palmer hasn't collected a first-place check on the regular circuit since Richard Nixon was president? Certainly not the galleries who followed him around when he was a mere millionaire. Now his estimated worth is something like $50 million, and if American capitalism can do that for a balding golfer with the yips, think what it can do for a young quarterback with movie star looks.

The question of course is backward. Companies want to know what athletes can do for them, not vice versa. Generally, they're interested in getting you, the consumer, to identify their product with a player or sometimes with a whole game.

Brand recognition and a warm, cozy feeling toward their company are what they're after, and they find the most ingenious ways to achieve those things.

What's more exciting than Magic Johnson in the open court? What's duller than motor oil? Valvoline found a way to put the two together.

The oil people placed a cutout of the grinning Magic in 276 auto parts stores and challenged the customers to try to outsmile the cutout. They took pictures of the contestants, and the winner got to go to the NBA finals for free. Valvoline had its biggest February ever in Southern California, and the Lakers won the NBA title. No wonder everyone was smiling.

Nobody really thinks Magic changes his own oil, any more than anyone expects to bump into John Madden at the hardware store. Or to see Dan Marino trying on Arrow shirts.

Arrow would like people to think about successful, energetic young men when they think about their shirts, so they hired Marino and made plans to sign up other athletes in other markets. Wearing Arrow doesn't help anybody throw sideline patterns, but it might make people feel so young they think they can. And everybody wants to feel young.

You may think people are too sophisticated to fall for this strategy, but if you're right, hundreds of high-powered businessmen are wrong—millions and millions of dollars wrong. The question in their minds isn't whether sports sells. It's which sports and which athletes sell best.

Not long ago, many company's sports marketing decisions were made on the basis of what the president or advertising director liked to do with his spare time. A lot of golfers and tennis players got a chance to endorse products because of that. They still do, but now it's for much more scientific reasons.

Ranking right behind Palmer in the *Sports Marketing News* survey of top endorsement owners is Jack Nicklaus. Then it's Boris Becker followed by Greg Norman. Two more golfers and a tennis player.

Athletes who play for teams don't show up on the list at all until Michael Jordan comes along in fifth place. The only other team player in the top ten is McMahon. That's not a coincidence, and it's not a new trend.

"Companies are more interested in equating their images with individuals than they are with team winners," said Robert Dowling, the editor of *Sports Marketing News*.

SPORT$BIZ STATS

Top Endorsers (1987)

Athlete	National endorsements	1987 estimated earnings
Arnold Palmer	Hertz, Paine Webber, Pennzoil, United Airlines, GTE, Toro, Loft Seed Co., Sears, Pro Group, Robert Bruce, Westin Hotels	$8,000,000
Jack Nicklaus	Bostonian Shoe Co., Hart Schaffner & Marx, Optique Du Monde, Pine Hosiery Mills, Warnaco	$6,000,000
Boris Becker	Puma, Coca-Cola, Deutsche Bank, Polaroid, UNICEF	$6,000,000
Greg Norman	Reebok, Spalding, Epson Computers, Hertz, Qantas Airlines, Daikyo Group, Swan Lager & Castlemaine, Akubia Hats	$4,500,000
Michael Jordan	Nike, Wilson, Excelsior, McDonald's, Coca-Cola, Chevrolet, Johnson Products, Ohio Art	$4,000,000

Note. From *Sports Marketing News*, November 9, 1987. Adapted by permission.

"The really successful endorsers can make three times as much money off the field as they can on the field, and most of them will turn down more offers than they accept, either because they don't believe in the product or they don't want to be overexposed."

At least part of the explanation for the popularity of golfers and tennis players among advertisers is that people who watch and play those games frequently have a lot of money to work with, either their own or their company's. What kinds of products and services do you see advertised during golf tournaments? Banks, brokers, insurance companies, expensive cars, and other upscale goods and services.

Besides, golfers and tennis players generally look good, speak well, get hurt less, and don't have to depend upon others for their success. Most important, they stay out of trouble.

There has been no shortage of brash, arrogant, and obnoxious tennis players over the years, and those endearing qualities have cost a few of them some corporate opportunities. But so far, there have been no reported cases of top performers in these sports doing drugs or doing time—the two things high profile athletes can't do if they want to make endorsement money.

Most basketball, football, and baseball players don't do them either, but enough of them do to make things tough on their teammates. Sometimes it's just safer for advertisers to go with games that have tidy pedigrees.

Overexposure isn't a problem for a great many athletes, but those who do experience it have to pay attention. Dowling's magazine polled 400 executives at corporations that sponsored sports in 1987 and asked them which athlete they would take if they could sign any jock in the world. First place went to Julius Erving, and he was followed by Nicklaus, Walter Payton, and Dennis Conner.

There were no votes for Palmer, Norman, Jordan, or Ivan Lendl, mainly because those fellows were already overexposed.

It doesn't seem to matter that Erving and Payton are retired, while Nicklaus hardly ever wins anymore and Conner only sets sail publicly when the America's Cup races are on. Winning isn't everything to advertisers. It takes something else to attract them. Dowling calls it "winning with style."

Erving and Payton are the epitome of grace and style, while Nicklaus and Palmer fairly exude truth, justice, and the American way. Would these guys cheat you?

Still, if the leading athletic product promoters all wore the same seamless, spotless personality, it wouldn't be too long before the American sporting consumer was bored senseless. That's why God and commercialism invented characters like McMahon and Madden.

They're among the top 12 national endorsers, according to the *Sports Marketing News* survey. Joining them are such varied personalities as Boris Becker, the German wunderkind; silent Ivan Lendl; sweet Chris Evert; and Jackie Stewart and Greg Norman, who talk funny.

The lofty dozen pulled down more than $45 million from corporate contracts in 1987, which kind of messed up the curve. Figure about 50 athletes will top $250,000 in endorsements in a year while another 100 will go over the $100,000 mark.

Greg Lustig, head of the Lustig Group sports agency that represents several big-league clients in their commercial dealings, says a variety of factors go into who gets how much from endorsements.

"The rates are determined by the demand for a player, the size of the market he plays in and whether he's involved in a national or local campaign," said Lustig. "The first thing I find out when an advertiser asks about one of my clients is what the budget is and whether he's shopping for people or if it's a done deal."

Lustig's clients include Buffalo Bills quarterback Jim Kelly, one of the hottest properties around in team sports. He said Kelly typically gets $5,000 for a personal appearance, $25,000 for appearing in a print ad, and $50,000 for a local commercial. A national commercial boosts the ante enormously—to between $125,000 and $150,000.

Contrast that to an athlete without much national appeal who Lustig says might get $300 to $500 for a public appearance and maybe pick up some clothes or the use of a car for saying nice things about a local merchant.

SPORT$BIZ STATS

Top Quarterback Endorsers (1987)

Quarterback	National endorsements	1987 estimated earnings ($)
Jim McMahon	Taco Bell, Honda, Kraft Foods, Adidas, Ebel Watches, LJN Toys, Revo Sunglasses	3,000,000
Phil Simms	Walt Disney World, York Barbell Co., Continental Airlines, Bell Atlantic, Drexel Burnham Lambert	900,000
Joe Montana	Sanka, Wilson Sporting Goods, Foster Grant, Ocean Spray, Mizuno Athletic Shoes	850,000
Dan Marino	Arrow Co., Pony, Isotoner Gloves, Chevrolet, Ryder Truck Rentals, Anheuser-Bush, MacGregor Sporting Goods	700,000
John Elway	Continental Airlines, Mizuno Athletic Shoes	250,000

Note. From Sports Marketing News, September 28, 1987. Adapted by permission.

That's a big difference, and most athletes would love to bridge the gap. To do it, though, they might have to change some circumstances that are beyond their control.

How do you get to be a star variety athlete from an advertiser's point of view? Well, you play well of course, but that's only the beginning. Other factors that can be just as important include these:

- **Appearance.** It helps to look good. In Bart Conner's case, it helped to look good all over.

  The Olympic gymnast signed a profitable deal with Jockey Underwear that got his body featured on 14 full-color, full-page ads wearing a kind of half-smile and not very much else. Maybe that's what's meant by media exposure.

  Jockey is something of a sports endorsement pioneer. Its first major endorser was the rotund Babe Ruth. In those days, full-page ads of guys in their underwear were not deemed suitable for mixed company, and it's probably just as well. That changed in 1979 when pitcher Jim Palmer first stripped down to bare essentials.

- **Geography.** One guy who will never get rich on his boyish demeanor and Greek god physique is Mike Ditka. He must look mean in his sleep. But the Chicago Bears coach is in the right place at the right time. It helps to live in an area where a lot of other people live and buy products and watch TV. Say Los Angeles, New York, or Chicago.

  Ditka, who has edged past Los Angeles Dodgers manager Tommy Lasorda as the top endorser among coaches and managers, reportedly makes more from outside income than he does from his $500,000 contract. It's one reason why he's never displayed much interest in changing teams.

  On the other hand, commercial opportunities can serve as a fine reward for relocating. When Andre Dawson left Montreal in 1987 to join the Chicago Cubs, he took a $500,000 salary cut, but he got a lot of it back in outside income.

  Montreal is a relatively small market to begin with, and half the people there speak French. Dawson was not among that half. In Chicago, he had no trouble turning his 1987 MVP season into a merchandising bonanza. To have any hope of doing that in Canada, he needed to be a hockey player.

  Like Wayne Gretzky. Of course calling Gretzky a hockey player is like calling Michelangelo a ceiling painter. Gretzky has been a national hero in Canada since he was 14, and that combined with his boy-next-door lifestyle and unparalleled talents adds up to the hat trick of endorsements.

  His agent says Gretzky has been with the same six corporations for a total of 27 years, and he's seen to it that he has something to say about

SPORT$BIZ STATS

Top Baseball Endorsers (1988)

Ballplayer	Major endorsements	1988 estimated earnings ($)
Andre Dawson	Rawlings, Converse, First National Bank of Chicago[a], Chevrolet[a], Pepsi[a], Tru-Link Fence[a]	325,000
Don Mattingly	RJR Nabisco, Franklin, Converse, Sports and Toys Concepts	300,000
Gary Carter	Nike, MacGregor, Newsday[a], Epyx, Franklin, Northville Oil[a]	250,000
George Brett	Wilson, Puma, Swingster Athletic Apparel[a], P. Leiner Nutritional Products[a], Vess Beverages[a]	230,000
Dale Murphy	Canon Camera, Nike, Rawlings, Oscar Mayer[a], Kinnett Drugs[a]	220,000

[a] Local account.

Note. From Sports Marketing News, May 23, 1988. Adapted by permission.

the product. When Gretzky endorses a cereal, he gets to help name it, shape it, decide what goes into it, and even design the box.

It's anyone's guess how much more of a corporate haul Gretzky will be able to make now that he's playing in the media-rich Los Angeles market. You get an idea of his impact from the reaction of the television people there. LA's Prime Ticket Network agreed to pay $2.4 million in additional rights fees to the Los Angeles Kings over four years so that they could swing the trade that brought Gretzky to LA from the Edmonton Oilers.

- **International appeal.** Gretzky's image has been projected as far east as Japan, which is one of the reasons he's in the multimillion-dollar endorsement class. But he still plays his game exclusively in Canada and the United States. If an athlete really wants to get into the heavy endorsement money, he has to take his show all over the world.

  One of the reasons Becker and Stewart rank so high on the commercial charts is that they are recognized internationally. Perhaps 900 million Chinese really *don't* know who won the Super Bowl, but a few of them might be able to tell you who the Wimbledon champion is.

- **Rules and regulations.** While Michael Jordan can plaster the Nike name all over his shoes, he can't wear anything else with a brand name on it as part of his uniform. Football players can't either.

Remember when McMahon was seen pacing the sidelines one Sunday wearing a headband bearing the Adidas logo? NFL Commissioner Pete Rozelle wasted no time explaining the fine points of the league's dress code to the Bears' quarterback and threatening dire consequences should he fail to comply with them.

McMahon responded at the next game by wearing a Rozelle headband, which Pete considered to be much more sportsmanlike conduct.

The NBA, if anything, is even more sticky about these matters. Coaches in that league can't even wear shoes with identifiable brands on them. Don Nelson made an issue of that a couple of years back when he was coaching the Milwaukee Bucks.

He wanted to wear referee's shoes during games because he said they were more comfortable than the standard loafers and wingtips. The problem was that the ref shoes all had big Converse stars on them, and the league said that was a no-no.

Nelson's answer was to put ugly gobs of tape over the logo, which of course gave Converse much better exposure than it ever could have gotten if people could have seen what was under the tape. It made Nelson look pretty funny, but Converse didn't mind.

Compare that policy to the one that operates in golf and tennis. Golfers can sell space on their hats and shirts. Tennis players can market their headbands, wristbands, and sleeves for about $100,000 apiece. Some, like Navratilova, do better.

There are some limits on the advertising that tennis players can tote around on their persons. They are allowed only two nonclothing, non-equipment patches in tournament play. But there's still plenty of room on a successful player's togs to get advertisers' messages across. And when the player walks off the court, the opportunities are boundless.

Steffi Graf, who is the world's No. 1 women's tennis player, makes $35,000 to $40,000 for each personal appearance, and appearances were just a small part of her estimated $4 million in earnings in 1987. Her $3.3-million endorsement income came from companies that make clothes, shoes, cars, audio equipment, cosmetics, fruit juice, and . . . oh yeah, tennis racquets.

- **Personality.** The product doesn't necessarily have to have anything to do with the sport. What matters is whether the games and the messages reach the customers. Graf gets them there in her own youthful, winning way.

  Then there's the John McEnroe approach. When Bic picked him to sell its razors, the company said it liked the excitable Big Mac not so much because he was a top tennis player, but because he had a talent for attracting media attention off the court. Shy John's never had any trouble doing that.

The best way for a golfer to attract attention is to win one of the world's major championships—the Masters, U.S. Open, British Open, or the PGA. Most experts figure that's worth around $500,000 in outside income. Winning a major lets you stand out from the crowd of other well-scrubbed, well-spoken, tan, fit, blond mashie magicians.

But if you project the right image, you don't have to win every big tournament. Take Norman, who is a kind of Crocodile Dundee of the fairways.

It helped him to win the British Open, but once he did that, it was more important that he was friendly, open, talkative Greg Norman, who seems to like everybody except an occasional reporter. Anybody who gets along with all reporters at all times is either canonized or brain dead.

Fuzzy Zoeller is another golfer whose personable style attracts galleries, and therefore advertisers. Palmer turned that into an art form, and he also had the good fortune to be in on the ground floor when companies were getting the notion that it was worth $7,000 to put their name on somebody's visor.

Companies like to make deals with promising young athletes so they can ride those budding careers right to the end of the rainbow. This involves some guesswork, however, and it's not unheard of for an advertiser to sign a long-term arrangement with a hot prospect and wind up spending several years in the rough with him.

- **Choice of sport.** It's even riskier to get involved with team athletes. There's no telling what's going to happen with those guys. Careers are shorter for them, and the room at the top of the team sport world is narrow and wobbly.

It's almost a law that World Series, Super Bowl, and NBA champions don't repeat. So although the ace left-hander on the world championship baseball club is a hot property all winter, his fame melts pretty quickly when his team goes on a 10-game losing streak the following spring. It doesn't make much difference how he's pitching either.

What's even worse is playing on a world championship team and having your accomplishments met by a collective, corporate yawn. It happened to the Minnesota Twins, who won the 1987 World Series, rode down the streets of Minneapolis in a ticker-tape parade, and then looked around and wondered where everybody went.

"I couldn't believe it," said Twins star Tom Brunansky. "You see a team win the Super Bowl or even the NBA championship, and they've got guys doing things nationally. It's almost like they still don't believe we've won."

Part of Brunansky's problem was that "they" don't live in Minneapolis. At least not many of them do. The Twins' relatively small market held down their endorsement opportunities. Some experts also said the players weren't aggressive enough in making themselves available to advertisers. They waited for the companies to come to them. They're still waiting.

But a final theory on why the world championship couldn't make the Twins rich was that they're baseball players. Just as it is generally acknowledged that team sports offer less outside income than individual sports, it is also believed that baseball is worse that way than other team sports.

Football is a little better than baseball for outside income, but it still isn't great. Brian Bosworth was easily the most prosperous NFL player drafted in 1987 in terms of outside income with well over $1 million. Next best was Vinny Testaverde with around $500,000.

Maybe a football player has more national appeal because his television exposure is national, rather than local. On the other hand, some qualified observers say fans have a tough time identifying with football players because they're "faceless." In other words, their helmets get in the way.

Quarterbacks usually make more outside income than other kinds of football players. Why? Ask a serious pro football fan to name the starting quarterback on every NFL team, and he'll probably come up with at least half of them. Ask him to name an offensive tackle or even a wide receiver from each team, and he'll come up with a faraway look in his eyes.

It's not enough just to throw the ball for a living, though. If you also play on a winning team, preferably a Super Bowl team, take one giant step forward. If the winning team hails from a big market, take another one. If you are a talented player on a winning team from a big market, and you're a little bit crazy—Bingo!

Your name is Jim McMahon, and you don't have to work one day longer than you want.

- **Race.** Following the 1988 Super Bowl, another quarterback began making his way up the endorsement ladder, and it should be sociologically illuminating to see how far he climbs.

  Just moments after dismantling the Denver Broncos' defense, Washington's Doug Williams told the world, "I'm going to Disneyland." He didn't do that out of a spontaneous urge to meet Mickey Mouse. And he didn't do it for free.

  A few hours after that, General Mills was churning out a million boxes of Wheaties with Williams's picture on it.

  Good start, but Williams's major claim to fame was becoming the first black quarterback ever to start in the Super Bowl. It's not something he promoted, but it is something reporters questioned him about constantly. The next question is whether it will get in his way commercially.

Nine months after the Redskins won the Super Bowl, Williams had earned a reported $127,500 in endorsements, which isn't bad for walking-around money but doesn't compare to the haul enjoyed by some of his white colleagues. For instance, McMahon took in $1 million after the Bears won in '86, and the Giants' Phil Simms picked up $750,000. Why?

To some observers, it's as plain as black and white.

"When advertisers decide to use an athlete in an ad they will almost immediately go to a white athlete," said Harry Edwards, a sports sociology professor at the University of California and a minority issues consultant to the baseball commissioner's office. In an interview in the Oct. 18, 1988, *Wall Street Journal*, Edwards went on to say, "These aren't people who consider this kind of thing to be racist. It just never crosses their minds."

Sitting on the other side of the fence, interestingly enough, is Tad Dowd, Williams's publicity manager. In the same *Journal* article, Dowd said, "It takes time, and they want to see you go to the next season." Dowd said Williams was forming a sportswear company that will make more money than all the other athletes' endorsements put together.

Williams's decision to take matters into his own hands by forming a company is a reflection of a growing trend in marketing athletes. Rather than waiting around for companies to decide whether they have any use for them, the really big jocks are starting to call their own shots.

Baseball's Pete Rose, for example, was smart enough to know just how fleeting fame can be, so he did some planning before he signed long-term deals that involved more than just commercials. He figured if he could get his name linked with a company in a general, promotional way, he wouldn't have to break Ty Cobb's hitting streak record every year.

Spud Webb's agent did the same thing for the Atlanta Hawks ministar, making sure that his client would cash in for several years on his 1986 slam-dunk title. Even when you're a 5'-7" favorite in the NBA, you can't be sure somebody even smaller and cuter won't come along. Like say, Muggsy Bogues.

Webb turned down a lucrative offer from Anheuser-Busch because he didn't think beer ads fit his image as a role model for kids. And Houston Astros pitcher Mike Scott, who has been accused from time to time of altering the surfaces of the baseballs he pitches, said no thank you to an ad campaign entitled "the right scuff." Image counts.

Smart athletes who deal with advertisers are less inclined these days to literally take the money and run. Kareem Abdul-Jabbar's latest two-year contract with Adidas is a case in point. He agreed to make some public appearances for the company and to be included in its newsletter and catalog. He also said he would participate in a program aimed at keeping Los Angeles kids in school. Adidas made the same move with Patrick Ewing in New York.

You hear about those things and you think kind thoughts about both the shoes and the player who has them on. That's the idea. While athletes represent companies, they're also concerned with how the companies represent them.

In this wonderful, media-mad society of ours, corporations and celebrities get more closely identified with one another all of the time. And the wrong identifications can be disastrous for either side.

So now who wants to be identified with Brian Bosworth? You might be surprised. When you think of the Boz, do you see a canny, farsighted business-man with an eye cast on the fiscal horizon? No? Think again.

The Seattle Seahawks' colorful linebacker has not just sought long-term deals like the one Rose and Webb have cut. He's started his own company to market personalized shoes and sportswear. This is taking the process one step further. Bosworth won't settle for an advertising contract or even a piece of the action. Bosworth is the action.

For the fastest growing action in sports marketing, though, we have to look past Bosworth, past Palmer, past any individual athlete in the world. More and more, companies are deciding it's not enough to promote their wares by enlisting a jock. They want to use a whole event, a whole game, or a whole league. What's more, it's not hard to find cooperative partners.

The NBA sells itself as the game of the young, upwardly mobile male, which just happens to be the kind of consumer many big companies are after. The league will be delighted to help companies use the NBA's image and prestige to get in touch with the right kind of customer.

In the process of course, the NBA makes money for its teams. It's the same in the other major sports.

Basketball, baseball, and football all have sophisticated marketing and licensing divisions. Basketball's is called NBA Properties, and it is big business indeed. From 1982 to 1987 the division grew from a staff of three to a staff of 30, and revenues rocketed from $1 million to $12 million.

That's meal money to Major League Baseball Properties, whose annual sales were between $450 million and $500 million in 1987. Football is in this market, too, with about $300 million in revenues.

Generally speaking, any item with a team or league logo on it—pennants, jackets, hats, mugs, whatever—is sold through the respective leagues' market-ing and licensing divisions. Sometimes they make nice profits on that stuff. Sometimes they give it away to get you to buy a ticket.

Let's say it's cushion day at the old ballpark. Turn that cushion around, and you're likely to see some company's logo on it. Now you know who paid for the cushion that you got for free. The team sold a ticket, the com-pany got some advertising, and you have been introduced to the wonderful, symbiotic world of "sponsorship."

Here's how that works. There are three basic ways a company can use sports to sell:

1. It can hire individual athletes to pump its products. Call that endorsement.

2. It can buy TV or radio time and have its commercials aired during sporting events. Call that advertising.

3. It can underwrite campaigns, events, or sometimes whole seasons and get its name identified with a particular sport, event, league, or team. That's called sponsorship, and it's growing like crazy.

As much as NBA Properties likes to sell trinkets, it gets even more excited about attracting sponsors. It had 20 of them in 1987, and it was out there looking for more every day. Example? Did you fill out an NBA All-Star ballot last year? There was the Miller Brewing Company all over the computer card. Miller paid to print, collect, and count the ballots, and in the process became the NBA Miller All-Star balloting sponsor.

Young, upwardly mobile males drink beer, and if Miller can get them to think a little bit about its product while they're thinking about basketball, its mission is accomplished. The leagues' involvement in this type of marketing is just the tip of a mile-deep iceberg.

Sponsorship is especially big for companies that sell products like beer and cigarettes, because they're pretty much shut out of the endorsement game. Active athletes, either by choice or necessity, don't promote those products.

It's not clear whether that's a formal rule or an informal arrangement, but it's there just the same. Athletes are role models, and role models wreathed in smoke and clutching beer cans are not furthering their cause with the product-consuming parents of America.

If you can't use an individual athlete to help you market your product, you can put a bunch of them together at a meet or a tournament and bask in their collective efforts. An August 1987 special report in *Business Week* magazine showed that 3,400 U.S. companies spent $1.35 billion to sponsor sporting events that year. Whole countries get along on less.

Phillip Morris alone allocated $85 million to sports sponsorship, according to that report. The other top five sports sponsors were RJR-Nabisco, Anheuser-Busch, Adolph Coors, and Coca-Cola. Lots of beer and tobacco there.

That $1.35-billion figure was four times larger than it was four years earlier when sports TV ratings were going through the roof. Now many companies figure they get more mileage out of their money if they identify themselves with the show rather than merely pestering people with their commercials.

It's not likely that any major American sport would disappear if corporate sponsorship dried up, but some of them could not continue to live in the manner to which they have become accustomed. A prime example is the Olympic Games.

The '88 Winter Olympics alone pulled in $350 million in sponsorship income. Next was auto racing with $276 million, followed by golf, tennis, and, of all things, marathon running.

There are all kinds of sponsors. At the grass roots, we have Joe's Corner Tap buying shirts for a local softball team. At the penthouse level, companies often pay for the privilege of having whole events named after them. That's called title sponsorship.

SPORT$BIZ STATS

Top Sponsors (1987)

Sponsors	Sports advertising ($ millions)	Event sponsorship, licensing, and related promotion ($ millions)	Total ($ millions)
Philip Morris Cos.	260	91	351
Anheuser-Busch Cos.	290	60	350
General Motors Corp.	291	19	310
RJR Nabisco	92	82	174
Ford Motor Co.	130	15	145
Chrysler Corp.	115	16	131
U.S. Armed Forces	115	0	115
IBM Corp.	92	10	102
AT&T	72	10	82
Gillette Co.	45	25	70

Note. From Sports Marketing News, February 15, 1988. Adapted by permission.

Some companies annex entire conferences. Phillips Petroleum once bought title sponsorship for the entire Big Eight Conference basketball season, including the championship tournament. Goodyear did the same thing with the Pac 10. In Goodyear's case the deal cost $1 million for three years.

Other places think smaller. You can't buy the Olympic Games. You can't even buy one of the Olympic teams. But you can claim your little piece of them for the right price.

If you would like to be the official left handlebar grip of the U.S. Olympic cycling team, come right ahead. But bring your checkbook. How's that for pure amateurism?

Some funny things happen on the way to the Olympic stadium if people aren't careful, however. For instance, the organizers of the '88 Winter Games spent $374,000 for ponchos to be worn by spectators at the opening ceremonies so as to provide a splashy TV backdrop. Coca-Cola helped foot the bill for the 60,000 ponchos and naturally emblazoned the Coke emblem right next to the Olympic logo on the front of the garments. Oops!

The emblem was supposed to go on the inside. Otherwise it violated the so-called Olympic ban on commercialization, which is a pretty ludicrous concept all by itself if you think about it.

Anyway, the offending ponchos had to be sent to the Calgary Correctional Institution where 12 inmates worked 10 hours a day unpacking them, turning them inside out, and resewing them so they could be used for the opening.

Nobody was laughing about that at Calgary, where sponsorship was a potent topic that carried both a high price tag and a fair amount of clout. Remember those ads that said "They don't take American Express" at the Olympics? They weren't kidding.

Visa spent more than $15 million as an Olympic sponsor, and one of the things it bought was an agreement that you couldn't buy anything on the grounds with an American Express card. So when you think about downhill skiing, maybe you'll think about Visa.

Subaru is hoping you'll think about cars. It wants to become synonymous with American amateur skiing, and it's devoted more than $50 million of its advertising budget to that since it began sponsoring the U.S. ski team in 1976.

Subaru picked skis. Culligan picked bikes. It paid to become the official drinking water of the World Cycling Championships. Different sports go for different sorts of products.

Back in 1916 Budweiser's idea of sports marketing was to sponsor a bowling team. Since then it has sunk money into auto racing, boat racing, football, basketball, baseball, hockey, soccer, triathlons, and even rugby. Anheuser-Busch officials say they get 50 sponsorship requests a week. Obviously they have to choose carefully.

Nowhere has sponsorship boomed more dramatically than in golf. When the '80s began, four PGA tournaments had title sponsors. By 1987, there were 29 of them, and some of those were on their second sponsor.

The same pattern is beginning to creep into football bowl games. It's no longer the Fiesta Bowl, it's the Sunkist Fiesta Bowl, with sponsorship fees topping $1 million. The Sugar Bowl has become the USF&G Sugar Bowl, with title sponsorship fees sweetening the pot to the tune of $2 million.

We may still have amateur sports in this country—although that's getting to be a more debatable proposition all the time—but there's nothing amateur about the way they're marketed.

The issue of corporations on campus is getting far more serious than anyone would have thought even 10 or 15 years ago. The biggest commercial controversy in amateur sports isn't sponsorship, though. It's shoes. Shoes are in a world of their own when it comes to sports marketing on both the amateur and professional level.

Next time you go to a college basketball game, take a look at what the players are wearing on their feet. Not only are the shoes all the same color, they're all the same brand.

Big money is involved in having collegians identically shod, and none of the money finds its way to the players. The NCAA is very touchy about having its athletes give even the appearance of endorsing products.

So who gets rich from the collegiate shoe scene? Coaches.

Mark Thomasshow, a corporate counsel for the Nike Shoe Company, says that the four or five top college basketball coaches in the country can earn as much as $200,000 apiece to sign endorsement contracts with shoe companies. Others in the top 20 can expect between $100,000 and $200,000.

Thomasshow points out that, unlike pro players, college coaches don't usually have agents making these deals for them. So they don't have to share the money with anybody.

Now what's that telling the athlete who's doing all the work? He's running up and down the court for tuition, room, board, and the love of old State U while his coach gets a couple hundred grand for an autograph and a few clinic appearances.

When a coach lives in that kind of financial neighborhood, his salary can become almost an afterthought.

The *Atlanta Journal* and *Constitution* got curious about this whole question and demanded to know what the football and basketball coaches at the University of Georgia were making in sports-related outside income. The coaches didn't want to tell them, but Georgia's open meeting law forced their lawyer to release some startling figures.

It came out that football coach and athletic director Vince Dooley made more in sports-related outside income than he did in salary. And basketball coach Hugh Durham's extracurricular activities were worth more than double his coach's paychecks.

Dooley's $95,000 salary and $4,500 "subsistence allowance" was supplemented by $103,000 from television and radio shows, $15,000 from a shoe company endorsement, $12,000 from speaking engagements, $5,250 from summer camps, and $2,406 from endorsement contracts with athletic equipment and clothing companies. Did somebody say "subsistence"?

Durham made $75,000 from the university to coach basketball, which was just $2,000 more than he brought home to talk about his team on radio and TV. He got another $40,000 from speaking engagements, $3,600 from a company that makes basketballs, and $1,500 from a uniform manufacturer. And, oh yeah, $36,000 from a shoe company.

North Carolina State's basketball coach Jim Valvano may not be the king of the coachly endorsers, but he's definitely among the leaders with an estimated $500,000 annual outside income to go with his $85,000 salary.

Just to give you an idea of the variety of opportunities open to people with Valvano's talent and personality—and face it, there are precious few people like Valvano—his outside income sources include a shoe company, a car company, the Washington Speakers Bureau, his own basketball camps, and several broadcasting interests. He also is half-owner of a company that creates corporate art.

Valvano acknowledges that his basketball job provided him with certain opportunities, but he points out that it was his own talent and personality that let him develop them. And he's not about to apologize for making money from honest work.

The athletes themselves don't seem to mind the coaches making all that money. They just want some, too.

Allen L. Sack, a sociology professor at the University of New Haven, passed out questionnaires to Division 1 basketball players, and 60% of the players told him they had no moral problem with taking money under the table.

They also thought they should get a share of the TV revenue the schools were making from their games. The professor didn't ask if they wanted a piece of the shoe action, too.

The NCAA's reaction to this kind of thinking is fairly predictable. There was a move in 1988 to get some kind of handle on coaches' outside income. A proposal was drafted that would require institution approval before a coach could take the money directly. To no one's great surprise, 77% of the university presidents surveyed were all for the idea, and 94% of the basketball coaches were against it.

The coaches fought off outright limits on outside income with a compromise measure requiring them to report what they made to school administrators. But they weren't really crazy about that either, because they figured the administrators would disclose what the coaches told them, thereby creating pressure for income limits.

That's led to an uneasy truce on the issue, which goes off in all sorts of directions anyway. For instance, some state ethics codes already require coaches to turn over the loot. And some coaches have been doing it all along.

Indiana's Bob Knight hands $100,000 in promotion money to the Indiana University Foundation every year, and North Carolina's Dean Smith gives half of his hundred grand to the university. Louisiana State University's Dale Brown won't take the money in the first place. Brown says he's been offered as much as $150,000 by one company, but he turned the deal down.

One of the legacies of Lefty Driesel's departure from Maryland during the Len Bias unpleasantness was a rule that Terrapin coaches could no longer have individual endorsement contracts.

Depending on what the schools do with the money, it's probably a good move. And it looks good politically for a public university to be able to snag all that extra cash for the taxpayer.

In 1984 the Virginia attorney general issued an opinion that any coach at a state-supported college who took promotion money was violating state conflict-of-interest laws. That didn't bother Cavalier basketball coach Terry Holland a bit. He was already giving the money to the university. But the ruling gave the school an idea.

Why not put the Cavalier shoe business out for bid? That's what the university did, and the result was a fat, five-year, $500,000 contract covering all sports, which was a good deal more than Holland was getting in the first place.

This should work fine as long as the school has winning teams. But how about the ones that haven't been to an NCAA tournament since the days of peach baskets and wooden backboards? Does anybody really want to be the shoe that went 0-26?

"I can't see Nike wanting to come in and have the Arizona coach be associated as a Nike coach when the program was 1-17 and last place in the

Pac 10 Conference,'' the University of Arizona's Lute Olson told *USA Today*. "They hired me, not the university.''

Whoever gets the money, the shoe companies will spread plenty of it around as they go toe to toe with each other for the minds and hearts of your sneaker-worshipping sons and daughters.

Take Bobby Cremins. Georgia Tech's coach didn't get that prematurely grey hair from worrying about how he was going to keep his feet warm. Cremins signed a deal with Nike that would pay him a reported $160,000 annually to make promotional appearances for the company.

Most coaches don't do that well. The average in 1987 was generally figured to be somewhere between $30,000 and $40,000 for Division 1 men's basketball coaches.

Women have come a long way, baby, but not on this road. Texas women's basketball coach Jody Conradt's $15,000 contract with Converse was tops in a group of only 15 women coaches who are in on the endorsement gravy. She got an extra $5,000 for winning the national championship in 1986.

The shoe companies do seem to be backing off the campus market a little bit as coaches' prices continue to go up, although Converse was still spending a reported $2 million on college hoops in 1987 and another $100,000 or so for football.

In addition to the money, the companies also have to provide four or five pairs of shoes per player per season as well as miscellaneous items like bags, sweats, and T-shirts. In return, the coaches do public appearances and clinics and in most cases dress their players in the appropriate tennies.

Surprisingly, the contracts don't all say the coach's team has to wear the shoes. Nike's endorsement contract just says the coach has to make the shoes available, tell the kids nice things about them, and suggest they wear them. Of course, coaches also ''suggest'' kids block out on rebounds and hustle back on fast breaks.

Other companies, such as Pony, don't leave any options. They require that the players display the product. They require quite a few other things, too, and it's all in black and white.

As leisure reading goes, a college coach's shoe contract is only slightly less gripping than a McDonald's menu. But there is some stuff in there that reveals what companies worry about when they go around recruiting campus spokesmen.

A typical Nike pact, for example, says if a coach's program is put on NCAA probation during the life of the contract, he gets only half of his money. A Pony contract says if his team is suspended, the deal is void.

And if the coach gets fired? ''See you later.'' That's in both the Pony and Nike contracts.

If he just changes jobs and goes to another Division 1 school, the company has 90 days to decide whether it wants to keep the coach under contract.

That has some interesting implications. What if Nike has a contract with a coach who changes jobs, and the school he goes to is one like Virginia, which has a deal with another shoe company? Do the players wear one Nike and one Converse? Or do the guards wear Nike and the forwards Converse while the centers go barefoot?

There can't be any doubt about what a college coach will wear. The contracts say he has to wear the company's shoes and nobody else's "anywhere in the world" that he coaches. It usually says he has to show up for some appearances and clinics and that he gets about $1,000 worth of shoes and merchandise.

And it says he has to behave. This is not a throwaway item. Let's give it to you from a standard Pony contract, legalese and all. Under "Special Right of Termination" the clause reads:

> Pony shall have the right to terminate this agreement at any time if the commercial value of coach as intended to be used pursuant to the terms hereof is substantially impaired by reason of the commission by coach or team of any act which tends to shock, insult or offend the community standards of public morals and decency.

It's pretty hard to shock, insult, or offend basketball fans in some communities, or Bobby Knight wouldn't be throwing chairs out onto the court. But a coach does have to watch his act somewhat.

He also has to watch his team's act, and that can be a much harder job. But for a hundred grand or so, it's not so much to ask.

One last thing about coaches' shoe contracts. When shoe companies sign a hot property, they like to keep him tied up. So the contracts have a clause that says after the term has expired the company can match a rival's offer. If Converse wanted to steal Cremins from Nike, and Nike could match the offer, Cremins couldn't change shoe companies.

The same thing goes for pro players, and the battles get pretty intense in this arena. That's because the identification is much stronger.

Most fans outside of North Carolina don't have a clue what kind of shoes a Tarheel wears, but if they watch television at all they must have caught Converse's Magic Johnson-Larry Bird shootout commercials. Jordan has been just as heavily exposed by Nike on TV. For a while, any kid who didn't have a pair of Air Jordans had to sneak into school and keep his feet under his desk.

Nike earned an estimated $110 million from Air Jordans the first year they came out. Then Jordan got hurt the following season, and sales plummeted to $5 million. Jordan's just fine now, and Nike is hoping a new line of his shoes will put them back into sneaker clover. The company was working on a 7-year, $19-million deal with Jordan.

Like college coaches, pro athletes have provisions in their shoe contracts that say they have to keep their noses clean. That can be interpreted in the most literal sense.

Among the things that will get a player's Pony contract canceled quicker than a Laker fast break is any drug offense conviction or suspension. A "moral turpitude" conviction will have the same effect.

Getting cut from the team does, too, and in some cases so does a strike. You don't suppose management is aware of that strike clause, do you?

Good things happen to an athlete who is having a good season. If he's famous enough for the company to put him on a poster, it pays extra. Maybe a dime a poster if nobody else is on it.

There are contract bonuses, too, for playing a lot of minutes or for making the all-star game. Like the teams themselves, advertisers have a rooting interest in the players they sign.

There was a time when just about anybody with two feet and a job on an NBA team could get $30,000 to $40,000 for wearing somebody's shoes. The average contract peaked at around $50,000, but then the companies pulled back.

There's still plenty of competition among the shoe companies in the NBA, but their approach is different. They go for big stars or players on teams that win a lot—or both.

By 1987, two years after Reebok started selling basketball shoes in the United States, it had a fifth of the NBA players under contract. Eight of them were Boston Celtics and seven of them were Atlanta Hawks.

But only 27 of the 70 players walking around in Reeboks were getting paid to wear them. Some of the others picked up a little appearance money from the company, and that's about all. For many NBA players, a shoe contract didn't give them anything but shoes.

This is not to say the well has gone totally dry. It just got shallower. While Reebok was No. 1 in athletic shoes, second-place Nike was still chalking up a reported $800 million in sales while hiring 500 endorsers to push 400 different styles.

Is it worth it? The marvelous thing about sports marketing, whether it takes the form of endorsements, advertising, or sponsorship, is that nobody really knows for sure.

Companies conduct exotic studies to determine whether the money they're spending on sports advertising, endorsements, and sponsorship shows up on the bottom line, and they have yet to come up with a definitive relationship.

Probably the only way to find out would be to stop doing it. That might work for the nuclear arms race, too, but nobody wants to take the chance of disarming unilaterally.

And so it is in marketing. Companies use sports because they're pretty sure the approach works and because everybody's doing it. Donald Dell, the former Davis Cup tennis player who now runs the biggest sports marketing firm in the world, once explained sports' attraction as a sales vehicle in a few well-chosen words.

"There are three common forms of entertainment in the world," said Dell in an interview with *Sports Marketing News*. "Music, sex and sports. Those three things know no boundaries."

And when you think about it, only one of them sells shoes.

Chapter
6
The Odds Fellows

High rollers and low lifes: Everybody into the pool

The doom in Dallas was matched only by the gloom in Vegas on that January day in 1979 when the Cowboys lost the Super Bowl.

The Cowboys were expected to lose the Super Bowl. There was nothing wrong with that. The Pittsburgh Steelers were four-point favorites to beat them. But that was precisely the problem.

The Steelers won the game, 35-31, thereby exactly covering the spread. It was a bookmaker's nightmare. By a mile-wide margin, more money is bet on the Super Bowl than any event in all of sports. And every penny wagered had to be returned.

Millions and millions of dollars, and maybe some of it was yours. Have you ever made a bet on a sporting event? Have you ever known someone who has? If not, you had better hurry back to the spaceship you arrived in.

Most people who follow sports at all and who have lived in this galaxy in this century have bumped into a wager or two along the way. You don't have to like it, but it's pretty hard to ignore. Gambling helps determine which sports get watched the most, which make the most money, and maybe a little bit how they got that way. We might as well know how it works.

If the '79 Super Bowl was an American tragedy for bookmakers, it was one they recovered from pretty quickly, because sports gambling is healthier now than it's ever been before.

What that means to the health of the sports themselves is another matter entirely. Plenty of people think the national obsession with gambling is a dangerous threat to the games. Other people see it as a harmless extension of the fun. Nobody thinks it's going away.

Lenny Del Genio, who manages the race and sports book at the Frontier Hotel and Casino in Las Vegas, sees it as a yuppie phenomenon. In a 1987 speech given at a sports business conference in Los Angeles, Del Genio estimated that sports betting in his city had increased by 8,000% in 10 years.

"I think betting on sports is part of the yuppie culture," he said. "They drink Perrier, drive BMWs, and bet on sports. They can study statistics, feed data into their computers, and then watch the event on television.

"They prefer to bet on sports because knowledge and study play a part. It's not just luck."

It's all so respectable and all so widespread. *Sports Illustrated* magazine reported the results of its own investigation into the scope of sports betting in the United States in its March 10, 1986, issue. The numbers were staggering.

According to the magazine, the Justice Department estimated that illegal sports gambling in 1966 was a $20 billion to $25 billion a year business. By 1984, a former organized crime investigator for the FBI figured the volume had grown to $70 billion. Pro football alone was attracting $50 billion a year in bets.

More conservative estimates of $30 billion annually in illegal betting would still produce a $5-billion profit for the people handling the action. That's a figure many international oil companies wouldn't mind seeing on their books.

Sports Illustrated quoted one expert as saying that Chicago bookies handled about $2 billion in sports bets every year, and a single football week in Dallas carried a $10-million handle.

Where horse and dog racing used to provide 85% of his business and sports betting 15%, a Chicago bookie told the magazine that now it's the other way around.

The effect of that was to drive betting underground and outside the law. Gambling on horses and dogs is legal in 36 states. Gambling on sports is legal in only one—Nevada.

The legal operators are doing just fine, too. The amount of money bet in Nevada is now around $1 billion. The '86 Super Bowl alone accounted for $35 million of that. Illegal betting on the same event was estimated at $1 billion.

Len Miller is an expert on the subject. The editor of *Gambling Times* magazine, he has written two books on gambling and appeared on radio and television talk shows all over the country. He's visited gambling centers all over the world. And the place he knows best is Vegas.

"Sportsbooks are legal only in the state of Nevada," he pointed out in an interview, and there are a total of 43 of them in Las Vegas, Reno, Lake Tahoe, and other Nevada casinos. Atlantic City casinos don't take bets. As a result, sports bettors throughout the eastern states make their wagers with illegal bookies.

"Betting at the sportsbooks ranges from five dollars up to hundreds," said Miller. "A $1,000 to $10,000 bet on a single game is quite usual and bets of $50,000 to $100,000 are not uncommon. The Super Bowl brings out the most action. One casino in Las Vegas had over 100 wagers by individuals of $100,000 each on the Super Bowl."

Recent legislation has slowed down some of these high rollers, according to Miller. The law says that any single bet of over $10,000 must be reported by the sportsbook. That's for Uncle Sam's benefit. Big winners don't like to brag on their tax returns.

Still, Miller says he's seen estimates that $400 million is bet in the Nevada books on football alone each year, and overall the casinos do about $1 billion annually in all categories of sports betting.

The big games are shown on huge television screens. The casinos take bets on horse races from major tracks all over the country. The races are telecast direct from the tracks as they're run, and bets are paid off on the racetrack tote board results.

Las Vegas sportsbooks do take bets by telephones, but only if the calls come from inside Nevada. "Bettors have money on deposit in their 'telephone accounts' and they call in their bets," said Miller. "Betting by telephone from outside Nevada is illegal. It's a federal offense, and the law is strictly enforced."

Not so strictly enforced are all of the office pools, parlay cards, and personal wagers put down all over the country. Those can't even be counted, let alone policed. There are legal parlay cards, too.

"These are mostly played by tourists who aren't into handicapping the games," said Miller. "They take a chance on picking a number of teams to win, but they have to pick a minimum of three games to win. To win big, they have to pick 10 straight winners.

"The cards are sold throughout Nevada. They're also quite popular for illegal activity all over the country."

The cards are luck. The bets on individual games are almost science. Or so think the people who place them. Especially the football gamblers. They love to test their knowledge of the game and its players against "the line" that comes out of Nevada every weekend.

The line or "spread" is really just a measure of the relative strength of the two teams expressed in points. In the '79 Super Bowl, the line said that Pittsburgh was four points stronger than Dallas. So if you bet on Pittsburgh, you couldn't make any money unless the Steelers won by five points or more.

If they won by four, the bet was a "push." Nobody won their bets, and nobody lost. By the same token, if the Cowboys lost by only three points, their backers cashed in.

A crucial factor then is who sets the line. Miller said most sportsbooks buy their lines from a service called Las Vegas Sports Consultants, which is run by a fellow named Michael Roxborough. Las Vegas Sports Consultants uses computers to keep track of all of the teams, rounding up the statistics and other important data required to decide who's going to win on a particular Sunday.

The service also has a staff of experts who stay alert for recent developments and who have a kind of sixth sense for this sort of thing.

Once the line is established, it's not carved in stone. It keeps changing from the time it's first put out until kickoff. And the service updates the sports-books from early line to final line.

It's not true that bookmakers take a bath whenever there's a big upset or when a team fails to cover the spread. The sportsbooks try to get an equal amount of money laid on each team. Sometimes they tinker with the line to accomplish that. It happened to one hotel in the '79 Super Bowl.

The hotel gave bettors 4-1/2 points with Dallas because it wasn't getting enough money on the Cowboys. When the Steelers won by only four, the book was left wishing it hadn't been quite so successful in attracting Dallas backers. It took a $500,000 bump.

There's a simple reason for the sportsbooks' desire to get money laid down evenly on a game. That's the way they make their living.

A bettor has to put up $11 to win $10. Let's say he's a low roller, and that's all he bet on his favorite team. If the team wins for him and covers the spread, he collects $21. That's his original $11, plus $10 for winning. So the bet costs the bookmaker $10.

But if the book has another guy betting against the first bettor's team, the second bettor loses $11. So the bookie is a buck ahead on the game. The percentage or "vigorish" in the bookie's favor is 4-1/2%. When the total bets start running into the millions of dollars, that 4-1/2% adds up fast.

Miller said the biggest sport by far in Vegas is professional football. It outruns the college sport by a wide margin. For one thing, it's just a very popular spectator sport. For another, there aren't nearly as many players, teams, and games for serious bettors to keep track of in the pro game as there are in colleges.

And then of course there's television. All of the NFL games are tele-vised either nationally or regionally, so anyone with a few weekend hours and the cash for a black and white set can become a part-time expert. No-body has to go to the racetrack, and nobody has to wait to find out how the game went. The tote board is right there in the living room.

Nobody doubts that television has played a major part in the explosion of both legal and illegal sports betting in this country. What's more, it is the most mutually beneficial of relationships.

The wide exposure of pro football in particular has helped make gambling popular. And widespread gambling has helped keep millions glued to their sets on Sunday afternoons, regardless of whether they have any particular love for the teams they're watching.

That's not a bad arrangement for the NFL, which relies so heavily on TV for its revenues. Good ratings translate into heavy advertising, which trans-lates into healthy income for both the networks and the league.

Perhaps it's not an accident that pro football is the only sport that pub-lishes injury lists every week. There are very specific categories for players who have had physical problems, listing their status from "probable" to "doubtful." Fans may like to know that stuff, but gamblers *have* to know it.

The presence of gaming "experts" like Pete Axthelm and, until recently, Jimmy the Greek also reflects football's awareness of the importance of betting on its sports. Everybody caters to it, including newspapers.

Most papers print the lines on every weekend football game, and the few that have tried to dispense with the policy have been driven to distraction by jangling telephones as readers express their displeasure.

Many of them are the same readers who call to confirm quarter scores, first downs, and other esoteric statistics following the weekend games. Maybe there has been a dramatic rise in the study of numerology in the United States. Or maybe the calls have something to do with sports pools.

While all of this is going on with the total knowledge and acquiescence, if not outright encouragement, of the sport, it creates something of a paradox. Some might even call it hypocrisy.

That's because pro football, baseball, and basketball all have very specific and very stringent rules about gambling on games. Players are expressly forbidden to do that.

For example, the NBA's uniform player contract says that any player who bets or even attempts to bet money or anything else of value on a league game can be suspended for an indefinite period by the commissioner. He can even be expelled for life. The commissioner's decision is "final, binding, conclusive and unappealable."

That's whether the game involves the player's team or not. Similar rules exist in major-league baseball and in the NFL where it's a violation to fail to report a bribe attempt, let alone accept one. Associating with gamblers or gambling activities "in a manner tending to bring discredit to the NFL" is also expressly forbidden.

And it's not hard to see why.

Once the sports fan gets even a whiff of the notion that games could be decided by anything other than the best efforts of the competitors, he starts to lose interest. And if players are betting, the fan can't help but wonder if they know something he doesn't.

The leagues also have security personnel who check out any reports of gambling by players. Critics think the owners could stand to hire a few more people to do that job, and maybe the ones who are doing it could be a bit more aggressive.

But the most important question they pose for football is if the league advertises injuries and condones handicapping in pregame programming, how much can it really frown on gambling?

Well, enough to want to keep its reputation clean certainly. All three sports are acutely aware of the importance of that, and all three have seen their images under attack by gambling-related incidents. So, for that matter, have the college games.

Baseball has been fighting this battle for more than a century. In 1877, a major-league team in Louisville bounced four players for throwing games.

And the celebrated 1920 Black Sox Scandal in Chicago left a bruise that the sport has never let itself forget.

Philadelphia Phillies owner William Cox was banned from baseball for life in 1943 for betting on his own team, and four years later Leo Durocher was suspended for associating with a gambler.

One of the most controversial steps former Commissioner Bowie Kuhn ever took was to order Hall of Fame players Mickey Mantle and Willie Mays to disassociate themselves from the game because they were in the employ of gambling casinos.

Kuhn's successor, Peter Ueberroth, later lifted those sanctions, but Kuhn at least had made his point.

Pro basketball was the 1987 victim of a leaky Phoenix grand jury that was investigating both drugs and gambling while spraying charges all over the country. Grand jury testimony that found its way into the local newspapers alleged that a couple of Milwaukee Bucks players gave a Phoenix nightclub manager winning betting advice before their game with the Suns.

Nobody claimed the game was fixed—just that the spread could have been manipulated. NBA officials viewed tapes of the game until their eyes crossed and couldn't find any evidence of that.

Neither could the grand jury, as it turned out. Eventually, the gambling charges fell away. Thirteen people, including three current and two former Phoenix players, but not including the two Bucks, were indicted on drug charges.

In the end, a waiter at the nightclub got 30 days in jail and five years' probation, and the NBA got a reminder of how vigilant it has to be about even the appearance of gambling involvement.

Not that the NBA has ever doubted that. There was even a time when it was too careful. Connie Hawkins was an 18-year-old freshman star at the University of Iowa when he became one of 47 players implicated in a 1961 college game-fixing scandal. As a result, the NBA wouldn't touch him for seven years.

Hawkins was never legally charged with anything, although he did make what he later said was a coerced confession to the New York district attorney's office, saying that he was offered $500 for introducing players to fixers Jack Molinas and Joe Hacken. Molinas was a former NBA player who had been kicked out of the league in 1954 for betting on his own team.

Hawkins played for the Harlem Globetrotters for a little while, and he had some spectacular seasons in the American Basketball League and the American Basketball Association. But he didn't get into the NBA until he threatened it with a $6-million, treble damage suit.

The modern day sequel to the Connie Hawkins story featured one John (Hot Rod) Williams, formerly of Tulane University and now of the Cleveland Cavaliers. That one didn't take nearly as long to resolve.

Williams was one of five Tulane players who were accused in 1985 of being party to a point-shaving scheme involving two Tulane games. He ad-

mitted that he had violated NCAA rules by accepting payments while he was in school and receiving $10,000 in a shoebox from a Tulane alum eager to help recruit him. But he denied he had ever helped shave points.

The Cavaliers did a little gambling of their own on Williams, but only figuratively. They bet he would be acquitted, and they took him in the second round of the 1985 college draft.

Williams wouldn't have slipped that low in the draft if it weren't for his legal problems. But the NBA had sent an advisory to every team in the league saying that he would be ineligible to play unless he was cleared of guilt in the point-shaving case. The Cavaliers decided he was well worth the risk. And the Cavaliers were right.

In June of '86, a jury cleared Williams of two counts of sports bribery and three counts of conspiracy to commit sports bribery. He had a new start in life, and the Cavaliers had one of the most promising young forwards in the league.

For its part, the NBA had done what was legally possible to protect itself from the stigma of gambling.

That apparently is what Commissioner Pete Rozelle was trying to do for the NFL in the late 1960s when he told Joe Namath to disassociate himself from his Bachelors III Restaurant because it was believed to be frequented by gamblers. And it's certainly what he was trying to do in the cases of Paul Hornung and Alex Karras in 1963.

Rozelle suspended both of them for a season for betting on games and associating with "questionable characters."

Hornung, the Golden Boy from Notre Dame and the Green Bay Packers, was the league's MVP in 1961. Karras was one of the NFL's premier defensive lineman as a Detroit Lion. None of that helped them much when Rozelle's staff decided that they had been wagering on games.

Nobody said they had done anything illegal, but Rozelle pointed out that the league's rules prohibiting wagers on NFL games were posted in every locker room. The implication was that if a player was smart enough to read he should have been smart enough to stay away from gambling.

Karras was accused of betting between $50 to $100 on at least six games between 1958 and 1963. He denied the charges, saying he never bet more than cigars and cigarettes on any game.

But the league didn't buy his version of the story. It also fined the Lions' management for not keeping better track of its players, and it later slapped six of Karras's teammates with $2,000 fines for betting on the 1962 NFL championship game between the Packers and the New York Giants.

While Karras denied all, Hornung pleaded guilty as charged. He said he was betting between $100 and $200 on games in an average week, but sometimes the stakes would climb to as much as $500.

His suspension cost Hornung around $50,000, counting his $35,000 contract and the $15,000 he could expect to receive in endorsements that year. Karras was a lineman, not a running back, and he was never as pretty as

Hornung, so he didn't lose as much money. He has insisted to this day that he was railroaded by Rozelle, who at that time was a young commissioner with only three years in office.

Twenty years later, Rozelle found himself facing a similar problem with much more money involved. The tragic case of Art Schlichter provides a ready answer for the critics of sports gambling when they're asked, "Who does it hurt?"

Like Hornung and Karras, Schlichter was suspended from pro football for gambling activities. Unlike those two, the former Ohio State and Baltimore Colt quarterback was a self-confessed pathological gambler who dealt in giant stakes. Rozelle suspended him indefinitely for gambling on at least 10 games in 1982 and for associating with illegal bookies.

It happened after the newspapers reported the arrest of four Baltimore bookmakers who had threatened to break Schlichter's passing arm if he didn't pay them the $159,000 he owed them. Schlichter said he had already lost $389,000 to those same bookies. The $159,000 was just the balance.

It was probably just a small percentage of his lifetime losings, too. Even Schlichter couldn't guess how much he had dropped on sports gambling in his lifetime, but the estimates have gone as high as $1.5 million. He started early.

His family owned a harness horse, and Schlichter liked to go to the track near his home. That seems to be where the problem began. At Ohio State, he would bet on college basketball games as well as horse racing. He branched out to college football games after he was drafted by the Colts.

Then it was on to pro football games before his habit and the league caught up with him. He admitted himself to a treatment center, and when the "indefinite" suspension ended in the summer of 1984, Schlichter wanted to resume his pro football career.

The Baltimore Colts became the Indianapolis Colts, and Schlichter became their starting quarterback. But he injured his knee in the 1985 opener, and he was placed on waivers in October. When no one picked him up, Schlichter was out of football again. He tried to get a job with the Buffalo Bills in 1986, but they cut him in training camp.

When the Colts let Schlichter go in 1985, rumors were flying that despite his treatment, he was gambling again. Schlichter denied them. But two years later, he was arrested and pleaded guilty to a misdemeanor criminal charge of sports gambling in Indianapolis. Police said he had bet more than $230,000 in 70 days.

In the spring of 1987 a Columbus television station reported that Schlichter had filed for bankruptcy protection with debts amounting to almost $1 million. The report said he owed $250,000 to Colts owner Robert Irsay and more than $150,000 on a bank credit card account.

There was one other small item—a $10,000 bill from the hospital where he underwent treatment for a gambling addiction that apparently never went away.

The sporting public obviously isn't as hooked on gambling as Schlichter was. But fans don't show any more inclination than he did to back away from the action. In fact the handle goes up every year.

Whether that represents a worrisome trend, harmless fun, or something in between is open to argument. One thing is sure: It didn't do Art Schlichter any good.

Chapter 7

Who's the Boss?

People are crazy, and owners are people

All you have to do is reach into your pocket and pull out $60 million to $70 million, lease a 60,000-seat stadium or maybe even build your own, hire four dozen highly skilled workmen at about $250,000 apiece, and figure on spending roughly every third year in one kind of court or another and every fourth year fighting a strike. Then die each Sunday in the fall when your side loses a contest over which you have absolutely no control.

Those are the requirements. Ulcers, heart attacks, and the animosity of thousands of strangers are optional.

If you are prepared to make these minimal sacrifices, then you're ready to answer the question once posed by Rankin Smith, chairman of the board of the Atlanta Falcons: "Doesn't every adult male in America want to own his own football team?"

Smith could be overstating his case by a few odd million Americans, and he had better be careful with that male stuff. There is an American female who happens to own a football team. But incredible as it seems, Smith may be pretty close to the mark.

Ask any American male who cares about sports at all, and he's likely to admit he wouldn't mind being John Elway's boss. Or Magic Johnson's or Mike Schmidt's, depending on the game he favors.

Go figure.

When the '80s began, all but five teams in the NBA were losing money. In 1987 no more than six or seven NFL clubs showed a profit. In 1988 baseball owners held their breath to see if a couple of arbitrators were going to set off a price war they feared would leave them awash in red ink.

In these perilous economic times, a great number of professional sports franchises offer all the golden cash flow opportunities of a lemonade stand.

And yet, anytime a major professional owner decides that enough is enough, a line forms at the door before the "for sale" sign comes out.

Some owners call that "the greater fool theory." It holds that no matter how costly or downright silly it might be to own a team, there's always someone just as rich as you are and probably sillier who's willing to take it off your hands. What's more, you always make a handsome profit when you sell. The problem is, that may be the only time you make a profit.

Most of today's owners didn't get into sports to make money, although once they're in, they're not opposed to the idea. They do get a little touchy when they start to *lose* money or when they feel somebody else is making it at their expense.

They have a variety of motivations for buying teams, ranging from sincere civic pride to outrageous ego gratification. But most ordinary people experience those drives in one degree or another. Owners aren't ordinary.

Although it may be that everyone dreams about owning a football team—or a basketball or baseball team—hardly anyone's dream comes true. The people who can make it happen for themselves are a very special breed. And they do have a couple of things in common.

One is that they are certainly not fools—greater or lesser. The other is they either have a considerable amount of money themselves or they have access to a considerable amount of somebody else's money.

Every year, *Forbes Magazine* publishes a list of America's 400 richest individuals, and the people who own sports teams were well represented on the 1988 list. Start with Ted Arison, the cruise ship magnate who bought the NBA expansion franchise in Miami and whose net worth was pegged at $1.6 billion. He zoomed past '87 leader Ed DeBartolo, Sr., the Pittsburgh Penguins' owner worth $1.4 billion. Rounding out the billionaires' club is August Busch, the owner of the St. Louis Cardinals, worth an even $1 billion.

Then the list goes like this: Jack Kent Cooke, Washington Redskins, $950 million; Joan Kroc, San Diego Padres, $745 million; Carl Pohlad, Minnesota Twins, $670 million; William Ford, Detroit Lions, $630 million; Alex Spanos, San Diego Chargers, $550 million; Paul Allen, Portland Trail Blazers, $540 million; Ted Turner, Atlanta Braves and Atlanta Hawks, $535 million; Richard Jacobs, Cleveland Indians, $440 million; Bum Bright, Dallas Cowboys, $400 million; Robert Lurie, San Francisco Giants, $385 million; Hugh Culverhouse, Tampa Bay Buccaneers, $330 million; George Argyros, Seattle Mariners, $250 million; and Gene Autry, California Angels, $230 million.

On the other end of the scale are some plain folks like the people who own the Green Bay Packers—all 1,800 of them. The Packers belong to 1,800 shareholders, none of whom has ever made a dime off a dividend. If the franchise is sold, the proceeds go to the American Legion post in Green Bay. What kind of party do you suppose the Legionnaires could have with $60 or $70 million?

This peculiar arrangement was arrived at in 1922 when the team was so broke it almost went out of business. So the citizens of Green Bay got together and bought stock in the team to keep it alive. All they received then, and all they receive now, for their stock is the notoriety of saying they own a football team.

No, owners are not all obscenely wealthy, but most of them are quite a bit better off than the average Packer shareholder. Or the athletes who work for them. Or you and me.

There was a time when you could buy into major-league sports for a song. Now it takes a whole opera.

In 1988 an expansion franchise in the NBA cost $32.5 million. The owners had to come up with that much before they even thought about paying operating expenses. Like players' salaries.

Existing franchises are much more expensive than that, with football teams carrying the biggest price tags of all. Whole conglomerates are buying franchises now. The *Chicago Tribune* owns the Chicago Cubs, and the Madison Square Garden Corporation (MSG) owns the New York Knicks.

That kind of thing can have hilarious consequences. Witness the Knicks' corporate search for a coach in 1987. By the time the vacancy had been batted around by all the nonbasketball people in the MSG board room, everyone but John D. Rockefeller had been mentioned as a candidate. Rockefeller was spared only because he was dead.

Most teams are still owned by people, not corporations. And the six-dozen-plus people who operate franchises in the NFL, NBA, and major-league baseball are about as interesting and diverse a group as you can find roaming offices anywhere in the country.

Almost all of them made their money doing something far more logical and predictable than running sports teams. Just about everything is. But there are a few like the Cincinnati Bengals' Paul Brown and the Los Angeles Raiders' Al Davis whose only business has been their sport.

Most of them made their own money. There are some remarkable rags to riches stories among them. There are also a few long-standing sports families, in which the sons and daughters inherited both their fortunes and their teams.

Sports owners tend to favor certain types of businesses. Real estate development and construction are big items. The odds are pretty good that you have spent some time in a shopping center built by the 49ers' DeBartolo or by Melvin and Herbert Simon of the Indiana Pacers.

Cars, broadcasting, and show biz are the other leaders. There are a half dozen lawyers, too.

There's really no limit to what these ambitious capitalists can do for you. They'll wine you, dine you, dress you, read to you, sing to you, fatten you up, and slim you down.

Hungry? Joan Kroc invites you to one of her thousands of McDonald's restaurants. If you're in the mood for a pizza, there's Monaghen's Dominos Pizza chain, or if you're into something a little tonier, Cleveland Cavaliers owners George and Gordon Gund offer the Rusty Scupper Restaurants.

A cocktail before dinner? Charles Bronfman of Seagrams Distilleries has a VO for you as well as a big chunk of the Montreal Expos. And to wash down your meal, there's Bud from Augie Busch's brewery or maybe some suds from John Labott Ltd., owners of the Toronto Blue Jays.

For that quiet evening at home, you can select a book published by Doubleday and Company. In his spare time, Nelson Doubleday operates the New York Mets. Or if you just want to sit and watch TV, Turner's cable empire is all around you. Catch an old movie and maybe California Angels owner Gene Autry is riding Champion again.

If you want to get away from it all, maybe Seattle Mariners owner George Argyos can help you. He owns an airline called AirCal. Or take a cruise on one of George Steinbrenner's ships.

The point is these people are touching your lives every day in ways you don't even realize. And they have been doing it for a long time. In most cases, longer than they have owned teams.

That is particularly true in the NBA. Before the mid-1980s, owning most NBA teams was the next best thing to flashing a roll of hundreds in a skid row bar. The risk far outweighed the satisfaction. That's probably why basketball owners kept coming and going.

Of the 25 owners in the NBA (counting expansion teams), 23 have taken over their teams since 1979. The longevity champ is Pollin, who assumed control of the Bullets in 1968.

No fewer than 12 NBA owners have purchased their teams since 1985. Contrast that to the NFL where only five clubs have changed hands since 1985 and just eight since 1979.

This might have a little something to do with the traditional profitability picture in the NFL. It's also rooted in history, family tradition, and probably just plain habit.

Wellington Mara's family bought the Giants in 1925, three years after Green Bay's fans saved the Packers. Art Rooney came along in '33 to claim the Steelers, and the Bidwill family has held on to the Cardinals through five decades and three cities starting in 1932.

Baseball boasts some families that have been around for a long time, too, like the Cardinals' Busch clan and the Dodgers' O'Malleys. The chairman of the board of the New York Mets is Nelson Doubleday, whose great-great uncle was a fellow named Abner. Yeah, *that* Abner Doubleday.

The major leagues kind of sit in between the conservative NFL and the active NBA when it comes to owner stability, although things are starting to move. In September 1988, publisher Edward L. Gaylord announced that he planned to buy the Texas Rangers for an estimated $80 million.

But enough of patterns and generalizations. Let's meet some of these movers and shakers in the world of sports. There will be no attempt here to introduce all of them. No group of 77 people is *that* interesting. Damn democracy, full speed ahead.

The Pioneers

"When I came into the league, there was no question who the NFL was," said Dallas Cowboys President Tex Schramm. "The league was George Halas in Chicago, Tim Mara in New York, George Preston Marshall in Washington, Curly Lambeau in Green Bay . . . and Art Rooney in Pittsburgh."

Schramm was speaking to the press one day after the death of Rooney on August 25, 1988. Now there are no more original owners in the NFL. When Rooney died at the age of 87, an entire era died with him—an era that wore leather helmets and passed the hat to make the payroll. He bought the Pittsburgh Steelers 34 years before there was a Super Bowl and 28 years before anyone had ever heard of a Dallas Cowboy.

Rooney was one of the guys who was present at the creation. Without them, the games would have a vastly different look today. Maybe their games wouldn't exist at all. We'll look at some of the pioneers who are still around today, but first let's start with "The Chief."

Art Rooney, *Pittsburgh Steelers.* You can't help but wonder what the patriarch of the Pittsburgh Steelers was thinking when NFL Commissioner Pete Rozelle suspended Alex Karras and Paul Hornung to keep the sport safe from gambling. A former semipro football player, the then-32-year-old Rooney bought the Steelers franchise in 1933 for $2,500, which just happened to be the proceeds from a profitable weekend at Saratoga Park racetrack.

This was a practical man. He named his team the Pirates and scheduled home games for Forbes Field, but then he discovered that the Commonwealth of Pennsylvania's blue laws prohibited Sunday games. Rooney's solution was to give free tickets to the superintendent of police.

He may have been the first man to sign a player to an outlandish contract, awarding the unheard of sum of $15,800 to a Colorado all-American in 1939. Maybe it wasn't such a bad idea. The guy turned out to be a U.S. Supreme Court justice, and the NFL needed all the help it could get in court. The Colorado kid's name was Byron (Whizzer) White.

Rooney had always been a hard loser. When his team went a whole season without scoring more than 10 points in a game, he sold it to a fellow named Alexis Thompson in 1940 and used the money to buy the Philadelphia Eagles. But he had a change of heart. Before the 1941 season began, he swapped the Eagles to Thompson to get the Pirates back. Subsequently, the clubs were merged and named the Phil-Pitt Steagles, which eventually became the Steelers.

With World War II creating a player shortage, that outfit was merged briefly with the Cardinals and called Card-Pitt, which naturally was unofficially dubbed the Carpets—the team everybody walked all over.

Paul Brown, *Cincinnati Bengals.*   If George Halas invented pro football, Paul Brown invented everything else about the game. He was the first one to hire a year-round coaching staff, the first to use game films, position coaches, and even 40-yard dash times.

There's a reason why pro teams time college prospects in the 40, although most of them probably don't know what it is. It's because Brown decided that 40 yards is about what a player needs to run to cover a punt.

Brown has never been a captain of industry. He's just a football guy. He got a Cleveland businessman named Arthur (Mickey) McBride, who was into taxicabs, radio stations, and real estate, to put up the money to form the original Cleveland Browns of the All-America Conference, and McBride named him the Browns' president.

Brown served as coach, general manager, and president of the team that was named after him for 15 years, and then Art Modell came along and bought the Browns for $3.9 million in 1961. Modell let everyone know that he would be quite content to let Brown run the show as he always had.

And he was content—for two years—then he fired Brown with six years still left on his contract.

Four years later, when the American Football League decided it would be awfully nice to have a franchise in Cincinnati, Brown put a group together to buy it and said at the time, "I feel like I can breathe again." He retired as the team's coach in 1976, but is still hanging in there as vice president and general manager.

Al Davis, *Los Angeles Raiders.*   Or is that the Irwindale Raiders? Used to be the Oakland Raiders, didn't it?

Davis has been around the pro football scene for more than 20 years, and while he's not exactly the same kind of innovator that Rooney and Brown are, he's certainly done some things that nobody ever thought of before. Suing the entire league, for example.

Of course he won the suit. Davis wins at just about everything he does, and he tends to step on toes in the process. Ask Los Angeles Rams owner Georgia Frontiere, whom he once accused of scalping tickets to the 1980 Super Bowl.

You know who does like him, though? Players, that's who. There are plenty of people in the NFL who would love to be Raiders because they think Davis pays his employees well and treats them fairly. Maybe because he's all football. Like Brown, he knows one business.

San Diego Chargers owner Gus Spanos once said, "He is probably the smartest man in professional football, if not the entire sports world."

The man responsible for the term "franchise free agency" was born appropriately enough on the Fourth of July in 1929. The son of a wealthy clothing merchant, he was raised in Brooklyn. He talks like he was raised in Brooklyn, too, and he certainly looks like a tough city kid. Hunter S. Thompson once said, "He makes Darth Vader look like a punk."

The youngest general manager-coach in pro football history, Davis was already the line coach at Adelphi College at the age of 21. He bought a 10% share of the Raiders for $18,500 in 1966 when they were an AFL club, and he later became commissioner of the AFL. Now he owns 27%, making him the largest shareholder in a franchise valued at $80 million.

Lamar Hunt, Kansas City Chiefs. Doesn't smoke, doesn't drink, and once said, "I happen to believe that one suit is enough for any man." Well, he has to spend his money on something if it isn't clothes, so why not the Chiefs?

The third son of the late Texas oil billionaire H.L. Hunt was nicknamed "Games" as a child, and he's spent his life living up to the name. A driving force in World Championship Tennis, he was also a stockholder in the Chicago Bulls and a part-owner of the Tampa Bay Rowdies soccer team. He spent his honeymoon with his second wife at the 1964 Winter Olympics.

Someone once called Lamar the playboy of the Hunt family, noting that while his brothers, Herbert and Bunker, were off making billion dollar oil deals, he was playing with teams. So he's made it a point to make money with his teams.

It is a great way to satisfy the competitive instincts of a former third-string end at SMU. "Average speed, but great hands," said long-time Chiefs coach Hank Stram of his ex-boss. "Good right hand with a checkbook," said network commentator Bud Collins.

The NFL knows all about that right hand. Hunt used it to write the checks that established the AFL. He was a tender 26 in 1960 when he started the Dallas franchise in the AFL simply because he thought Dallas needed a football team and nobody in the NFL wanted to let the city have one.

Later the leagues merged, and Hunt moved his club to Kansas City. It has been doing quite well ever since. Maybe even a little better than Hunt himself, whose family has experienced some unpleasantness in the areas of silver and oil. But he's still worth around $250 million, and given his simple tastes, he should get by—despite the sentiments once expressed by his older brother.

As Bunker Hunt once put it, "A billion dollars isn't what it used to be."

William Bidwill, St. Louis, er, Phoenix Cardinals. The oldest continuous franchise in the nation dates all the way back to 1898. In 1920, it became one of the two charter members of the NFL, along with the Chicago Bears, and 12 years after that it became the property of the Bidwill Family.

Charles Bidwill, William's daddy, bought it, and William joined the Cardinal organization in a somewhat limited capacity at the age of 11. The team moved from Chicago to St. Louis in 1960, and two years after that, Bill and his brother Charles, Jr. assumed control of the team from their mom, Violet.

Bill bought out his brother in 1972, and since then he has given the good people of St. Louis two divisional championships and a play-off appearance in 1982.

Not only that, but according to the Cardinals press guide, William Bidwill has remained "continuously involved in the support of various civic and charitable organizations in the St. Louis area."

When your roots run that deep, there's only one logical course of action. You move to Phoenix.

August A. Busch Jr., *St. Louis (baseball) Cardinals.*   One of the reasons Bidwill found it so easy to forsake St. Louis was that it's Augie Busch's town. At least, it's the baseball Cardinals' town. While the baseball club was filling up that too-small stadium, the football team was looking at empty seats, especially when it started to make noises about going somewhere else.

August Busch became president of the Cardinals when his dad's brewery, Anheuser-Busch, bought the team in 1953. A lot of Budweiser has flowed through the streets of St. Louis since then, and Busch wouldn't mind seeing some more spilled in recognition of his beloved Cardinals. "My ambition is, whether hell or high water, to get a championship baseball team for St. Louis," he said.

Of course, he's already done that, but the man never gets tired of winning. At 82, he became the first American to win the Queen's Cup coaching title for precision horse and carriage driving.

He's been widowed, divorced twice and remarried, and he has 10 kids. He ran the brewery from 1946 to 1975 when his son August III took over, and he's still chief executive officer of the baseball team. Drives the Clydesdales, too.

Utility Players

If you have to be crazy to own a sports franchise, what do you have to be to own two? Schizophrenic? How about three? And throw in a stadium, arena, or racetrack while you're at it. Hey, there are actually people who have all that stuff.

The NFLPA put together a cross ownership chart in 1981 showing how football moguls are also involved in baseball, basketball, soccer, racetracks, radio-tv, hockey, and stadiums. And while they were at it, they showed how the owners in those areas were involved in the other areas.

The chart looked like one of those airline route maps with everybody going in every direction and hoping they get home without falling off the end of the earth. You have already heard about Hunt and his tennis, baseball, and soccer ventures. Well, that's only the beginning.

Some guys just want to own *something* athletic. Like Minnesota's Max Winter. He was a co-owner and general manager of the Minneapolis Lakers when there was such a thing. When they moved to Los Angeles he jumped at the chance to form a syndicate that purchased an expansion franchise for the Vikings.

Other guys seem to want to own *everything* athletic. It's probably because they're big sports fans and they can afford to indulge their hobby. Or it could be that when cities are trying to keep or attract franchises, these are the fellows they look to.

Seattle SuperSonics owner Barry Ackerley was asked one time if he wouldn't also like to own an expansion hockey team in Seattle. His reply: "You have to be crazy to own one of those things. I may be crazy, but I'm not stupid."

The people who own more than one franchise are neither. For instance:

Jack Kent Cooke, *Washington Redskins.*   OK, so it's just one team, but he has race horses, too. Any discussion of multiple sports owners has to begin with Cooke, because this is one man who has done it all.

He undid most of it in 1979 when he sold the Los Angeles Lakers, Los Angeles Kings, and the Los Angeles Forum to Jerry Buss for $68 million, completing the largest sports transaction in history. That gave him plenty of money to participate in the largest divorce in history.

Cooke had been married to his wife Jean for 40 years when they went before Judge Joseph Wapner. That's right, the People's Court. He awarded Jean in the neighborhood of $50 million, assuring both partners a place in the *Guinness Book of World Records* for the largest divorce settlement ever.

If Cooke's business ventures were all as stable as his marriages, he wouldn't own a season ticket to the Redskins, let alone the whole team. A year after he divorced his first wife, he married sculptor Jean Maxwell Williams, but that broke up in a year.

Then in July of 1987 he was wed to 31-year-old Suzanne Martin. He filed for divorce three months later, but there were some complications. While Cooke was cheering his Redskins on in the Super Bowl, his estranged wife was giving birth to a baby girl. Named her Jacqueline Kent Cooke.

Little Jacqueline should have enough money to get through college. Although *Forbes* lists Cooke's net worth at $950 million, friends of his say he's working on his second billion. Among the things he owns are the *Los Angeles Daily News*, several cable television companies, extensive real estate holdings on both coasts, Elmendorf Farm (which he is hoping will produce a Kentucky Derby winner for him some day), and a Redskins franchise worth an estimated $100 million.

Nobody handed any of this stuff to him either. The Canadian-born Cooke began his business career selling sets of $39.50 encyclopedias door to door in Saskatchewan during the Depression. If he'd had his choice, he would have played the clarinet and saxophone, but neither he nor his family could live on that.

"That's all I wanted to do," Cooke recalled during a press interview at the '88 Super Bowl. "Had I been endowed with more musical talent, I'd be a professional musician today." Instead he's an amateur musician who spends his spare time composing songs.

Not that he's composed many. He's never had much spare time. By the time he was 30, he and fellow entrepreneur Roy Thompson had teamed up to buy a bunch of newspapers and radio stations that made Cooke a millionaire.

He became a sports owner for the first time in 1951 when he bought the Toronto baseball franchise in the International League. Four years later, he tried to buy the Detroit Tigers. No sale, but Cooke was on his way. In 1965 he bought the Lakers and then the Kings, and then he built the Fabulous Forum for them to play in. When he sold all of that, he used the profits to buy the Chrysler Building in New York.

He also spent $5 million to underwrite the first Muhammed Ali-Joe Frazier fight in 1971. When a man deals in those kinds of figures, Cooke's purchase of the Redskins looks like a trip to the corner newspaper stand. He acquired 25% of them for $300,000, and he bought the rest for about $10 million and now calls the team "an expensive hobby." He doesn't figure they'll ever make money until they have a domed stadium.

But he's enjoying them anyway, and he is a most enthusiastic hobbyist. He's been known to pull up a chair on the sidelines next to Coach Joe Gibbs during freezing days at practice, which doesn't seem to surprise Gibbs very much.

"Mr. Cooke, he's the big boss," says Gibbs. "He has the gold, and he makes the rules."

Jerry Buss, *Los Angeles Lakers, Los Angeles Forum, Los Angeles Lazers, Los Angeles Strings.*   Of course Cooke doesn't have *all* the gold. Dr. Jerry Buss, as he likes to call himself, had earned more than enough from his real estate business to buy Cooke out in LA. He picked up Cooke's 13,300-acre ranch in the bargain.

Why did Cooke sell? Because Buss was offering more than he thought all that stuff was worth. Why did Buss buy? "Because I've been a sports nut since I could remember," Buss told reporters.

"There's a lot of crapshooter in me," Buss went on. "If I handle it right and produce some winners, I can do rather well economically."

You don't notice anybody starving with the Lakers, do you? Buss has always had a knack for doing rather well economically. He grew up in Kemmerer, Wyoming, a mining, sheep ranching kind of place, and he had to work as a kid. That didn't leave any time for sports. You might say he's making up for lost time.

Buss earned a PhD in chemistry from Southern Cal, which explains where the Dr. comes from, but doesn't explain how he got into real estate. He was working in the aerospace industry when he met an engineer named Frank

Mariana in 1958. The two discovered they had a mutual interest—making money.

They scraped together $1,000 to invest in an apartment building, and one way or another they have parlayed it into millions in property in California, Arizona, and Nevada.

World Team Tennis, the league most people don't know anything about but has such a knack for attracting big money like Lamar Hunt's, snared Buss in 1974. It was his first sports investment. He went on from there to buy the Major Indoor Soccer League Lazers and all of Cooke's stuff. He lost his taste for hockey in 1988, though, when he sold the Kings to Bruce McNall.

Buss doesn't run all these enterprises himself. That's what families are for. His daughter Jeanie operates the Strings, and his son Jim is president and general manager of the Lazers.

Buss has also put together something called ''Prime Ticket,'' which is the first cable sports network in California.

What do you watch on Prime Ticket? All of Jerry Buss's teams of course, plus a few other people's teams. You can usually watch Jerry Buss himself, too. He's the grey-haired guy in the jeans chatting with all the other celebrities who go to the Lakers' games. And he's having a great time.

John J. McMullen, *Houston Astros, New Jersey Devils.* No, George Steinbrenner isn't the only shipping tycoon in big-league sports. A U.S. Naval Academy graduate, McMullen launched his private maritime career in 1968 when he became chief executive office of the United States Lines, Inc. He has sailed smoothly from there into a number of other businesses. McMullen estimated that he once owned or controlled 17 corporations.

So how could he get by on one team?

He entered the sports world in 1973 when he joined the Steinbrenner group that bought the Yankees from CBS in 1973, but he exited quickly after working with Steinbrenner for a while. As McMullen put it at the time, ''Nothing is more limited than being a limited partner of George's.''

So six years later, McMullen headed a group of 25 investors who bought the Astros from the Ford Motor Company for $13 million. The first full year that McMullen was in Houston, the Astros won their division championship, whereupon the new boss fired the Astros' president, Tal Smith, prompting a stockholders' revolt that almost landed in federal court.

In 1982 McMullen formed another group and purchased the sorry Colorado Rockies of the NHL, whom he promptly moved to his home back east and renamed the Devils. ''I'm far more knowledgeable on baseball than hockey,'' he said at a news conference called to introduce the team's new ownership. ''There's no similarity.''

That showed a basic knowledge of the game right there. The Astros' new president, Al Rosen, described McMullen as ''a leader type, someone who is always visible, especially in times of adversity.'' Rosen ought to know.

He's the guy who replaced Smith while McMullen's co-owners were threatening to take him to court. Talk about adversity.

"He makes decisions quickly," Rosen was quoted as saying. "He has tenacity. Empire builders like him don't reach that level of success without it."

Abe Pollin, *Washington Bullets, Washington Capitals, Capital Centre.*
Pollin is fond of saying that 30 million people have come to his house, which probably makes him the biggest Washington entertainer since Pearl Mesta.

He started building his house in 1973, finished it 15 months later and gave it a catchy name—the Capital Centre.

Pollin needed some place for his basketball team to play, and this was the place. He and two partners bought the Baltimore Bullets for $1.1 million in 1964. That may not seem like much now, but it was a record at the time. Four years later, he bought out the co-owners.

But sole ownership of one team wasn't enough to quiet Pollin's sporting blood, so he tossed his hat into a ring of 11 other candidates for a National Hockey League expansion franchise. Jimmy the Greek made him a 600 to 1 shot to get the team, but the Greek has been known to blow a few. Besides, the odds weren't too much longer than they were against Pollin's 44-38 Bullets winning the NBA championship in 1978.

Not bad for a plumber's kid. Pollin used to get up early in the morning to work as a laborer in his dad's plumbing and contracting business. Twelve years after graduating from George Washington University in 1945, he started his own construction business. He won a bunch of awards for construction and design and then became the first man in Washington to build a swimming pool on the roof of an apartment building. What's next? A swimming team?

George and Gordon Gund, *Cleveland Cavaliers, Minnesota North Stars, Minnesota Metropolitan Center, Cleveland Coliseum.*   Unlike McMullen, George Gund knew a thing or two about hockey before he bought an NHL franchise. He organized the first hockey team at Case Western Reserve University and went on to play for a city league called the Cleveland Falcons.

He and younger brother Gordon are cochairmen of both their teams and both of the places they play in. It does cut down on squabbles with the landlord.

George has extensive banking interests, real estate interests, and a cattle ranch as well as a big chunk of the Rusty Scupper Restaurant chain. Likes movies, too. He's chairman of the board of the San Francisco International Film Festival.

A Cleveland native with teams in two Midwestern cities, where do you think George lives? San Francisco of course.

Gordon is chief executive officer of the family business, which is named the Gund Investment Group. He's a Harvard grad, and like his brother, he's into western art in a big way. He's president and trustee of the Gund Collection of Western Art. Since the Gunds took over the staggering Cavaliers from the always entertaining and unpredictable Ted Stepien, the franchise has been setting attendance records. Clevelanders are getting the picture.

Jerry Reinsdorf, *Chicago Bulls, Chicago White Sox.*   From time to time, professional sports owners get booed, usually when they fire a popular manager or fans think they're not spending enough money to make their team a winner. To Reinsdorf, that would be no big deal. He's knows what it is to be *really* unpopular. He used to work for the Internal Revenue Service.

The former IRS attorney is also a CPA. He put all those initials together and built a real estate empire called the Balcor Company, an American Express affiliate that has about $6 billion in investments.

He and Eddie Einhorn led a group that bought the White Sox in 1981, which served a very practical purpose for Einhorn. It gave him something to put on TV. Einhorn, a former CBS executive producer and president of TVS, created Sports Vision in Chicago, a cable TV network that carried the Bulls' games and other Chicago sporting events.

Four years after he and Einhorn bought the White Sox, Reinsdorf bought controlling interest in the Bulls.

Show Biz

When you put aside all the sweat, civic pride, and symbolism, there's only one reason for big-time sports to exist. They're there to entertain you. Jocks are in the entertainment business, and so are team owners.

Some of the owners were in it before they got into sports, and it was the most logical thing in the world for them to branch out to clubhouses and locker rooms.

Danny Kaye was in on the ground floor of the Seattle Seahawks. Danny Thomas was in the original Joe Robbie group that got the expansion franchise for the Miami Dolphins. Cyndi Lauper managed a wrestler. Scratch that last one, we're talking about sports.

And what's the biggest entertainment medium of all? You're looking at it every time you flick the switch on your television set. People in the tube business, like Einhorn, recognize good programming when they see it. Or take Ted Turner . . . we will eventually, but let's warm up to that task first. It's a big job.

Gene Autry, *California Angels.*   Of course we're going to start with Gene Autry. After Don Meredith departed Dallas, how many singing cowboys were left?

"When I started out, I didn't know any more about running a baseball team than I knew about building a submarine," Autry has said. When he started out in baseball, the Angels were an expansion team that operated at the bottom of the American League standings. So the enterprises weren't so dissimilar after all.

Anybody who's ever seen an old Western movie knows about Gene Autry and his trusty horse, Champion. A chance meeting with Will Rogers got Autry into the radio business, which got him into the movie business, which got him named the top box office western star for eight years in a row. All of which got the rest of us "Rudolph, the Red-Nosed Reindeer" and other epic musical delights.

You want to know how big Gene Autry was? Why, he was the first movie star to endorse a product. It was a mail order guitar.

He was also described by *Fortune* magazine as Hollywood's No. 1 businessman, a reputation he earned by building an electronic empire called Great West Broadcasters. It owns radio stations in Los Angeles, San Francisco, Seattle, Portland, and Detroit, a pay TV company, two TV stations, a 10-acre movie and television production center, and a national agency for selling radio time.

So what does he know about baseball? As Autry himself explains it, he knows enough to "hire the best people you can find, give them trust and loyalty and pay them top money." With that philosophy he is back in the saddle again. He's never been out of it.

Art Modell, *Cleveland Browns.*   Modell has upon occasion been called the NFL's most respected owner.

He was only 36 years old when he purchased the team for $3.9 million, but he had been around. A high school dropout at the age of 15, he went to work as an electrician's helper in a Brooklyn shipyard. He went to night classes to get his high school degree, and then after a stint in the Navy, he enrolled in the New York City Television School.

That's where Modell found out he was pretty good at the electronics game. He produced one of the first daytime television shows in the country. He went on to become an executive partner for the L.H. Hartman Company of New York as well as the president of the NFL from 1967 to 1970.

He's also a board member of the Churchill Downs racetrack and of course the NFL Broadcast Committee. It is at least partly through Modell's efforts that broadcasting has been very, very good to the NFL.

Sidney Schlenker, *Denver Nuggets.*   Sooner or later Schlenker is going to settle on a team, and maybe this is the one. He and associate Allen Becker bought the Nuggets in 1985 after Schlenker had served as president of the Houston Astros and a minority owner of the Houston Rockets.

You notice the Houston pattern there, do you? Well, that's where the man is from and where he made his fortune. Schlenker founded PACE Management Company in Houston in 1960 and got involved in theaters and concerts. He also developed a couple of television stations in Houston and Dallas, but he sold those.

Now he's got the Nuggets, and if you have ever watched Coach Doug Moe's offense, you know that's entertainment.

Richard Evans, *New York Knicks, New York Rangers.* Evans doesn't actually own either of these teams. The Madison Square Garden Corporation does, and it's owned by Gulf and Western. But when executive decisions are made, this is the guy in charge.

He is president and chief executive officer of the MSG Corporation, which includes four groups. One of the groups is MSG Sports, which includes the Knicks and Rangers, but does not include Madison Square Garden boxing, which is part of MSG Communications, which doesn't seem to make much sense . . . but what the hell, this is New York.

Before becoming CEO, Evans spent 20 productive years in the entertainment field and none in the sports field, unless you count a term as president of the Leisure General Corporation in Atlanta. He was with Radio City Music Hall Productions, where he put the famous hall back on its feet with a lineup of concerts, special events, and theatrical productions.

He's also worked for Walt Disney Productions and Ringling Bros. Barnum and Bailey, and cynical New Yorkers claim that that background showed through in the Knicks' 1987 search for a coach. Could be, but Evans finally settled on Rick Pitino, and it looks as if he made the right choice.

Ted Turner, *Atlanta Braves, Atlanta Hawks, CNN, WTBS.* Where do you begin? There's a sign on Turner's desk that says "Lead, Follow, or Get Out of the Way." This man doesn't follow anything but his teams and his business investments. And nobody can remember the last time he got out of anyone's way.

He won the America's Cup sailing championship, bought the Hawks and Braves, launched the first cable TV superstations and the first 24-hour TV news network, tried to buy CBS and settled for Metro-Goldwyn-Mayer instead, staged the Goodwill Games in Moscow, and claims to be the only man in the world to have flown with both the presidents of Cuba and the United States on their Air Force One airplanes.

It all started with billboards. Turner's father, Edward, made himself a millionaire with outdoor signs and Ted took over the business. Rescued it actually. His father, a hard-driving man, died in 1963 when Ted was just 23 years old, and the son discovered that his father had sold the enterprise he expected to inherit.

Turner threatened to go to court and place new billboards directly in front of the ones that didn't belong to him anymore. The new owners canceled the deal, and Turner built the billboard company into an $800-million fortune.

From there it was on to WTBS, the cable superstation he used to turn the Braves and later the Hawks into household names all over the country. WTBS (now called TBS) is worth an estimated $28 million, but Turner had bigger things in mind. His CBS acquisition offer forced the network to buy back $1-billion worth of its own stock. When that fell through, he purchased MGM for $1.5 billion because he needed the film library for WTBS.

If there's anything Turner hasn't done in the world of sports, entertainment, and just plain power, it's only because he hasn't gotten around to it yet. Makes you wonder why he hasn't gotten into politics.

Of course, he explained that once, too, saying, "I would only run for president if it was the only way I could get the country to turn around." Now if he could get the Braves to turn around. . . .

Tell It to the Judge

There's one place where professional sports owners spend almost as much time these days as they do watching their teams play. That would be the nation's courtrooms.

Somebody's always suing somebody, and at least a handful of the owners should feel right at home in that environment. Not only are there lawyers and ex-lawyers at the controls of franchises, but there's also a judge.

Robert J. Parins took over as chief executive officer of the publicly held Green Bay Packers after ending a 15-year career as a circuit court judge. It's only fair that he and other legalistic types should be exposed to the trials of pro ownership. That's called poetic justice, isn't it?

Edward Bennett Williams, *Baltimore Orioles.*   When Williams died on August 13, 1988, both the legal world and the world of pro sports lost a fearsome battler. He defended Teamster leader Jimmy Hoffa, former Texas Governor and U.S. Treasury Secretary John Connally, mobster Frank Costello, former CIA Director Richard Helms, Communist hunter Sen. Joseph McCarthy, Congressman Adam Clayton Powell, and presidential aide Bobby Baker. Oh yeah . . . George Steinbrenner, too.

Who's Who? devotes three whole inches to Williams's career, and that's small type. A *Washington Monthly* article once listed him as one of the 10 most powerful people in Washington, although Williams himself had said his clout was overrated.

Maybe, but he was treasurer of the Democratic Party a few years back, and senators, ambassadors, and presidents had been known to show up in his owner's box. He is also credited with winning an antitrust exemption for the NFL so that it could swallow the AFL. Williams said he had never lobbied for sports.

"Someone out there thinks wonderfully of me," he said at the time. "I assure you I do not have that kind of influence."

For more than a decade, Williams fought the cancer that finally killed him, undergoing seven operations. "Either it's going to beat me, or I'm going to beat it," he said.

In his will, he gave the option to sell or retain the Orioles to his widow, Agnes.

Joe Robbie, *Miami Dolphins.*   Robbie has it all figured out. He put up everything he owned, including the Dolphins franchise, to build the $100-million Joe Robbie Stadium in Miami. It's the first major sports stadium to be funded entirely with private money, and Robbie says he'll have it all paid for by the year 2016. He'll be exactly 100 years old then. Happy birthday, Joe.

If that seems like fuzzy thinking, you have to remember that Robbie wanted to be a sportswriter once. He was sports editor of the Sisseton, South Dakota *Journal-Press* at age 14. But then he turned to a life of crime—criminal law that is.

As is the case with many attorneys, Robbie took a fancy to politics. He served a term as a state representative in South Dakota and then as state Democratic chairman before running for governor. He lost. Then he moved to Minnesota and ran for Congress. Lost again.

He didn't lose, though, when he went after the Miami expansion franchise in 1965. He and comedian Danny Thomas led a group that put up $7.5 million for the team and got it. Three years later, Thomas sold out.

A little skulduggery ensued as one of Robbie's limited partners entered secret negotiations to move the team to Seattle. Robbie caught wind of the strategy and gathered up a group of Miami businessmen to buy out the dissident.

Maybe he learned something from that, because Robbie has been careful to put people he can trust in positions of authority. People like his daughter and three sons, who all work in the Dolphins' front office. What about his wife, you say? Well, Robbie also bought the Minnesota franchise in the Major Indoor Soccer League, and made his wife Elizabeth the active owner of that team.

He is also working hard to bring major-league baseball to Miami. Now that he has this shiny new stadium, he knows he needs to put more than the Dolphins and the Strikers in it. Otherwise he won't get the thing paid off until he's 200.

William Davidson, *Detroit Pistons.*   It's been quite some time since Davidson actually practiced law, but he did receive his Juris Doctor's Degree from Wayne State University near Detroit. He's been too busy saving companies since then to spend much time in court.

Davidson gave up his law practice after three years to take over a wholesale drug company and save it from bankruptcy. He turned that around in a few years, then took over a surgical supply company and did the same thing. The family business, the Guardian Glass Company, was the next enterprise to require Davidson's healing talents. He wiped out its debts and renamed it Guardian Industries, and it has lived happily ever after.

Much the same can be said of the Pistons, although it took a good deal longer than three years to breathe some life into that mummy. Davidson bought the club from Fred Zollner, who had founded it in Fort Wayne in the 1940s and moved it to Detroit in 1957. Since adding some heavy talent and moving their games into the huge Pontiac Silverdome, the Pistons have become the NBA's runaway best sellers.

They're in their own arena now, and the future looks so bright for Davidson and his team, it's almost criminal.

Hugh Culverhouse, *Tampa Bay Buccaneers.*   If there is a secret to the success of a man who has accumulated $330 million through real estate and a prosperous law practice, it has to be persistence.

Culverhouse tried to buy the Los Angeles Rams in 1974, but he couldn't make the deal. So he just kept trying. When the NFL decided to go to Tampa in 1974, it awarded the franchise to a construction baron named Tom McClosky. Two weeks later, McClosky withdrew his bid, and Culverhouse was there with $16 million to pick up the pieces.

That same dogged determination has served Culverhouse well as a leader in the labor negotiations with the players' union and of course as the long-suffering owner of the Bucs.

Tampa Bay had a big year in 1982 when it made the play-offs, but that's been about it for this perennial tail-ender. Still, after the Buccaneers finished 4-11 in 1987, Culverhouse said, "I feel we're on the right track. The number of wins, other than in a financial way, makes very little difference to me. What's important is making the play-offs and then the Super Bowl."

Then he announced a $3 ticket hike. "The '90s will belong to the Bucs," the wire services reported him as saying. Presumably, to their fans, too, but they'll have to pay in advance.

So You Wanna Buy a Car?

There must be some reason why so many pro sports owners are either in the automobile business or have been at one time or another. It would be grossly uncharitable to suggest it takes a special kind of talent to convince people that a lemon is the chariot of their dreams, so it must be something else.

Maybe it's the ability to take a variety of moving parts and blend them into a smooth, well-oiled machine. Yeah, that's it.

William Clay Ford, *Detroit Lions.*   If we're going to talk about cars, let's not mess around. You might say the Ford family has been in the business for a while. The Ford Motor Company has sold more than 35 million cars since William's grandfather, Henry, founded the company.

William was named chief executive officer in 1978, some 22 years after he got involved with the football team. He used to go to the Lions' games with his dad, Edsel, when they played at the University of Detroit. Ford became a club director in 1956 and the team president five years after that. Then in 1963 he bought the club for a piddling $4.5 million.

Just your average sports nut, Ford was the captain of both his soccer and tennis teams at Yale. He was even nationally ranked as a tennis player until a couple of Achilles tendon operations relegated him to the showroom.

One of Ford's best moves as owner of the Lions was to take the team to Pontiac in 1975 where it could play to houses of 80,000 in the shiny new Silverdome. He also brought the 1982 Super Bowl to Pontiac. What he'd really like to do is bring the Lions to the Super Bowl, but every time the team gets near the play-offs, the wheels come off.

Norman Braman, *Philadelphia Eagles.* If you're in the market for a Cadillac, Rolls-Royce, BMW, Maserati, or Porsche, this is your guy. He has a whole string of dealerships across Florida and in Denver. They sell more than 25,000 of those and other up-scale machines every year, accounting for a gross volume of more than $500 million. Not bad for a guy who used to sneak into the Eagles' games.

Braman's dad was a barber, who emigrated from Poland to the United States, and his mom came here from Romania. He once served as a water boy at the Eagles' training camp. Then when the regular season started, he would slip into Shibe Park when nobody was watching, because he couldn't afford a ticket.

By 1985 he could afford the whole team. That's when he bought out his brother-in-law's 35% share of the club to become sole owner. The money was no problem. Braman made his first million in the pharmaceutical and cosmetics business, sold out, moved to Florida, and three years later bought a Cadillac agency. From there it was just a short ride to multimillion-dollar prosperity in other luxury autos.

President Reagan nominated Braman to be commissioner of the U.S. Immigration and Naturalization Service in 1981, but he politely declined so he could devote his time to his cars and his Eagles.

Charlie Thomas, *Houston Rockets.* This will make your day. Thomas is the only professional sports owner who ever helped Clint Eastwood become mayor of Carmel, California.

That's right, he's a friend of old Dirty Harry, and he campaigned for him in Carmel, which is right next to Pebble Beach, where Thomas has a home.

He also seems to have a home in Houston. He bought 54% of the Rockets for $12 million in 1982 and has held onto them ever since. The team has had six other owners, and none of them stayed around that long.

Thomas used to make $40 a week as a parts runner. Now he makes more than that. He must, because he owns 43 dealerships, Charlie T's Restaurant, and a whole bunch of real estate, ranches, banks, hotels, insurance, and TV properties.

***Larry Miller**, Utah Jazz.*   Here is a man who knows how to make a pitch. He started selling cars in the Denver area in the early 1970s, and he parlayed his marketing skills into 10 dealerships in Utah, Idaho, and Arizona. He also used to be one of the better fast pitch softball players around, and he still sponsors some of the nation's top teams.

Miller bought half the Jazz in 1985, and then he bought the other half in 1986 to keep the team from being sold to a group of investors who wanted to move it to Minneapolis.

He reasoned that if the Jazz moved, Salt Lake City wouldn't see major-league sports again any time in this century. Now there's a notion he wouldn't have any trouble selling at all.

***Tom Benson**, New Orleans Saints.*   The creator of the notorious, not to say infamous, "Benson Boogie" had them dancing in the streets of New Orleans in 1987 when his Saints finally made it to the play-offs. Of course they're always dancing in the streets of New Orleans, but the team almost waltzed right out of there in 1984 before Benson organized a group that bought the club for $70.2 million.

When the Boston Celtics clinch a victory, Red Auerbach lights a cigar. When the Saints win, Benson does this thing on the sidelines that he calls a "jiggle shuffle," which poses no threat whatever to Michael Jackson but is dearly loved by some of the same fans who used to put bags over their heads at New Orleans' games.

Benson knows Louisianans. He was born in New Orleans and educated at Loyola College. But he started making his money in Texas when he bought a San Antonio Chevy dealership in 1962. That acquisition has grown into Benson Automotive World, which boasts 36 different franchises and provides the wherewithal for a variety of other Benson projects, like a stable of race horses and a game preserve for exotic deer and antelope.

The impact of the Saints' first winning season ever on Benson's auto business was pretty exotic, too. Sales at his 14 dealerships around New Orleans dropped about 20% in October and November. But Benson figured sales were down all over the country for that period. And he kept on dancing.

A Woman's Touch

There are still chauvinists around who think a professional sports owners' meeting is no place for a woman. What's more, there was a time when the women who are entitled to attend those functions would have agreed.

Georgia Frontiere, Joan Kroc, and Marge Schott didn't grow up yearning to own a major-league team. All three are widows, and two of them inherited their franchises when their husbands died. But once in the driver's seat, they didn't climb down either. And each has brought her own style to the task of running a club.

Georgia Frontiere, *Los Angeles Rams.*   The will came as quite a shock in Los Angeles after Carroll Rosenbloom died in a swimming accident in April of 1979. Everyone expected the team to be turned over to Rosenbloom's son Steve, but everyone was wrong.

Carroll bequeathed 70% of the club to Georgia, whom he had wed 13 years earlier after ending a 25-year marriage with his first wife. His five kids, three by his first marriage and two by his second, got 6% apiece. Steve remained the team's "football manager," but that arrangement would last only as long as he got along with his stepmother.

Turned out not to be very long at all. Frontiere wasn't much interested in being a figurehead, and when Steve gave long-term contracts to some of the Rams' front office people and stripped Don Klosterman of his authority as general manager without consulting the boss, she canned him.

Klosterman replaced Steve Rosenbloom, and the Rams' new owner tried to make up in enthusiasm what she lacked in experience. At least everybody on the team knew who she was. She wore a powder blue jogging suit to her first minicamp, where she chatted with Coach Ray Malavasi and played catch with quarterback Pat Haden. Summer camp in August found her attempting field goals while clad in a white pantsuit.

The Rams have experienced few dull moments since Frontiere took charge, but then they didn't have very many with the colorful Rosenbloom running the show either. He was her sixth husband. The seventh is music arranger Dominic Frontiere, whom Georgia wed in 1980. She filed for divorce in 1988.

About the time she married Frontiere, Georgia landed in the middle of one of the NFL's most celebrated intrafamily squabbles. Naturally, Al Davis was involved, too. The Raiders' owner publicly charged the Rams' owner with scalping tickets to the 1980 Super Bowl.

The allegations were made in depositions submitted when Davis sued the NFL for blocking his move from Oakland. He also accused Commissioner Pete Rozelle of taking part in the deal, introducing still another endearing element in their already warm relationship.

To give you an idea of how messy the whole Raiders move got, a former Rams employee later said he had been instructed by Frontiere to bug her house. Mel Irwin said she told him to listen in on conversations involving Rozelle, among others. She denied it.

The lady isn't shy. She can be seen at times on the sidelines on game days offering encouragement to players, coaches, doctors, whomever. And she has had some prominent guests watch the games with her in her stadium box.

She's active in a number of civic causes, including a drug awareness program in the Los Angeles and Orange County schools. And she has plenty to do. Along with the Rams, she inherited a whole raft of business ventures, a big stock portfolio, and oil leases that were estimated to be worth $300 million to $500 million.

It's safe to say that as long as Frontiere owns the Rams, Southern Californians will have Georgia on their minds.

Joan Kroc, *San Diego Padres.*   When Raymond Kroc of McDonald's hamburger fame died in January of 1984, his widow and third wife Joan declared, "I don't know a darn thing about baseball."

She may not have known much about milkshakes either, but she's had to learn. Joan Kroc's own claim to fame before her husband died was her active support of drug and alcohol treatment centers and rehabilitation programs. Her Cork program is a pioneer in the field.

Seattle Mariners owner George Argyros tried to buy the team from Kroc at one time, but that deal fell through when he had trouble getting rid of his own club. So Kroc still owns the Padres, but they're not the only enterprise that occupies her time. They're not even the most important one.

Raymond Kroc used to be a large contributor to conservative causes. He supported antiabortion campaigns and Republican presidential candidates among other things. His widow has headed off in a different direction.

The grandmother of four has devoted a great deal of time and hundreds of thousands of dollars to campaigns aimed at preventing nuclear war. Said one San Diego journalist: "She is taking positions Ray Kroc would never support."

Responded Joan: "I love this country very much, and I am willing to fight for it, and this is how I am doing my fighting now."

Marge Schott, *Cincinnati Reds.*   What does a 170-pound St. Bernard do at a press conference? It keeps Marge Schott company.

The dog sitter shortage being what it is, Schott took her pet, Schottzie, along on that December day in 1984 when she announced that she had purchased the Reds for $13 million. She had been a minority stockholder since 1981, and as she put it, "I couldn't stand the thought of the Reds moving somewhere else."

Schottzie subsequently became the team mascot and got his picture taken a lot. Schott likes animals. She has three St. Bernards, and she once took a dancing bear to a formal party. "It's pretty hard to get a date when you're a widow," she explained.

It's pretty hard to take someone like that seriously, too. But anyone who doesn't is making a terrible mistake. When Schott's husband died in 1968, he left her an auto agency, two brickyards, a pig iron plant, a half-finished shopping center . . . and a landfill. "I am the Betty Crocker of garbage," she declared.

Schott admits she was tempted to run away from all that responsibility. Instead, she appointed herself chairman and president of Schottco Corporation and commenced to battle some long-standing stereotypes.

For instance, General Motors declined to put the auto franchise in her name because she was a woman. She let the company know that women can get things done, too, when the new Opel came out. Rather than having the first model delivered to her showroom, she hired a scruffy looking crew to maneuver it into her front hall at home. Then she sent a picture of her accomplishment to GM. She got the franchise.

This is not a prototype women's libber by any means, though. She pronounces Ms. "Mess." The daughter of a lumber baron, she married Charlie Schott in 1952 and settled into the life of a society matron. She was having a great time, and her only real sorrow was the discovery that she couldn't have children.

Then her husband died at the age of 42, and she became a businesswoman by necessity. She was moved when her late husband's executives showed up at the funeral, but she says she fired them when they filed expense accounts for the time they spent there.

Schott's hardheaded business sense has helped rescue the Reds from the brink of fiscal disaster, where they were teetering when she bought the club. Overpaid players rile her, and so do prima donnas. One day one of her players showed up in skin-tight leather pants and announced he was a born-again Christian. "But Schottzie knew," she said. "The dog didn't like him, and I decided to root for the lions."

Mainly she roots for the Reds. Asked about women she admires, Schott said, "The ones I admire most are wives and mothers. All I ever wanted to do was stay home and have kids."

Now she has 25 of them—all in Reds uniforms.

"It's My Ball"

Anytime a businessman invests several million dollars in an enterprise, he tends to think he should have a little something to say about how the shop is run. Most of the time, sports owners hire specialists to take care of day-to-day operations and are content to be consulted and stroked occasionally by their coaches, managers, and front office people.

Those are coaches', managers', and front office people's favorite owners. But there are other types; ones who expect their managers to be on the other end of the phone when they get a notion to make a call. They have a great deal to say about trades, and sometimes they even offer some forceful suggestions on who should be in the lineup.

There are several of these folks in fact. The following are three leading examples. It's no coincidence that you read about them all the time.

Harold Katz, *Philadelphia 76ers.* The deal that sent Moses Malone from the Sixers to the Washington Bullets was probably not the worst trade in the history of the NBA, but the good people of Philadelphia will rank it right up there until a sillier one comes along.

When Katz fired coach Matt Guokas midway through the 1987-88 season, he insisted that Guokas had approved all the trades that were made during his coaching reign, including the Malone swindle. Guokas just said they were committee decisions, and he was on the committee.

Veteran Sixers' watchers, however, say Katz has the ultimate veto power on all swaps. And he and Moses let anyone with the price of a newspaper know they were not best friends. The owner is generally "credited" with getting rid of his all-star center, a transaction that sparked a few other transactions that basically left a proud team sinking fast toward the bottom of the Eastern Conference.

That hasn't particularly delighted Katz either, and he is not averse to visiting the 76ers' locker room to let his employees know how he feels about things.

The latest account of Katz's involvement came after a game the Sixers lost to Chicago in 1988. According to newspaper reports, he was so incensed by the players' postgame laughing and joking that he went into a rage in the coaches' office, slamming his foot into a door and declaring "I'm sick and tired of losing. I'm sick and tired of the general manager. I'm sick and tired of the coaches." All of the above were there to witness the tantrum.

But then Katz, a longtime Sixers' fan, didn't buy the team to watch it lose. He had two things in mind when he purchased it for $12 million in 1981. He wanted the 76ers to win an NBA championship, which they did in 1983, and he wanted to make the operation profitable, which happened in 1987. Katz knows a lot about turning a profit.

He established a weight loss center in 1972, which grew into something called Nutri/System, Inc., which he was able to sell for a reported $87.5 million in 1984. That is a nice piece of change for a man who had to take over the family grocery business when his father died and he was just a high school kid.

It was probably easier for Katz to sell his company than it was for him to buy the 76ers. At least then he didn't have Barbara Katz to contend with. Barbara sued to block her estranged husband's purchase of the team because she said it would hurt her divorce settlement.

She later dropped the suit, but before she did, she claimed Katz only wanted to buy the club for "personal aggrandizement and ego gratification."

So why else would anyone buy a basketball team?

Robert Irsay, *Indianapolis Colts.*   The man who introduced the midnight moving van to professional sports had a few marital problems of his own in 1985 when his wife sought to make the Colts part of her divorce settlement. Harriet Irsay didn't want to run the team, she wanted to sell it to a group of Indianapolis businessmen and claim a portion of the profits.

She later dropped her attempt to gain control of the franchise, thereby denying the world one more off-beat installment in the unconventional ownership history of the Colts.

Irsay didn't really buy the team at all. He traded for it, swapping the Los Angeles Rams to Carroll Rosenbloom for the then Baltimore Colts. And then in March of 1984, he literally spirited the Colts out of Baltimore under cover of darkness, hiring a fleet of moving vans to pull up to the team's offices and moving everything to Indianapolis before anybody could show up to stop him.

It was not the NFL's finest hour, but then Irsay has provided a few other episodes that his more conventional colleagues would prefer to forget. When the team was still in Baltimore, Irsay regularly suggested personnel moves to coaches Mike McCormack and Howard Schnellenberger, and it was widely reported that he tried once to send in plays from the owner's box during a game.

After the club had moved to Indianapolis, he walked into the locker room during a game in Los Angeles to suggest changes to Coach Frank Kush, and he more or less forced Coach Ron Meyer to change quarterbacks in the fourth quarter of a game with New England.

None of this has made Irsay very popular with fans, coaches, or players, but he might prefer success to popularity anyway. He has certainly enjoyed that in the business world. He made a tidy fortune in the heating and air conditioning business in the Chicago area and later sold that corporation to go into construction and development.

The rest of Irsay's background is the subject of debate. *Sports Illustrated* wrote an extensive article on him in December of '86, disputing just about everything he had said about himself, from his religion to his war record. Irsay threatened to sue the magazine for $100 million, but then he changed his mind.

George Steinbrenner, *New York Yankees.*   "When I was a kid," former Yankee third baseman Graig Nettles once said, "I wanted to join the circus and play baseball. With the Yankees, I got to do both."

It's been like that with the Bronx Bombers ever since George M. Steinbrenner III put together a group of financial heavy hitters to buy the team from CBS at the bargain price of $10 million. That was in 1973, nine years after the network had paid $13.2 million for the club.

At the time of the purchase, Steinbrenner said, "We plan absentee ownership as far as running the Yankees is concerned. We're not going to pretend we're something we aren't. I'll stick to building ships."

Right.

The rest of the group, which included general partners like John DeLorean, Nelson Bunker Hunt, Gabe Paul, and Michael Burke, did get out of the way. But it was Steinbrenner's way they were getting out of. A former assistant football coach at Northwestern and Purdue, he is extremely partial to winning.

And so in the pursuit of success, this "absentee owner" has changed managers 16 times and pitching coaches an even two dozen times, including four occasions in a single season. Those 16 managerial changes have included just nine managers, however. The equation is obscured by the fact that he's hired Billy Martin five times.

Martin got the job when Steinbrenner became disenchanted with Lou Piniella in 1987, partly because the owner wanted to chew out his manager by telephone and Piniella wasn't available to take the call. Piniella was kicked upstairs where he became general manager, then resigned that post and became manager again halfway through the 1988 season. And now he's out again.

Even a busy signal would be enough to set off the volatile Steinbrenner, who's been known to send rookies back to the minors for making an error. When pitcher Doyle Alexander lost six straight starts in 1982 Steinbrenner ordered him to undergo a medical exam. "I'm afraid some of our players might get hurt playing behind him," he explained.

Steinbrenner admits sometimes that he acts hastily, but he usually tries to make amends when an error has been committed. Maybe that's why he ordered 50,000 Yankee Yearbooks removed from the concession stands in 1981 because he didn't like his picture.

Some things can't be made to go away. One of those was his 1974 conviction for violating election laws with his contributions to the 1972 Nixon campaign. He was charged with 15 counts, eventually pleaded guilty to one, and paid a $15,000 fine. Part of the charge was that he tried to influence and intimidate employees into lying to a grand jury.

Steinbrenner has applied twice for a federal pardon, and he may get one yet.* In the meantime, his national standing can't be all that bad. U.S. Olympic officials signed him up after the medal-thin 1988 Winter Games to try to get the U.S. teams back on track.

His main endeavor has been to get the Yankees back on track. To that end, he spent millions on free agents, which some of his colleagues claim knocked baseball's salary scale all out of whack. But George could afford it. He inherited the American Ship Building Company after his father turned it into the family fortune, and he made it even more profitable than it was when he got it.

Many of his imbroglios involve millionaire outfielder Dave Winfield, whom Steinbrenner once dubbed "Mr. May" because he didn't think he could count on him in October. Winfield wrote a book about his experience with the Yankees. It did not get rave reviews from the owner.

Reviews on Steinbrenner are what you would call mixed. Lots of people can't stand him. On the other hand, there are guys like New York Mayor Ed Koch, who says, "George Steinbrenner is a tremendous asset to the city of New York. There's no question he plays hardball, but after all, that's his game."

Yep, and the Yanks are definitely his team.

---

*Editor's note. George Steinbrenner received his federal pardon just before President Ronald Reagan left office.

Chapter 8

The Right Moves

Why franchises are worth so much that they don't have to sit still for anything

There are lots of ways to figure the value of a professional sports team, but nobody ever thought of measuring it with oil tankers until Vincent Piscopo strolled onto the scene in Chicago.

Like Bears fans everywhere, Piscopo read daily about the nasty family fight being waged by the heirs of George S. Halas for control of their favorite football team. The scrap reached its climax in December of 1987 when a couple of real estate developers named Neil Bluhm and Judd Malkin offered $17.5 million for roughly one fifth of the Bears' stock.

That might seem like a lot of money to most people, but not to Piscopo, a self-described "exporter of everything" who explained vaguely that he was "involved in biotechnology in Europe."

Piscopo also wanted to get involved with the Bears. So much so that he said he would buy the whole team for a minimum of $90 million, payable in three tankers of light crude oil.

That's two million barrels per tanker, at the going rate of $18.60 a barrel, and Piscopo calculated that if oil prices jumped to $25 a barrel, the deal would be worth $150 million.

"If they ask me, I could prove this is a bona fide offer," said Piscopo. They didn't ask him.

Some of the details of the offer were presented to a Cook County circuit judge, but the executor of the Halas estate said Piscopo never put his bid in writing. What's more, one of the attorneys involved in the dispute contended that the would-be Bear owner's involvement in petroleum products wasn't quite as extensive as he claimed. The lawyer said Piscopo ran a gas station.

Vince didn't get the team or even a part of it. Neither did the developers as it turned out. Halas's daughter, Virginia McCaskey, exercised a right of first refusal and snatched up the stock for the price offered by Bluhm and Malkin.

It might have been fun watching the outgoing Bears' owners trying to find some place to park their tankers.

We were denied that experience, but the Chicago court capers did provide us with something almost as rare—a glimpse into the books of an NFL team.

The judge eventually determined that $17.5 million was a reasonable price for 20% of the Bears, a decision that would have sent George Halas, Sr., into catatonic shock. Papa Bear bought the franchise in downstate Decatur, Illinois, in 1920 for less than the price of a rowboat. For $100 to be exact.

But that was before the Bears won the Super Bowl. Indeed that was before there was a Super Bowl. In 1986, the year the Bears became champions of the football world, they had reported revenues of $28.05 million and profits of $2.05 million.

There may not have been that much money in all of Decatur in 1920. And if there was, nobody was going to make much of it by putting on football games.

As they say, that was then, and this is now. The experts estimated the 1988 value of the Bears franchise at somewhere between $80 million and $90 million if the family ever decides to sell out. And even then, the team would be underpriced, according to Stephen Halas, George's grandson and one of the principals in the suit.

"What value can you put on the Statue of Liberty?" asked Stephen. "That is what the Bears is."

Despite the grammar, his point is well taken. He just has the wrong landmark. A more accurate comparison would be Fort Knox.

Every team has become solid gold, but only at a very special time. That time is the precise moment when its owner decides to put it on the market.

That is the central truth of the sports franchise business in the 1980s. Never in history has there been a sellers' market anything like this one.

With that comes a great paradox. Buying a team is a fine investment. Running it is a marginal business. In most cases, owners can't get rich on teams until they sell them. But then they're not owners anymore, and what fun is that?

They were dancing in the front offices of major-league baseball when 18 of the 26 franchises either made money or broke even in 1987. The industry as a whole showed an $11.5-million profit, marking the first time in the '80s that baseball didn't finish in the red. Commissioner Peter Ueberroth was predicting 20 clubs would make money in 1988.

However, with a few exceptions like the Los Angeles Dodgers, nobody was talking about gigantic profits. Take that $11.5 million and split it 26 ways, and it comes to something less than $500,000 a team. Most of the owners can make that much in their real businesses before spring training starts.

They don't split it 26 ways either. They should, but that's a different story.

There were ominous signs on baseball's economic horizon in 1988. The reason the sport had managed to stop losing money was that it had cut its payroll by a significant amount in the past year. It would have preferred to do that again in 1988, but there was serious question whether the game could pull it off without suffering some major legal bruises.

Owners paid active players around $308 million in 1986 and less than $296 million in 1987. They were able to tighten up because they had called off their bidding war for free agents. But that got them into trouble with the players association, which said there was collusion among owners to hold down salaries.

When an arbitrator agreed with the union, things started to get loose in the free agent market again. That old spendthrift George Steinbrenner sent shivers through the industry when he signed St. Louis Cardinals star Jack Clark.

Soon the owners began lobbing million dollar contracts at .240 hitters again, and by the summer of '88, a second collusion decision had gone the players' way. The owners weren't favored to win the third one either.

Milwaukee Brewers president Bud Selig may have been speaking for many of his colleagues when he said, "If you could guarantee that I wouldn't make a dime or lose a dime on my team in the next ten years, I'd sign that contract right now, shake your hand and go home happy."

If you had made that same offer to most basketball owners in the early '80s, they would have taken you home with them, fed you a nine-course meal, and put you up for the night.

In 1983, NBA teams lost a collective $15 million. A couple of years before that, there were only seven profitable franchises in the whole league. But by 1987, the NBA was $1 million in the black, and Commissioner David Stern said that in 1988 all but two or three teams made money.

Basketball turned things around with a salary cap and a much improved television package. Still, the future is not guaranteed. A new CBA with the union will send average salaries close to $1 million by 1990, and some owners are concerned that revenues won't keep pace with payrolls.

The only league in which almost all of the owners have gotten used to making hefty amounts of money from their teams is the NFL. That situation went south in 1987, compliments primarily of the player strike.

It has been reported that just seven NFL teams turned a profit in '87. There might have been more if the league hadn't spent so much time and money in court. First the owners were nailed for $30 million for unsuccessfully trying to block the Raiders' move to the Los Angeles Coliseum. Then it cost them $26 million in legal fees to bury the upstart USFL.

The clubs with the highest payrolls got slugged the most. It used to be that television revenues alone covered the cost of paying the help in the NFL. But the network package was going down at the very same time salaries were going up, which is the worst possible kind of seesaw for sports owners.

Adding to the generally gloomy picture from the owners' point of view was a union lawsuit challenging the college draft and restrictions on player movement.

If the union won and if a few more teams like the Washington Redskins signed other teams' free agents, there could be players moving all over the league. And what would that do to salaries and the NFL profit picture?

Nobody can really answer those questions unless or until all of these events come to pass. But there is considerable evidence to support the notion that operating a team, even in the gilt-edged NFL, has become a tough racket. Sports has become a tough racket. Still profitable in the long run, but tough.

Teams will remain gold-plated commodities as long as people desperately want them. And everybody wants teams. Owners want teams, cities want teams, and politicians want teams.

Even bad teams.

Look at the Seattle Mariners. George Argyros bought the club in 1981 for $11 million, and he claims to have lost $30 million on it over the next five years.

His investment has been rewarded with six straight losing seasons, on top of the five losing seasons the previous owners enjoyed. Bad deal, right? Nope.

When Argyros decided he had enough of losing in Seattle, he decided to try losing in San Diego. He offered to buy the Padres from Joan Kroc for a figure somewhere between $55 million and $60 million. The sale appeared to be all set, but first Argyros had to get rid of the Mariners.

Baseball frowns on one owner controlling two teams, even if the teams are in different leagues. What if they meet in the World Series? In the case of the Padres and the Mariners, that was a possibility by the year 2050 or so, but Argyros wanted to sell the Mariners anyway. Or so he said at the time.

The deal with Kroc eventually fell through, allegedly because the National League owners weren't too crazy about admitting the tight-fisted Argyros to their lodge. Still Argyros kept making noises about getting out from under the Mariners' situation in Seattle.

He had an attendance clause in his lease with the county that said he could move, but first he had to offer the club to local interests at fair market value. And what was fair market value for the Mariners? According to independent appraiser Arthur Andersen & Company, a lusty $58.6 million.

That's $58.6 million on an original investment of $11 million made six years earlier for a club that had never had a winning season. Outrageous? Commissioner Ueberroth thought so, but not for the reasons you might think.

While the politicians were awaiting the appraisal, Ueberroth wrote a letter accusing them of making "a clear effort to belittle baseball." And he said if they didn't treat the team better, he might allow the Mariners to move to a different city. This became a favorite Ueberroth soliloquy.

The county did do some belittling in its communications with the appraiser.

The higher the price of the Mariners, the more it would cost for local interests to buy out Argyros, or at least buy in with him. So the county people pointed to embarrassing little items like bad trades and truckloads of losses while trying to hold down the value of the Mariners.

The strategy must not have worked, because Argyros's original asking price was believed to be in the $35 to $40 million neighborhood before the appraisal came through to tell him his property was worth much more than he thought it was.

The appraiser didn't care so much about wins and losses. He liked the way the Mariner management did business, reining in the payroll, shying away from guaranteed contracts, and not paying a lot of deferred compensation to players who didn't work for the team anymore.

Economy is important, especially to owners who are operating in smaller markets. They can earn much less from radio and TV than, let's say the New York Yankees, because they don't have nearly as many households to draw from.

But that doesn't make the electric bill any smaller for them. Most important, it doesn't mean their players are willing to work for less.

There are enormous payroll disparities among major-league teams, and they don't have much to do with the size of the teams' markets. The Yankees were paying their players an estimated $18.8 million in 1988, but the Yankees could afford it. The Kansas City Royals, on the other hand, were putting out $14 million in salaries, and it was much tougher for them to remain profitable at those rates.

Next to last were the Texas Rangers with a $6-million payroll, and the Rangers had the rich Dallas-Fort Worth television market to help carry the freight. They should have been doing just fine, even if the team was pretty grim.

The Mariners' payroll was fourth from the bottom at $7.2 million, and maybe that's why they finally made some money in 1987. That seemed to make Argyros much happier about everything. At last report, he said he had no intention of moving.

OK, that's a bad team. Now how about a good one? One that wins a lot, draws from the biggest population center in the world, and has media exposure that goes on forever? How 'bout them Mets?

The Doubleday Publishing Company bought the Mets in 1980 for what at that time was the princely sum of $21 million. It was princely because the original owners got them in 1962 for the expansion franchise fee of $1.85 million.

When Doubleday was acquired by a company in West Germany in 1986, Nelson Doubleday and Fred Wilpon took over ownership of the team. And the price tag on the Mets at that time? How does $95 million sound? That may not be the Statue of Liberty, but it's at least the Empire State Building.

What we have here is a trend. From 1971 to 1976, eight major-league

SPORT$BIZ STATS

Major League Payrolls (1988)

1988 major league payrolls based on opening-day rosters, including players on the disabled list (rounded off to the nearest 100,000):

	Payroll ($)	Average salary ($)
New York (AL)	18,800,000	673,791
Los Angeles	16,000,000	641,480
New York (NL)	15,100,000	633,096
Boston	14,300,000	551,195
Kansas City	14,000,000	561,108
Baltimore	13,400,000	518,060
Philadelphia	13,600,000	547,520
Chicago (NL)	13,300,000	535,193
St. Louis	13,000,000	448,103
Detroit	12,900,000	518,122
Minnesota	12,500,000	523,027
San Francisco	12,400,000	478,557
Houston	12,300,000	474,064
Toronto	12,200,000	451,989
Atlanta	11,600,000	465,346
California	11,600,000	464,795
Oakland	10,200,000	395,384
Montreal	9,600,000	371,466
San Diego	9,400,000	378,166
Cincinnati	9,100,000	351,073
Milwaukee	8,500,000	334,980
Cleveland	8,300,000	221,907
Seattle	7,200,000	290,798
Chicago (AL)	6,300,000	264,268
Texas	6,000,000	215,933
Pittsburgh	5,800,000	237,540
Totals	**297,400,000**	**447,291**

Note. From "Average Salary Increases 9.6 Percent," by H. Bodley, *USA Today*, April 6, 1988, copyright 1988, *USA Today*. Adapted by permission.

franchises were sold for between $8 million and $12 million each. In the next five years, nine clubs changed hands for between $12 million and $30 million apiece. And then things warmed up.

From 1982 to 1987, eight teams went for an average of $40 million. Recent examples are the Minnesota Twins, who sold for $45 million, and the Detroit Tigers, whose price was $53 million. The lowly Texas Rangers were on the market at an appraisal value of $75 million.

The pattern is about the same in basketball. For instance, when Larry Weinberg had finally had enough fun running the Portland Trail Blazers, he sold them to computer wizard Paul Allen in 1988 for a record $70 million. Weinberg bought the Blazers in 1971 as an expansion franchise for $3.5 million.

The league has expanded twice since the Trail Blazers got in, and the entrance fee just keeps going up.

Dallas entered the NBA in 1981 for $12 million, and everybody thought the Mavericks were being ambushed in broad daylight. In 1987, Minnesota, Charlotte, Orlando, and Miami agreed to pay $32.5 million apiece for the right to get their new teams' brains beaten out until they had been around long enough to win a few games. Normally that takes three or four seasons.

If the expansion teams beat anybody at all in those first couple of years, it will probably be teams like Phoenix. The Suns have been pretty bad for the past couple of seasons, and then a local drug scandal made them look a good deal worse.

But Suns General Manager Jerry Colangelo wasn't discouraged. He led a group that bought this woeful outfit for $44.5 million in 1987. The original owners had purchased it in 1968 for $2 million.

The Colangelo purchase was labeled the richest in the history of the NBA. One month after it was made, an out of town businessman who declined to be identified offered Colangelo's group $60 million for the Suns. He turned them down.

Hey, if the Phoenix Suns are worth $60 million, then the Boston Celtics must be worth twice as much, right? Just about.

An empty seat in the Boston Garden has become about as rare as a Robert Parish smile, and the Celtics' management decided all of that loyalty should be rewarded. Besides, the team needed a little working capital. So it offered a piece of the action to the public, putting 2.6 million shares of Celtic stock on the New York Exchange.

The fans ate it up. They bought the shares for as much as $18.50 a share. The owners gave up only 40% of the franchise, so they didn't lose any control. But they netted $48 million on the deal. And the team they bought in 1983 for $15 million was now worth $119 million on paper.

The new citizen owners were feeling pretty good about the whole deal, too. The Celtics showed a 1987 profit margin of 19.8% compared to IBM's 9.3% at the time. The only trouble is as IBM gets older, it seems to get better. That's not the case with the Celtics.

The Detroit Pistons ambushed Boston's aging aggregation on the way to the 1988 NBA finals, and the Celtics weren't a great bet to make it back to the top in 1989. As a result, playoff revenues appeared to be on their way down. So was the price of the stock. By June 13, 1988 those $19 shares were worth $13 on the New York Stock exchange.

Most NFL teams weren't doing nearly as well as the Celtics or IBM in 1988, but the value of the franchises wasn't losing any ground. It's hard to tell in football, though, because teams don't go on the market as often.

There was a flurry of activity in 1984, however, when Pat Bowlen bought the Denver Broncos for $70 million, and Bum Bright purchased the Cowboys for a Texas-sized $60 million, plus $25 million for Texas Stadium operations. Then things heated up again four years later.

When oil and real estate took a dive in Texas, Bright found the Cowboys to be kind of an expensive toy. It was widely reported that millionaire Marvin Davis offered Bright between $150 million and $160 million to take the team and stadium operations off his hands, but the deal fell through.

By the fall of 1988, Bright still had the club on the block, and the price had gone up. He was asking for approximately $100 million for the franchise, $50 million for Texas Stadium operations, $20 million for the club's Valley Ranch headquarters and $34 million for team-related debts.

That may seem high for a declining team in a troubled league, but these were not lonesome Cowboys by any means. Team President Tex Schramm, who had an 8% interest in the franchise, hired a Wall Street investment banking firm to find investors who could meet Bright's price. They didn't have to look long.

Up to the plate stepped former Postmaster General Robert Tisch with an 0-2 count on him. Tisch had tried to buy the New England Patriots, and then, according to the September 12, 1988 edition of *Sports inc.* magazine, he tried to buy the Tampa Bay Buccaneers. So why not the Cowboys? Pete Rozelle, Tisch's good friend, was hoping it wouldn't be strike three.

The commish said he was encouraging his tennis buddy to join the league because he would do a terrific job with the Cowboys.

While the financiers were diddling in Dallas, they were selling in Seattle. The Nordstrom family decided in August of 1988 to spend more time on their chain of upscale fashion stores, and that gave them less time for the Seahawks. The family sold the team for $80 million to California land developer Kenneth Behring and his partner, Ken Hofmann, another Californian.

The Nordstroms had been the Seahawks' majority owners since they joined the league in 1975 for the $16-million franchise fee, and the good people of Seattle were very comfortable with them as the custodians of their favorite football team. The comfort index dropped dramatically when this pair of Californians took over. Behring insisted he wasn't interested in moving the team. Let's just say the fans are watching closely.

In Massachusetts, the fans are always watching closely. Look away for a minute, and they're bound to miss something outlandish. The curious case of the New England Patriots deserves a more thorough inspection if for no other reason than to prove that a sports franchise can be turned into a financial disaster, just like any other enterprise. It just requires more effort.

Meet Billy Sullivan, who got some partners together in 1959 to put up a piddling $25,000 to acquire an AFL franchise in Boston. A very prudent purchase.

Over here is son Chuck Sullivan, administrator, music lover, and executive vice president of the Patriots, who managed to lose just as much as his father on the team and assorted other ventures.

And finally there's son Patrick, general manager and treasurer of the club, who kept his own wallet in his pocket.

The Sullivans created great anxiety among the brotherhood of NFL owners in strike-plagued 1987 because for a moment or two, it looked as if they wouldn't meet their payroll. That would have made free agents of 45 professional football players. The crisis was averted when Commissioner Pete Rozelle freed up some contingency funds to get the Pats paid, but that only quieted the other owners' nerves temporarily.

Rozelle made it clear that he didn't know who would own the Patriots in 1988, but it sure wouldn't be the Sullivans.

Chuck Sullivan acknowledged that the team had lost $12 million in the past season, and he listed its liabilities at $42.7 million, compared to $4.6 million in assets. Actually, things may have been worse than that. When the franchise finally sold, some observers said its debts just about equaled its selling price.

How can anybody cook up that much fiscal hash out of an original $25,000 investment? Particularly when everybody else has either made money or stayed close to even.

Well, it wasn't easy, and it wasn't fun. It had something to do with stockholders, stadiums, racetracks, and even Michael Jackson, the singer.

The Sullivans' real problems began when after a decade or so of life as Boston orphans, they decided they needed a home of their very own. Nobody wanted to build them one in Boston, so they bought some land 20 miles away in Foxboro and put up a place for a parsimonious $6.7 million.

The Schaefer Brewing Company picked up 25% of the tab in return for having its name put on the place. Schaefer Stadium was born in 1971; the Boston Patriots became the New England Patriots; and sports-loving Bostonians thought very highly of the Sullivans.

Well, not all Bostonians. Some of Billy Sullivan's original partners became disenchanted with his leadership, and they dumped him from the presidency in 1976. Son Chuck reacted by concocting a deal that allowed his dad to buy out his dissident partners. They had to borrow money to do it, and the collateral was the team. The buyout put the family about $11 million in the hole.

Five years later, the Sullivans paid $12 million to buy sole control of Schaefer Stadium and rename it Sullivan Stadium. At the same time, they also agreed to pay $1.5 million a year to lease a harness track next door. And they sank a little deeper into debt.

Things just got worse in 1982 when the players declared a strike that nicked some owners a little and the debt-ridden Sullivans a lot. Then Chuck thought he saw a way back to profitablity.

He had done a little music promoting in his time, and he decided to back Michael Jackson's epic 1984 Victory Tour. This time he used Sullivan Stadium as collateral. The venture ended up costing him roughly $20 million and a mild heart attack.

Even in 1986 when the Patriots went to the Super Bowl, they lost $9.6 million. They lost a couple of lawsuits, too. The shareholders whom the family had bought out in 1976 decided they had been underpaid. They filed three suits and won two of them in 1986 to the tune of more than $3 million. A year later, the third suit resulted in a $7-million judgment against the Sullivans.

And of course in 1987 there was another costly strike.

Enter a group of businessmen headed by Francis Murray of Philadelphia. He lent the Sullivans $21 million in a few different installments and gained an option to buy the team for $63 million in the process. The logical conclusion to this tale would have the financially foundering Sullivans dumping the team on Murray and riding sadly but wisely into the sunset.

But the Sullivans kept backing away every time Murray tried to exercise his option. So Murray sued.

About that time, the banks were all clamoring for the money they had lent the family, and the stadium came within an eyelash of being sold at auction. Only a bankruptcy filing delayed the auction.

With the entire situation threatening to burst into flames, who should come racing onto the scene but a Fireman?

Paul Fireman, the chairman of the Reebok Shoe Company, joined Murray in a 51-49% arrangement that would have given him control of the Pats. The NFL owners unanimously approved the conditional sale, and New England pro football appeared to be on the brink of normality at long last. Did you notice that word "conditional"?

Fireman didn't want the Patriots unless he could also buy Sullivan Stadium. He figured the place was worth $18 million tops. No sale. Fireman missed an NFL deadline for acquiring the stadium; the Sullivans backed out of the negotiations; Fireman sued, and the Pats were up for grabs again.

Next up was Connecticut industrialist Victor Kiam. When Fireman's deal disappeared, Kiam entered into an agreement with Bill Sullivan, Jr., to gain controlling interest in the team. He got it for an estimated $85 million, while Murray was allowed to buy additional stock.

So what have we learned from the strange saga of the New England Patriots? Well, the lesson is about demand.

Here was a club with its stadium in hock and debts of more than $60 million that had been dropping money faster than a one-armed wide receiver. And yet a line of high-powered potential purchasers was forming at the door.

At one time or another, Tisch, Marvin Davis, and New York real estate mogul Donald Trump also expressed serious interest in buying the Pats.

Does that mean people are crazy? Certainly. Most pro owners would cheerfully admit to that. Fellows like Fireman and Kiam know they can invest their millions in far more profitable ventures than a football team.

But fellows like Fireman and Kiam didn't pile up nine-figure net worths by being dumb either. And the Pats wouldn't have been a dumb investment for the simple reason that they knew they could have some fun with the team and still get their money out whenever they wanted.

When teams start losing too much money or not making enough, their owners tend to do one of two things. They sell out, or they move out, which is what more and more owners are either doing or threatening to do.

A third possibility is for owners to demand local concessions to keep them from taking their show someplace where it will be better appreciated.

It's not a new scene. Walter O'Malley played it back in the '50s when he took the Dodgers from Brooklyn to Los Angeles. But it's a bigger scene today because there is so much more competition for franchises.

An amazing amount of competition in fact. And it's taking place in every area of the country in every sport.

In football, the USFL lived just long enough to give a number of cities a brief taste of pro ball, and not even very good pro ball at that. But absence makes the heart grow fonder.

Phoenix, home of the old Arizona Outlaws, swiped the Cardinals from St. Louis, while other USFL stops like Memphis and Jacksonville would call up the militia if they thought they could conquer an NFL team.

Similarly, Oakland has never gotten over the loss of the Raiders, and Baltimore is still smarting over the midnight ride of Robert Irsay with the Colts. St. Louis is pining for somebody to replace the Cardinals.

Then there are cities like Sacramento that have never had a team but want one now. Even Montreal is after an NFL franchise now that it has said au revoir to the Alouettes of the Canadian Football League.

Basketball is the same way. The NBA has just put franchises in Minneapolis, Charlotte, Miami, and Orlando, leaving three or four other suitors waiting.

The pressure in baseball may be greater than it is in basketball and football combined. There aren't any bad baseball towns anymore.

The lowest attendance in the major leagues in 1988 was 848,089. That's how many people paid to watch the Atlanta Braves, the only team that has failed to draw 1,000,000 since 1985. Remember when a million fans was a big year for a baseball team?

So who wants a baseball team? Only Indianapolis, Vancouver, New Jersey, Columbus, New Orleans, Sacramento, Denver, Washington, Phoenix, and any city in Florida big enough to dock a boat.

There are a couple of factors involved in all of this eagerness, and one of them is about image. Civic leaders have decided that their towns can't be considered big league unless they have big-league teams playing in them. They're more than willing to pay for the distinction.

Why? Let's ask Michael S. Megna.

Megna is corporate vice president of American Appraisal Associates, a national leader in appraising sports franchises. American Appraisal not only tells teams what they're worth, but it also has a very good idea of what they mean to the economy of their cities.

"The only area in which there hasn't been a dramatic increase in the value of teams is hockey," Megna told us. "Basketball, baseball, and football have gone up significantly in the last 10 years.

"It's tied into two key factors. One is the increase in national exposure given to sports through the media. The other is the increase in the desire of people to participate in sports as spectators. They have more leisure time and more money to spend on leisure activities. Average people spend about $80 when they go into a stadium and bring somebody along.

"I talked about what teams mean to cities to the chairman of the board of Westinghouse. He said it was very simple. He said, 'How can I bring people to Pittsburgh to work for Westinghouse if I can't tell them we have a major league community?' Now you want to translate that into dollars. It can't be done. But that's not the important thing. It's the desire. The image."

John Christison, the director of Orlando's entertainment facilities, put it another way in a Jan. 1988 *Sports Marketing News* article.

"I can tell you without hesitation that I'd rather have 42 rock shows than 42 NBA dates in terms of the bottom line, because there's no question that the rock shows are going to make more money," said Christison.

"But is Orlando recognized on the nightly news because it did David Bowie? Probably not."

Cities all over the country agree. The city of Phoenix figured an NFL team would pump between $40 million and $60 million into the local economy. The particular team it chose was the Cardinals, and the St. Louis Convention Bureau estimated that losing them would cost up to $4.5 million a game.

That probably sounds about right to the city of Green Bay. The Packers did an economic impact study in 1987 and came up with a figure of $35 million a year. That's in a town of fewer than 80,000 people.

Football doesn't raise as much money for a city as baseball does, because a football team has only eight home dates during the league season compared to 81 for baseball. Basketball has 41 home games a year, but they're played in smaller places.

So if a city wants to be big league and it can have only one team, its best bet is baseball. Then it's football and basketball.

That's for regular-season activities. Special events change the picture dramatically. Minneapolis calculated that $93 million was injected into its local economy from the '87 Series, while St. Louis's take was about $105 million.

Not bad, but it's not the Super Bowl. Pasadena pulled in $190 million from the 1988 Super Bowl and wasn't even close to the record set by New Orleans at $226 million in Super Bowl XX.

Keep in mind, there's a "multiplier effect" built into all of this. Experts take the spending directly connected to the game and multiply it by two or maybe two and a fraction, figuring that will account for the additional dollars that circulate around town from purchases made by local businesses and from labor, materials, and services.

Not everybody agrees with these figures. There are experts who say people in cities without professional teams will spend their money on the other things the city has to offer. It is useful to remember who pays for these studies.

In many cases it's the teams. And the teams aren't going through all of that effort to prove they're just an amusing little frill.

The numbers can vary pretty widely, depending on who's crunching them. But the studies are fairly consistent on what goes into calculating the amount of revenue a team generates for its home town.

It almost always involves ticket sales (which means rent and/or taxes), concessions, parking, hotels, restaurants, transportation, and licensing and advertising. In other words, it's anything that gets money spent locally that wouldn't get spent if the team wasn't there. And anything that puts people to work.

Let's take a quick look at a couple of those studies—one done by the Montreal Expos in 1983 and one done by the Milwaukee Brewers in 1987.

The Expos figured their impact on the Montreal economy to be about $100 million in 1983, and that's direct money without the multiplier.

They start with the 2,000 summer jobs they create every year for people like beer vendors, ushers, and ticket takers. Then there is the $1.25 million paid in amusement taxes on ticket sales of $15 million a year, $8 million in concessions, $2 million in souvenirs, and $10 million in advertising sales for the stations that broadcast the games.

When a team is doing well, everybody wants a piece of the action. The Expos were earning another $2.5 million from businesses that bought advertising in its magazines, put signs up in the stadium, or bought a spot on the scoreboard.

The team advertised, too, spending $1 million on ad and public relations agencies and another $600,000 on printing contracts. The Expos also sold rights to their logo to companies that used it to help generate sales of $4 million.

Visiting teams have to eat, too, and they have to get around. They were leaving about $1.25 million behind, not counting what they contributed to airport revenues.

But the most important visitors of all were the fans who lived outside of the area and came to town just to watch the game. The club said about 25% of its attendance came that way, and each of those fans was spending an average of $150 on meals, gas, and accommodations during his or her stay.

There is also the matter of player salaries, which the Expos' study didn't specifically identify. If a city can get its players to stay home in the off-season, they do wonderful things to the tax rolls and local shopping spots.

That's Montreal in 1983. Four years later, the Brewers calculated their impact on the Milwaukee economy to be more than twice as much as the Expos' figure. The Brewers arrived at a $212-million total by adding $153 million in sales, $47 million in wages, and $12 million in taxes.

Rather than breaking it all down again, let's just note that they paid

$11.2 million in salaries, while visiting teams and media spent about $300,000 locally, and nonresident fans dropped approximately $34.5 million into local cash registers.

In a city like New York where everything costs more, the numbers get even bigger.

If a new stadium or arena is factored in, team owners say the numbers can go right through the roof. "Propaganda!" cry the critics.

Robert A. Baade, an economics professor at Lake Forest College near Chicago, prepared a report for the Heartland Institute, a nonprofit, nonpartisan research group specializing in state and local policy issues. The Institute released the report entitled, "Is There an Economic Rationale for Subsidizing Sports Stadiums?" in February of 1987. Baade's answer was a resounding no.

He said new jobs aren't created by stadiums at all. They're just shifted from higher skilled to lower skilled occupations.

He also said the money spent at sporting events is just money that normally goes to some other activity and that in seven of the nine cities he studied, each city's share of regional income actually went down after a new stadium was built.

The report must not have made many best-seller lists because new stadiums continue to pop up like mushrooms all over the country. In the war for big-league teams, they are the most popular kind of ammunition.

Cities have always sparred with one another in the athletic arena. Only the prizes have changed. The rivalries used to be for bragging rights—"My team's better than your team." Now they're for the franchises themselves.

Critics say the most dramatic result of this all-out sellers' market in sports is teams taking cities hostage. Franchise owners reply that in this era of out-of-sight salaries, they need every edge they can find.

In either case, owners don't mind the trend toward municipal combat a bit. Even if they don't want to move, they have an impressive amount of leverage in dealing with local governments for better rent agreements, stadium renovations, or brand new ballparks.

A successful season and a whirling turnstile are no guarantees that a club will stay around. Look at the 1987 pennant races. The Giants won the NL West for the first time ever and all but promised they'd be gone in a couple of years if they didn't get a new place to play. The Twins won the World Series and hinted darkly about a move to Tampa if something couldn't be worked out with their lease.

The battle is even being waged in spring training. The Chicago Cubs draw 160,000 fans a year for their Cactus League games in Mesa, Arizona, making them a prime target of the tourist industry in Florida. And while the Floridians were talking to the Cubs, they were also trying to lure the San Diego Padres from Yuma and the Cleveland Indians from Tucson.

When the Cubs' lease in Mesa was up, five different Florida cities called them with offers of free land and/or free stadiums. Arizona businessmen figured the best defense was a good offense. While trying to hang onto the Cubs, they also extolled the virtues of training in the sunny Southwest to the Minnesota Twins, St. Louis Cardinals, and Philadelphia Phillies, all of whom spend their springs in Florida.

Why the sunshine war? Because spring training attendance has set records for the past six years, going from 1.4 million in 1981 to 1.9 million in 1987. The governor of Florida claimed that the 18 teams that trained in his state fetched between $500 million and $1 billion annually in tourism revenues.

The Arizona people doubt those figures, but they don't doubt that they have to stay on their toes to keep Florida from luring all of their teams away.

"We're in a dogfight with Florida over the Cubs and the other major-league teams in Arizona," said Dave Workman, one of the Mesa businessmen working to hang onto the Cubs. "Community leaders are determined to keep the teams here."

Determination is commendable. Cash is indispensable. If cities are willing to volunteer piles of the stuff to secure the advantages of a professional team for just six weeks, think what they'll do to keep one all year long.

That's something the management of the football Cardinals set out to discover in 1987, and the result was a bitter war between Phoenix and St. Louis that illustrates how these municipal confrontations come about.

How bitter? Listen to the loser:

"For the first time in modern NFL history, the league has voted to abandon an NFL community. Twenty-eight years of fan loyalty deserves better. By its despicable conduct, the NFL has chosen to sanction the franchise free agency that Mr. Rozelle so feared in 1984."

That was the mayor of St. Louis talking after the Cardinals formally deserted his city.

Mayor Vincent T. Schoemehl gets a C in arithmetic for his statement, but an A− in history. The Cardinals experienced 26 years of fan loyalty in St. Louis, not 28. The last two there were pretty lonely.

His Honor is right on the money with the part about franchise free agency, however, if modern NFL history can be dated after 1960.

A few teams had changed addresses since then, but not as a result of a league vote. When Robert Irsay decided to move the Colts from Baltimore to Indianapolis, and when Al Davis took his Raiders from Oakland to Los Angeles, they neglected to ask permission from the other owners.

Davis's case was the one that brought about the term "franchise free agency" after the league lost a suit seeking to prevent the transfer. Ironically, the last team to move with the legal blessings of the league was none other than the Cardinals in 1960. They abandoned Chicago to go to St. Louis.

While Schoemehl was appalled by the team's 1988 flight to Phoenix,

SPORT$BIZ STATS

Sports Structures of the '70s

Structure	City	Year opened	Cost ($ millions)
Veterans Stadium	Philadelphia, PA	1970	6.5
Three Rivers Stadium	Pittsburgh, PA	1970	35
Riverfront Stadium	Cincinnati, OH	1970	44
Sullivan Stadium	Foxboro, MA	1971	6.7
Texas Stadium	Dallas, TX	1971	35
Arrowhead Stadium	Kansas City, MO	1972	63
Rich Stadium	Buffalo, NY	1973	19.9
Pontiac Silverdome	Pontiac, MI	1975	55-58
Superdome	New Orleans, LA	1975	163
Giants Stadium	E. Rutherford, NJ	1976	302*
Kingdome	Seattle, WA	1976	60

*Includes racetrack.

Note. Information compiled from *Sports inc.The Sports Business Weekly*, March 14, 1988 and July 11, 1988. Adapted by permission.

he shouldn't have been shocked. The *St. Louis Post-Dispatch* had written three years earlier that there was a better than 50-50 chance the Cards were on their way out.

The newspaper quoted team attorney Thomas Guilfoil as saying he and owner Bill Bidwill had met with Phoenix-area officials that year.

The major itch team officials seemed so eager to scratch was 54,392-seat Busch Stadium. It was the second smallest in the league, and the fact that it was named after the owner of the town's baseball team says something about the football club's status there.

Seating capacity wasn't a terribly pressing problem in 1988, however. While the baseball Cardinals were drawing three million fans on their way to the World Series, the football birds were averaging about 30,000 people a game. There were plenty of seats.

Also plenty of problems. The 1987 strike didn't help matters, nor did a strong local perception that the Cards were getting ready to fly out of town anyway. Besides, it was a bad team.

When fans are unhappy about something, the only real way they have to make their feelings known is to stay home. So an informal boycott developed. Attendance wasn't all that impressive the previous year either. At least not for football. "Let's face it," said Cardinal linebacker E.J. Junior, "we're a football team in a baseball town."

Bidwill might have seen his way clear to stay put if plans for a $170-million domed stadium hadn't fallen through. After that happened, he turned down a compromise offer for a $117-million open-air facility. Meanwhile, Baltimore,

SPORT$BIZ STATS

Sports Structures of the '80s

Structure	City	Year opened (or date projected)	Cost/ estimate ($ millions)
Metrodome	Minneapolis, MN	1982	76.5
Hoosier Dome	Indianapolis, IN	1984	82
Joe Robbie Stadium	Miami, FL	1987	102
Miami Arena	Miami, FL	July 1988	52.5
Charlotte Coliseum	Charlotte, NC	August 1988	52
The Palace	Auburn Hills, MI	August 1988	70
Arco Arena	Sacramento, CA	September 1988	40
Orlando Arena	Orlando, FL	December 1988	40
Bradley Center	Milwaukee, WI	October 1988	50

Note. Information compiled from *Sports inc.The Sports Business Weekly*, March 14, 1988 and July 11, 1988. Adapted by permission.

Memphis, Jacksonville, Columbus, and Phoenix all wanted to talk to Bidwill about his unappreciated football team.

The state of Maryland said something about a dome, while the city of Columbus pointed out that Ohio State's Buckeyes always filled their cavernous 85,339-seat stadium. The Ohioans offered the Cards a generous five-year interim lease on the place.

Bidwill wanted a dome eventually. To sweeten the pot, a Columbus station offered $500,000 annually to televise the team's preseason games.

Jacksonville had the 80,000-seat Gator Bowl lying around idle on Sundays, and it offered to guarantee sellouts for the Cardinals there for 10 years.

The Jacksonville people had tried the same pitch on the Houston Oilers, offering a 10-year, $125-million revenue guarantee. The Oilers used it to negotiate a new lease from the Houston Sports Association that gave them all of the revenues from 72 new skyboxes to be built at the Astrodome. Cost: just $60 million.

Meanwhile in St. Louis, Bidwill kept listening, and time kept passing. He had until January 15, 1988, to let the league know whether he planned to move. A week before the deadline, St. Louis fattened its offer by saying it would build the team a $5-million practice facility and office complex and charge only nominal rent. It would also continue to work toward a new downtown, indoor stadium.

Not bad. But no matter what anybody else came up with, Arizona kept topping it. Not one, but two, local groups were dedicated to bringing a team to the Phoenix-Tempe area.

One of them, quarterbacked by former Green Bay Packer great Bart Starr and former American Football League Commissioner Joe Foss, had an expansion franchise in mind. When the Cards started looking west, Arizonans saw no reason to wait.

Bidwill said he wouldn't move his club for less than $7 million. "No problem," said a consortium of 40 Phoenix-Tempe businessmen that did not include Starr and Foss. They put up $10 million for starters.

And they did mean starters. Phoenix was hoping to build a $160-million downtown dome to accommodate the Cardinals and a major-league baseball team it didn't even have yet. In the meantime, there was 70,491-seat Sun Devil Stadium, home of Arizona State University.

The Phoenix incentives came out to around $20 million by the time everything was put together. The proposal would give the Cardinals 90% of all ticket revenues, based on a price of $20 a ticket for the regular seats at Sun Devil.

They would also receive all of the money from 500 special loge seats priced at $500 apiece, and they would split the parking and concessions revenues with the university. Wait, there's more.

Sixty luxury boxes priced at $40,000 each were to be added to Sun Devil Stadium, and a $5.5-million practice facility was to be made available.

The luxury boxes were bound to go in a hurry because they had air conditioning. September in Tempe does not provide an ideal atmosphere for watching football games. September in Tempe does not provide an ideal atmosphere for anything a human being would do on purpose.

That was not Bidwill's problem. Bidwill didn't have any problems on January 15, 1988, when he announced he was heading west. All that was left was the voting and a last-ditch effort by St. Louis to keep its team.

On March 15, a 27-member group called Civic Progress was allowed to make a one-hour presentation to the owners before they voted. It offered to build a 70,000-seat domed stadium with 65 skyboxes to be sold for a guaranteed $40,000 each, and the team would also receive added concession revenues. "It was a very strong presentation," Bidwill acknowledged.

In other words, "Nice try," but all it got St. Louis was some vague encouragement from Rozelle, who said the city was a prime expansion site in the future.

The owners voted 26-0, with two abstentions, to let the Cardinals have their way. Abstaining were Miami's Joe Robbie and Al Davis of Los Angeles. Robbie was a good friend of rejected suitor Foss. Davis was being sued by the league at the time, and he was just protecting his legal interests.

Bidwill did a little of that himself. He agreed to a 10-year lease at Arizona State, with two additional 10-year options. But he wasn't expecting to keep his team on campus nearly that long.

He had an escape clause that would let him move to the proposed downtown dome as soon as it was built. He also admitted he had the option to move again.

"But if you think I'm going to go back in that room and go in front of those other owners again . . . ," said Bidwill. "I don't think I want to do it again. Our obligation is to Phoenix."

Legally it might be argued that his obligation was still to St. Louis, since the Cardinals' 30-year lease on Busch Stadium didn't expire until 1995. But in their recent rush to more prosperous pastures, pro sports teams have never tripped over anything as small as a lease.

Nobody knows that better than the cities that have lost teams or have had teams threaten to desert them. Even towns like Pittsburgh, which has zealously supported pro football for more than half a century, realize they can't be too careful.

The Steelers sued to break their lease at Three Rivers Stadium in 1984 on the grounds that the city allowed the USFL Maulers to use the facility. The city sued right back when the team cut its rent payment from 10% of ticket sales to 5%.

They finally settled on a new deal that keeps the rent at 10% but with a cap of $850,000. More important, it extends the lease until 1999.

Allegheny County Judge Ralph Cappy supervised the negotiations, and when they were over, he made a little speech that indicates just how defensive cities have become in the national struggle for pro franchises.

"I think this serves notice on the rest of the country," said the judge. "These have been the Pittsburgh Steelers, are the Pittsburgh Steelers and always will be the Pittsburgh Steelers. Stay out of our territory. Don't fool around with our club."

Forbidding stuff, but one can't help but wonder if that warning would have made much of an impression on Bidwill or Irsay, or more important, to Phoenix and Indianapolis. Especially Indianapolis.

Indiana has long been recognized as the unofficial national capital of basketball, but until recently it was decidedly minor league in the other sports. Then Indianapolis made up its civic mind to change all of that by pioneering a brave new trend in franchise speculation.

It could best be described as "Pay now, play later."

With a great deal of help from local industry, the city built a brand new downtown stadium, complete with dome, plenty of seats, and all the modern conveniences except one. It didn't have a tenant.

The citizens were patient, and one night a caravan of trucks pulled up carrying all the earthly possessions of the former Baltimore Colts. Now the Hoosier promoters go to bed every night hoping they'll awaken to another convoy carrying a major-league baseball team.

And if they can do it, why can't other cities?

Cities like Sacramento where work was set to begin in 1988 on a 45,000-seat baseball stadium if Greg Lukenbill could just get the environmentalists out of his hair. Lukenbill planned to put the stadium right next to the 17,000-seat arena he was building for his NBA team.

Or cities like Orlando. The people there put up a 15,200-seat facility and saw their efforts rewarded with an NBA expansion franchise. And in St. Petersburg where construction began on the $65-million Suncoast Dome, which would seat 43,000 for baseball and more than 20,000 for basketball.

St. Pete didn't have either a baseball or a basketball team when it started digging the hole. What it had instead was a healthy rivalry with neighboring Tampa, which also was in the market for baseball.

However, hundreds of miles to the north, a battle was brewing in Chicago, where the White Sox thought local politicians were dragging their feet on plans for a stadium to replace venerable, but rickety, Comiskey Park. The word was the Sox were looking south for answers.

One unidentified team official told the *Chicago Sun-Times*, "I think there's a 50-50 chance we're going to go (to St. Petersburg), and it tears my stomach out. We don't want to leave, but we're getting pushed and pushed and pushed by the politicians."

And they were pushing right back, with the friendly assistance of Ueberroth. The commissioner who said he wouldn't do anything to stop the Mariners from moving if the city of Seattle didn't behave said the same thing about Chicago. He wouldn't try to stop the Sox from moving.

When a baseball team is trying to gain leverage with local government and business leaders, it doesn't hurt to have some outside muscle standing alongside wielding a crowbar. And Ueberroth is an eager helper.

The people in St. Pete understood that kind of stuff. If they were at all tempted to jump up and down and shout, "The White Sox are coming! The White Sox are coming!" they showed admirable restraint.

A. Ray Smith, one of the leaders in the drive to bring baseball to St. Petersburg, captured the mood when he said, "You know and I know that there's not one chance in a hundred that the White Sox are going to leave Chicago after the long history they've had there. It's just a ploy to wake up the local politicians."

In other words, a bluff. But if this is a poker game, it's the worst kind for cities negotiating with pro franchises, because only one side has to show its hand. And there are so many bidders.

Probably the most revealing comment anyone has made on the pressures cities are feeling to get or keep teams came from a fellow in Denver named Steve Katich.

Katich, the executive director of the Denver Baseball Commission, told his city council that it would have to pick a site and have both a design and a financial plan for a new $70-million stadium before baseball would even consider expanding there. This, despite the fact that the Broncos' Mile High Stadium was originally built for baseball and Denver has been waiting for a team for decades.

"It doesn't matter that we have been trying longer to get a team," said

Katich. "It's not like the meat market where you get a ticket and wait your turn. Let's face it, we are competing with cities who are blessed to be in economic communities that are better than ours."

Or at least as good. And there are so many of them. In 1988, two dozen of the nation's 60 largest cities were building, planning to build, or thinking seriously about building sports complexes that would cost $100 million or more.

The obsession was taken to its illogical conclusion in California where the town of Irwindale, 18 miles outside of Los Angeles, gave Al Davis a nonrefundable check for $10 million.

In return, it got a nonbinding agreement from Davis to move his Raiders there. The city also said it would secure financing for a new $100-million, 65,000-seat stadium. As of July 1988 Davis and Irwindale reportedly were haggling over the financing.

Most cities aren't quite as adventurous as Irwindale, but they are willing to gamble millions of dollars that the attendance boom in baseball and basketball will go right on booming and that it will return to football. When they don't fill their new parks for games, they figure they can fill them for concerts and circuses.

Many cities figure the best scenario of all would be a stadium or arena that could house two tenants, a football team in the fall and a baseball team in the summer. Many cities may be wrong about that, though.

Cincinnati has such an arrangement, and it's been very profitable. Also very troublesome. The Reds generated $2.9 million in 1987 revenues at Riverfront Stadium; the Bengals brought in another $1.4 million; and the place hardly ever stood empty.

The courts stayed pretty full, too, while the two teams fought with each other and with the city over their separate leases. They have been to court to contest the scoreboard and the luxury boxes, and it wouldn't amaze anyone if they were back for new disputes centering on scheduling and the stadium restaurant.

In 12 cities, the major-league baseball teams share stadiums with NFL clubs, and some places have had three big-league teams under the same roof. Seattle's Kingdome housed the Mariners, Seahawks, and Sonics for awhile. Pontiac's Silverdome had the basketball Pistons and the football Lions.

Rarely are co-tenants the best of friends. Dates, parking revenues, concessions, and advertising are all potential fracas creators.

But that hasn't discouraged intrepid civic planners. Not when they have this new toy to dream about—the retractable dome.

The retractable dome is the ultimate foil for Mother Nature. A roof that comes and goes at the push of a button, offers warmth for football fans, sunshine for baseball buffs, and cash for construction workers all over the north.

Toronto plans to open its $304-million retractable dome stadium for the

Blue Jays in 1989. Phoenix, Cleveland, and San Antonio are in the drawing board stage. Of course only Cleveland has a baseball club, but why get bogged down in details?

Well, maybe a couple of details require a certain amount of attention.

Ueberroth deals with both of them in a set of guidelines he issued outlining the essential ingredients for operating a successful baseball franchise. The commissioner urges a privately owned, baseball-only stadium with natural grass and adequate lighting.

The man said baseball only. And if it can't be that, he wants the stadium priority to be baseball use.

He also said "privately owned," and this is a very large item indeed. Stadiums are becoming incredibly expensive. Local government units either can't afford them or don't want to try.

Look what's happened to prices. Veterans Stadium went up in Philadelphia in 1970 for $6.5 million before most people had gotten around to building domes. Dallas followed with its partially covered Texas Stadium a year later for $35 million, and then Pontiac added Teflon lids to the recipe with the $55-million Silverdome in 1975.

New Orleans probably wishes now that it had thought of that. The conventionally topped Superdome cost $163 million the same year the Silverdome went up for barely more than a third of the cost.

By the late '80s, the only thing that could be built for under $100 million was a circus tent. It cost almost that much to renovate the old places. And Toronto's $304-million tag seemed to be the wave of the future.

City and county governments are being careful not to get swamped by that wave. With certain notable exceptions, such as irrational Irwindale, they are showing more inclination all the time toward limiting their involvement in the stadium business and leaving more of it to private enterprise.

With leases being weighted more in the teams' favor every year, the governments can't make much money from rent. And the cities can derive most of the same economic and booster benefits from having a big-league team if somebody else pays to build the ballpark.

Politicians like big-league teams a lot, but they love votes more. And the voters were sending them messages from New Jersey to San Francisco with stops in Columbus and Miami. All of those cities turned down referenda for publicly subsidized sports palaces in 1987.

Maybe they were looking at New Orleans where the Superdome was running an operating deficit reported to be as high as $3 million to $5 million every year. That stadium is in dire need of a baseball team to fill some of the seats in the summertime, but New Orleans is not considered to be a front-runner for expansion.

Neither is Sacramento where Lukenbill is willing to take the risk the city government won't take. "Major league status is worth the financial outlays if you have that kind of money laying around," said Mayor Annie Rudin. "But when you have other things going begging, it's not."

Making things even tougher for public financing of stadiums is the new federal tax law that says bonds issued to build sports facilities are no longer tax exempt. Twenty-five projects that had already been started were grandfathered out of the tax change, but bonds issued after December 31, 1990, are on their own. The interest rates on those were jumping from 6% to 10%.

In a climate like that, the safest course seems to be cooperation. Cities may not be able to build stadiums by themselves, but that doesn't mean they can't help.

Toronto provides a sterling example of that. The plan there called for $30 million to be raised from municipal taxes, $30 million from lottery proceeds, and $5 million each from 15 corporations that buy the rights to things like supply contracts.

The city will also sell $15-million sponsorship tiles on the stadium "Wall of Fame" and issue another $15 million of preferred stock.

San Francisco is also seeking a cooperative arrangement. The city would dearly love to keep the Giants, even though the referendum for a new stadium flopped. A task force there offered to name a new stadium after anyone who was willing to put up $20 million to help build it. As Shakespeare said, "What is in a name?" Evidently not $20 million. So far, no takers.

In Chicago, the Bears have said they'll spend $130 million of their own money to build a 70,000-seat, open-air stadium on the city's west side. But they want public and other private financing to take care of the $30 million needed to replace the housing they need to knock down to make room for it.

And in Atlanta, local businessmen got together on a marketing drive to raise 70% of the $158 million needed for a new 72,000-seat stadium for the Falcons. The other 30% was to come from public funds. The private part would be raised by leasing executive suites and club seats.

That project was slowed down when the leases to the suites didn't go as quickly as expected. And once again, the team was threatening to move somewhere else.

The obvious reason why threats like that usually prompt some kind of action is that there aren't enough franchises to go around. Supply may never catch up with demand. But there is a considerable amount of pressure being exerted to close the gap.

The NBA has just grown by four teams, and that league will need a few years to catch its breath before getting any bigger. There aren't enough players to go around as it is. Worse yet, there aren't enough referees.

Football has three angry former franchise holders to deal with when it decides to grow. Rozelle has already told St. Louis that it's a leading candidate for a new club now that the Cardinals are gone, while Baltimore insists it's interested *only* in an expansion team. The city does not care to do unto others what has been done unto it.

Oakland says it has identified no fewer than seven potential ownership groups that could pay more than $60 million for an expansion franchise and $30 million more to run a team that could make Davis and the Raiders just a bitter memory.

Also very interested are Jacksonville, St. Petersburg, and Montreal. That's six candidates for two spots at the most. Rozelle has said he expects to put two expansion teams on the field within two years after a new CBA has been reached with the players.

Baseball is the sport that seems primed to make the biggest move. It's also the one that's feeling the most heat.

Don Fehr, executive director of the players' union, has charged that baseball owners like to keep a few hungry cities on hold, so that existing teams can use them as leverage in dealing with their cities. Fehr said the owners have made franchises "artificially scarce."

"If every market has a team, then it would be next to impossible for an owner to announce 'I am unhappy here, and I will leave you high and dry without another team unless you satisfy me,' " explained Fehr while he was in Washington to present a study commissioned by the union.

The study examined 23 markets that Fehr said are pursuing a baseball franchise.

The owners' response to the charges was that the union was simply trying to create jobs for players. If that's true, they're not the only ones.

A confidential report revealed by *Baseball America* magazine in its June 1988 edition says a group of "very successful entrepreneurs" has targeted 22 cities as sites for a third league that could begin as soon as 1990.

The new league would be called the Professional Baseball Federation, and the magazine said the PBF wouldn't be interested in merging with anybody. The organizers want their own show, and they want to put it in some of America's biggest markets.

Meanwhile back in the world as we know it, Ueberroth has said that once new labor and television contracts are negotiated in 1989, the major leagues can add as many as six teams for a franchise fee of as much as $40 million apiece.

That's what the commissioner said. But come April 1, 1989, he won't be the commissioner anymore. In September of 1988, National League President A. Bartlett Giamatti was elected to succeed Ueberroth, who stepped down voluntarily. And Giamatti didn't share his predecessor's enthusiasm for welcoming members into the National League club.

In fact, he declared himself "tepid" on expansion, although he did say the subject would be discussed after the TV and labor contracts were worked out.

That was not exactly what the United States Congress wanted to hear, and it's usually a good idea for baseball to tell our national legislators what they want to hear.

Next to tax cuts, nothing makes representatives look better than bringing a pro team to their own city or state. Quite a few of these politicians are fans, too, and they think it's about time somebody replaced the Senators in Washington, D.C.

When they're really feeling ugly, they can make scratchy, unpleasant noises about ending the illogical exemption baseball enjoys from federal antitrust laws.

So it behooves baseball, and every other game for that matter, to keep national legislators happy. It's not difficult to figure out what that takes.

In November of 1987 a group of 15 senators and one representative formed a task force to "encourage" baseball expansion. They sent letters to Ueberroth and league presidents Bobby Brown and Giamatti reminding them of the free market system and how they would like it to operate in their states as it relates to the sporting industry.

They also held a press conference where everybody showed up wearing blue baseball caps inscribed with the name of a city. Everybody but Florida Senator Lawton Chiles. He said he would have to wear three caps—one each for Miami, Tampa, and St. Petersburg.

It's a pity the senator didn't have three noggins to put them on. The way the country is losing its head over pro sports franchises, we may all need that many before long.

Chapter 9

The Bottom Line

Paying the bills . . . and Kareem's and Fernando's, too

The Toronto Blue Jays have developed the ultimate solution for fans who can never find a hot dog vendor when they need one.

Room service.

Picture yourself propped up in bed sipping coffee while outside your window George Bell is pounding a hanging curveball over the left-field wall. The roar of the crowd is your wake-up call. Good morning. You are a guest in the sumptuous Toronto SkyDome Hotel.

There are 364 suites in this posh hostelry, which has been built right into the team's new, $304-million, 54,000-seat playing palace. Seventy of them overlook the field from either side of the scoreboard. Watch the game live while the kids play in the pool. When the pitcher goes to the showers, so can you.

Strange things are happening to the national pastime. A day at the ballpark used to mean green grass, sunshine, maybe a few beers, and the crack of the bat. You can still get all of the above in most places, although the grass is missing in some parks. But if you want to spend a bit more, there are plenty of extras for sale.

Baseball, football, and basketball teams throughout the United States and Canada are hoping fans will want to spend a bit more. In fact, they're depending on it. They need the money.

It's true that nobody ever watched from a hotel suite while Babe Ruth circled the bases at Yankee Stadium. Perhaps those were better days, but who's to say? They were certainly different days, and the biggest change since then has come in the economy of sports.

In Ruth's time, a team's whole payroll might have come to less than the average salary paid to one player today. Ticket sales were the only main source of revenue for club owners.

169

That was before radio, and more important, television came along to boost professional sports into an entirely different economic atmosphere. Some baseball teams make more from broadcast rights than they do from the live gate. All NFL teams do.

Average fans, if there are such animals, are starting to feel less and less important to their favorite teams. Do teams really need ticket-buying fans when they can rake in millions from the networks? If they love the fans, why are they raising prices all the time?

Owners swear on their mothers' graves and their teams' account books that nothing is more important to them than the loyal follower who walks through the turnstile with family in tow. And maybe they mean it. But they also know they can't live by gate receipts alone anymore.

Not in these times. And not at these prices.

To stay alive, every team has to feed on two main sources of income. One is the live gate, including ticket, concession, and souvenir receipts. The other is broadcast revenue.

And now the sports world is on the verge of adding a third essential ingredient to its daily diet—luxury accommodations for the well-heeled customer.

The teams that can make all three revenue sources work for them will succeed in this era of escalating expenses and stupendous salaries. The teams that can't will be sold, or moved, or both.

To get an idea of how franchises feed at these three separate troughs and who fills them, it's best to look at them one at a time. Let's start with the newest one.

Luxury Seating

Whenever teams talk about building new stadiums or refurbishing old ones, the conversation doesn't go very long before getting to this. It's the fastest-growing source of revenue in sports, and it's not calculated to make that average fan feel any better about his or her place in the entertainment market.

Average fans know they're never going to sit in one of these air conditioned minipalaces, and they're not sure why anyone else has to. But owners feel they're at war with a modern changing market, and they can only win with the most modern armaments. That's where upscale seating comes in.

It goes by a lot of different names: executive suites, luxury boxes, sky boxes, ego seats. What it comes down to is VIP treatment at a price. A considerable price.

Luxury boxes have been used to build whole stadiums. They have lured some teams out of town and kept other teams home. They started modestly, spread slowly, and then took off like a rising fastball. And they're here to stay.

Toronto's high-tone hotel might serve as the grandiose conclusion to the trend, except that somebody's bound to top the Canadians sooner or later. It will take some imagination to do it, however.

Twenty corporations agreed to contribute several million dollars apiece to build a new home for the Blue Jays, complete with a retractable roof that can open and close in 20 minutes as well as an 800-seat, three-tiered restaurant and bar. The hotel with the stadium view was an afterthought.

Right next to the stadium was a 35,000-square foot piece of land just sitting there not doing anything. The developers got to thinking about that and decided the stadium would be much more profitable if there were something going on there 24 hours a day.

Before long, Toronto wasn't talking about a baseball park anymore. It was talking about a live-in amusement park that also offered a health club, a 25-meter swimming pool, an indoor track, a miniature golf course, and a 150-seat movie theatre.

And luxury boxes. Lots of luxury boxes. After all, not everybody can stay in the hotel.

The SkyDome has 161 luxury boxes priced between $100,000 and $225,000 per season under 10-year leases. And that doesn't even include the price of a ticket. Nor do the fans who lease the boxes get to use them for special events. Should the World Series or Olympics come to Toronto, that would cost extra. The tenants also have to provide their own furniture and finance the interior finishing.

Arrangements like that vary at different stadiums and arenas. So do the amenities. But the suites all contain the basics: bars, restrooms, carpeting, and a varying number of seats in case anyone wants to take time out from the party to watch the game.

Toronto fans who found the boxes just a little out of their range, but who still wanted something extra, signed up for the new stadium's club level. That offers 5,800 extra-wide seats and a carpeted concourse leading to a veranda that overlooks Lake Ontario. The extra seat width helps to accommodate a wallet large enough to handle the $2,000 to $4,000 each occupant is charged. They were sold out long before the stadium was finished.

Eventually, every big-league stadium and arena in the country probably will offer features like these. And the whole thing started barely more than 20 years ago.

Naturally, it started in Texas. In 1965 the Houston Astrodome, which is also responsible for the dubious blessing of artificial turf, opened with 55 luxury boxes. The next year Busch Stadium in St. Louis followed suit with 39. And then stadium architects seemed to neglect the suite life for the better part of a decade.

Only about 30% of the luxury boxes in today's parks were built in the '70s. The rest came in the '80s when salaries soared and cities warred for pro franchises. Houston is an outstanding example of the latter.

The Astrodome, once labeled the "Ninth Wonder of the World," had slipped somewhere into the bottom 100 in the wonder department as far as Oilers owner Bud Adams was concerned. The only thing he was wondering about was where his team would play in 1988.

He made a very convincing shopping trip to Jacksonville, Florida, where local interests were offering not only the sun but several million dollars to get the Oilers to move. No one will ever know how much Adams really wanted to move to Florida, but the negotiations provided him with important leverage in Houston where he got a brand new lease.

The Houston Sports Association agreed to build 72 new skyboxes for the Oilers priced at $30,000 to $45,000 per season. And all the revenues go to the football team. That comes to about $2.9 million a year or just under $30 million over the life of the 10-year lease.

Poor Jacksonville got nothing. It was not a great winter for Jacksonville, which made an equally attractive and equally futile pitch to the St. Louis football Cardinals. While the Oilers provide an illustration of a team that boxes kept home, the Cards provide one of a team that boxes lured away.

They went to Arizona where the Phoenix Sports Alliance guaranteed them $7.1 million from the rental of 60 suites. The suites were to be finished by 1989 at Arizona State's Sun Devil Stadium where other elite seats were planned as well. A 5,000-seat middle deck priced at $500 a chair would generate another $2.5 million, and 22,000 chair-back seats were going for an extra $100 apiece and bringing in $2.2 million.

St. Louis made a last ditch offer to keep the Cardinals with luxury seats of its own, but that came too late. The team was anticipating an even sweeter deal in the future when Phoenix planned to build a downtown stadium for both football and baseball that would offer even more luxury box revenues.

This may all sound like a genteel form of municipal blackmail, but it does recognize the realities. If you want a team, build boxes. The Los Angeles Raiders and Washington Redskins are the only clubs in the NFL that don't have luxury suites, and they'll have them before long.

Miami has the most luxury suites in the NFL with 216 at Joe Robbie's brand new place, while the New England Patriots have the least with 42.

As of 1987 the most expensive ones to rent were the 60 that Denver Broncos owner Pat Bowlen put in recently at $80,000 each, while the cheapest were the $9,500 models at the Pontiac Silverdome. The Lions built those in 1975 when the stadium went up, and they're still quite a bargain as boxes go. Green Bay and Indianapolis have $10,000 base prices.

The suites have anywhere from a dozen to three dozen seats, and sometimes the tickets are included and sometimes they're not. The really lucky suite leasers get amenities like parking, closed circuit television, and refrigerators.

Dallas even offers computers that tie into the scoreboard to provide player statistics to the occupants, and it has power windows that shut out the noise at the touch of a button. Fans who really get attached to their luxury boxes can buy them instead of lease them. For between $300,000 to $1.5 million they can literally live with the Cowboys. They don't even have to cut the lawn, and they can usually resell at a profit.

The price is high but the need is great. And that goes for all three sports.

Dallas is one of several cities that has built a stadium or arena from the proceeds of luxury suites. That's what financed the construction bonds for the Cowboys, and that's what's going to pay the freight in Miami where Dolphins owner Robbie has privately financed his stadium. It's the same way in Auburn Hills, Michigan, new home of the Detroit Pistons.

The Pistons have been setting NBA attendance records for the past two years in the spacious Silverdome. But that's a football stadium, and they're just tenants there. Owner William Davidson wanted his own place, so he broke ground in 1986 in suburban Detroit.

One of the first things he did was get some help naming the place. The Pistons ran a contest offering a lifetime pass to the fan who came up with a name for their new building. The winner was "the Palace at Auburn Hills."

It doesn't have quite the same ring as, say, the Parthenon or the Eiffel Tower, but it's descriptive enough. Davidson's glorious new edifice cost a king's ransom to build. The $70-million arena features 180 suites with some as close as 20 rows from courtside.

Those choice spots go for $120,000 annually. More modest luxury accommodations can be leased for a mere $30,000. And when everything is filled up, the team will make almost $12 million a year from the suites. At that rate, the $70-million construction cost could be wiped out before Isiah Thomas retires.

Robbie didn't need any help naming his new stadium. He called it Joe Robbie Stadium. People who can raise $100 million to build a ballpark can name it anything they want. Robbie expects to pay the mortgage off from the revenues generated by preferred seating.

He's figuring on $29,000 to $65,000 a year for each of his 216 luxury suites, plus another $600 to $1,400 apiece for 10,000 other premium seats. Those include some of those wide-bottom seats that are so popular in Toronto.

The gross comes to $18 million a year, which is more than half of most NFL teams' annual revenues.

It's not necessary to build a new place to get luxury suites. In most cases, teams can add them to existing structures. It can even be done in basketball arenas.

The Utah Jazz plays in the 12,212-seat Salt Palace, which is one of the smallest arenas in the league. The team's management has been working with the city to add 350 permanent seats, including 100 of the ego variety.

To qualify for one of those, a fan has to join the Jazz 100 Club. The first 20 members get into the club for $15,000. Then it's $20,000 for the next 20, $25,000 for the 20 after that and on up by $5,000 increments until the happy 100 are all together. They each pay $10,000 a year in dues, and the Jazz nets a tidy bundle from a small building. Fans can resell their memberships and keep the profits.

In baseball and football, there is usually much more room to upgrade facilities. And quite a few teams are telling their landlords in nice and not so nice ways to do exactly that.

Shea Stadium in New York recently underwent a $36-million face-lift that featured 46 skyboxes. The Mets expected to make about $1 million a year on the new boxes, which is half of the total receipts. The other half goes to the city.

That is an important point. Teams aren't the only ones that prosper from ego seats. Occasionally, they don't prosper from them at all.

Some teams keep all of the revenues from luxury seating. Some share the take. Others just get the price of the tickets but none of the rent. And some don't get a dime—at least not directly.

It depends on who built the boxes and why. If a city or county puts up a stadium, it may need all of the proceeds to pay off the construction costs. Even then, the team benefits financially from playing in a new place.

If private developers or local governments add boxes, they arrive at some kind of deal with the team on what will happen with the revenues.

For instance, the Indianapolis Colts get the first $500,000 from suite rentals, with the other $900,000 going to the Hoosier Dome's capital improvements board. The New Orleans Saints are buying the Superdome suites from the city as they come up for renewal.

Generally speaking, that's a local matter that teams and cities have to thrash out for themselves. They do it when they sign their leases. That's also when they divide the money from the second main source of pro sports revenues.

Gate Receipts and Concessions

Football depends less on the live gate than the other sports, and that's probably a good thing. It's the only game that fewer people paid to see in 1987 than in 1986. The average NFL attendance in 1987 was 54,315, compared to 60,663 in 1986. The league blamed it on the strike, which is a reasonable assumption although not the whole story.

An average of 32,706 fans per game were gullible enough or idle enough to pay full price for semipro football or, as the owners called them, "replacement games" during the 1987 strike. Nonstrike games drew an average of 59,717.

That last figure is pretty good, but there is evidence to suggest that football fans do get tired of picket lines.

In 1981, the NFL set an attendance record of 60,745 spectators per game, and it's never gotten that high again. There was a 57-day strike in 1982 that knocked the average gate down to 58,472 the following year, and the league has been trying to get back to the 1981 level ever since.

It got close in 1986 and then another strike came in 1987. Owners watched the turnstiles anxiously in 1988 to see what the damages were.

Not just their own turnstiles either. NFL teams share gate revenues. During the regular season, home teams get 60% of the receipts and the visitors get 40%. Baseball shares on an 80-20 basis, while the home team keeps everything in basketball.

The strike wasn't the only thing that created ill will between football owners and fans. The Cardinals' apparent intention to move out of Missouri in 1987 must have had a little something to do with St. Louis crowds dipping under the 20,000 mark.

And when a bad team entertains a lame duck team, you get something like the 15,909 who turned out for the Cards' game at Atlanta in November of 1987. More than 18,000 season ticket holders stayed home from that one.

Perhaps the most frightening statistic for the NFL is the trend in Dallas, where America's team has drawn fewer Americans every year since 1983. And still the Cowboys raised their ticket prices from $19 to $23 in 1988.

Even if the NFL rebounds to the 60,000-per-game level again, its gates will have flattened out for the past seven or eight years—at a time when baseball and basketball are booming.

One million fans used to be a seasonal goal for most major-league baseball teams. Now everybody does at least that well. The 1988 St. Louis Cardinals topped one million before June 1. But one million isn't even enough to stay out of the red any more. Clubs have to get somewhere between 1.5 million and 2 million to break even or turn a profit. And they're doing it.

Total attendance in both leagues in 1988 was over 52 million, compared to about 45 million three years earlier. The gate went up every year in that span, and that total gain was 16%.

As impressive as baseball's attendance gains have been, basketball's are even better. The NBA's gate jumped 31.3% and set a record every year from 1983 to 1988. Average attendance was at 13,419, up from 12,795 in 1987. Almost everybody rode the wave, with 15 teams gaining fans, five losing, and the rest staying the same.

Detroit, playing in the immense Silverdome for the last year before heading for its own new building, became the first team in NBA history to draw more than one million fans at home. The Pistons pulled in an official 1,066,505. They had to paper the house to do it, however.

Club officials admitted the total included the number of tickets sold, rather than actual attendance. They were selling blocks of tickets to businesses for a buck or two a game, and the blocks sometimes amounted to 10,000 tickets.

There may never be another NBA team that draws one million fans in a season. The Pistons will lose about 30,000 seats when they move into the Auburn Hills Palace. But they'll also have a much better deal on rent and concessions. Their owner built the place, and a team can't get a better deal than that.

The NBA will miss the dome. The top 10 crowds in league history, starting with the 61,983 announced for a 1988 game with Boston, were achieved at the Silverdome.

Maybe baseball and basketball attendances are on the rise while football gates have leveled off because attendance is so much more important to the first two sports. Football officials would probably argue that point, but it's pretty obvious that baseball and basketball are much more creative when it comes to getting fans into the stands.

When was the last time a pro football team had a ladies' day? Or gave away a wristband or a pair of sweatsocks?

Or a 200-pound cake of ice?

Football teams play 16 regular-season games and apparently figure the significance of the event will fill the seats. About the only thing they do to spice things up on game day is hire a bevy of local beauties and let them dance to music on the sidelines.

Baseball and basketball, on the other hand, have to get their fans into the habit of going to a lot of games that aren't likely to have any immediate, earthshaking effect on the standings.

Sometimes they recognize that that requires a little more than the product. And those times can produce some delightful results—the kind that used to be provided by the late Bill Veeck, the undisputed king of shenanigans. He gave away the 200-pound block of ice.

As the owner of three different major-league teams, Veeck also gave away guinea pigs, burros, suntan lotion, and 500 jars of iguana meat. All a fan had to do was pay his way into the park, and there was no telling what Veeck might have in store for him. One befuddled customer received 50,000 assorted screws, nuts, and bolts.

The one thing Veeck wouldn't give away was tickets. He reasoned that was all he had to sell. His reasoning has been adopted through the decades in baseball, and some owners have tried to out-Veeck Veeck.

Minnesota may have taken things as far as they can go when it declared Halter Day in 1978. The lucky ladies in attendance were given halter tops emblazoned in strategic places with the word "Twins."

If you think that's bad taste, how about the Washington Senators' Mother's Day promotion? Every mom got a can of Right Guard deodorant. The Senators subsequently left town. So much for the sweet smell of success.

Basketball's answer to Bill Veeck is Pat Williams. NBA fans can't wait to see what he'll do to attract attention to his expansion team, the Orlando Magic.

In previous stints with Atlanta, Chicago, and Philadelphia, Williams has staged Big Feet Night, Skyscraper Night, and Weightlifter Night. He's also featured racing pigs, wrestling bears, and Arlene the Hot Dog Eater.

Big Feet Night coincided with a visit from Bob Lanier and his size 21 shoes. Anyone with shoes over size 13 got in free. Any man over 6′ 4″ and any woman over 6 feet got a pass to Skyscraper Night starring Seattle's

7′ 4″ Tom Burleson, and anyone under 5′ 10″ was a guest at Mite Night with Nate Archibald of the Kansas City Kings.

All fans 250 pounds and over were invited to Weightlifter Night. Four of those fans were placed on a table at halftime, and weightlifter Paul Anderson tried to get them off the ground. The table broke.

Arlene the Hot Dog Eater was supposed to eat 76 hot dogs at intermission of a 76ers' game. She swallowed 78 instead, in addition to 21 peaches and 10 Cokes.

The pig races were something Williams and the 76ers' janitors would have preferred to skip. The porkers were quick enough, but they weren't housebroken.

Williams's last official promotion at Philly was the first annual Don Nelson Coat Throw. Nelson, then the coach of the Milwaukee Bucks, was at the Philadelphia Spectrum coaching against the 76ers when he became so incensed over a referee's call that he ripped off his sport coat, whirled it through the air in an ever-widening arc, and sent it skidding down the court. He and his wardrobe were ejected.

After the game, Williams dug through the trash can in the visitors' locker room where he salvaged Nelson's tattered coat. The next time the Bucks came to town, he had dozens of fans parade to the floor at halftime to see if they could throw the coat further than Nelson had. The NBA office wasn't amused, but Nelson was. He offered to play the winner.

Most promotions in both basketball and baseball are tamer than Williams's or Veeck's. The standard of course is Ladies' Day, which, legend has it, started in 1889 with a handsome young Cincinnati Reds pitcher named Tony Mullane. Every time Mullane pitched, the stands were filled with ladies. So the Reds began letting them in free when their favorite was scheduled to start.

That might seem counterproductive, since the ladies were going to attend anyway, but baseball doesn't necessarily look at promotions that way. A giveaway night can do two things: It can make a potentially dismal crowd respectable, or it can make a good night great.

So, contrary to popular belief, baseball teams don't always schedule their special days and nights for games against weaker opponents. They have lots of seats to fill. On the other hand, basketball teams, with smaller arenas, are more likely to do it that way.

Ever wonder how a baseball team could afford to give away bats to every fan 14 and under who comes to a designated game? Bat Days, after all, are among the most popular promotions in baseball. Just about everybody has them.

The answer is the bats don't cost the team a thing. They're paid for by a sponsor. Maybe two sponsors. Look at the bat, and you'll see somebody's company logo on it. It could be a soft drink company or a hamburger chain.

The companies pay the teams for the right to put that logo there. What they're really paying for is the right to be mentioned on every radio and television commercial the team buys to advertise Bat Day. Sponsors are buying exposure. They get their names mentioned, and they get to be associated with the team.

The bats, by the way, only cost the sponsors about $2.50 apiece because they can buy them in huge quantities.

Still, that's a fairly high-priced item, and often a team will get two sponsors to back an expensive promotion. There's no problem finding them. It used to be that the teams themselves would split the cost of a promotion with a sponsor. Now they find potential sponsors waiting in line.

Just five or six years ago, teams budgeted giveaway nights on the loss side of the ledger. Now they're profit makers. And the bigger the market, the more they can make on them.

The most popular giveaway items aren't necessarily the ones fans can use the most. Usually they're the ones fans think are worth the most. Everybody wants a good deal, even if it's on an item they can't use.

Milwaukee Brewers vice president Dick Hackett, the man in charge of his team's promotions, says he never wants to give away cheap merchandise. For one thing, it doesn't do anything for the team's image. For another, it might start getting thrown around. Very few teams have ball days anymore. Potential missiles.

Bats, jackets, and cushions go over big. Kids' promotions are best on Sundays. Adults on Friday nights. Beer? Maybe never.

Teams used to have 10-cent beer nights all the time, but the Cleveland Indians had a memorable experience with that particular promotion a few years ago, and everybody is suds-shy now. The fans found the product to be such a bargain that many of them consumed more of it than they could handle.

Then they turned on both the visiting Texas Rangers and the umpires. The umps got tired of holding things up while sloshed fans were escorted off the field, and they finally forfeited the game to the Rangers.

The whole problem of customers becoming intoxicated by more than their teams' success is being seriously addressed by major-league teams these days. Some of them have designated certain areas of the stadium as family areas where no beer is sold. To make that work, the areas have to be available in all price ranges. And that can get tricky.

Selling beer is much more important to some clubs than others. The same goes for parking, peanuts, popcorn, and hot dogs. A team's cut of concession revenue depends on its lease, and there are as many different leases as there are teams.

Often it's a cooperative venture. The landlord and the tenant arrive at a percentage deal. The Brewers, for instance, have an arrangement with Milwaukee County that gives them all concession revenues until attendance reaches one million. Then the county gets 10%.

A few hundred miles away, the Minnesota Twins were giving up 35% of all concession revenues to the Metrodome management. Owner Carl Pohlad thought so little of that deal that he terminated it as soon as he could.

Anybody who thinks hard bargaining over concession money is fighting over peanuts hasn't noticed what's happened in the ballpark food business lately. Total sales at busy ballparks run into the millions of dollars, and the question of who gets most of that money is no small matter.

There are only a dozen or so major companies in the concession business, although that group has added some high-powered members—companies like McDonald's and the Marriott Corporation—in the past few years.

The traditional arrangement was for the concessionaires to buy their own stands and equipment in return for a contract that gave them a percentage of their sales. That percentage sometimes went as high as 80%, leaving the rest to the stadium, which might or might not share it with the ball club.

With more competition in the concession business comes better deals for stadiums and sometimes their teams. And of course if the team owns the stadium, it's better yet.

As long as the lines are reasonable and the food is passable, most fans don't care very much who's cooking it. They do care what it costs, particularly if they have brought along two or three eating machines known as kids.

An April 1988 *Money Magazine* survey revealed what it costs at various ballparks to take a family of four to a baseball game. It included the price of four choice tickets, parking, a pennant, a cap, a T-shirt, a program, four hot dogs, two sodas, two beers, a pretzel, peanuts, and popcorn. If the menu is making you a little ill, wait till you see the tab.

Believe it or not, the cheapest place to take the family in the major leagues was Dodger Stadium, where you could get away for $65.75. Next was Kansas City at $69.60, and then everybody was over $70. Tops was Boston at $89.95.

Teams sell everything from T-shirts to turf, and business goes most briskly when the club is winning. The Minnesota Twins claim their souvenir sales following the 1987 World Series were four or five times greater than anyone's ever experienced after a Series. Homer Hankies alone hit the one million sales mark before Christmas.

For a real down-to-earth pitch, look at Chicago. When the Bears decided to remove the artificial turf from Soldier Field and replace it with natural grass, they figured they could use some seed money. So they took the turf out, piece by small piece, and put it up for sale. And to help them sell it, they enlisted the services of that noted horticulturalist Walter Payton.

Some of the stuff was mounted and marketed as 12-inch by 12-inch plaques bearing Payton's picture and a list of his rushing records. Some of it was used as a centerpiece in 40-inch by 28-inch fine art works fashioned with scenes from Payton's life.

Some of it was even being rented out as a dance surface to be used at parties. The Chicago park district was hoping the souvenir turf would net about $700,000, which would cover the cost of putting the real grass in at Soldier Field.

None of this creative merchandising has done anything to drive down the price of your ticket, however. That's going up in every sport at every level.

According to the NBA, the average ticket price in 1987 was $7.10, which was 40 cents more than 1986 and better than twice as much as it was in 1976 when the average was $3.45. You might need a telescope and a guide to help you find the floor from that $7.10 seat.

Top prices in the NBA ranged from $18 in Milwaukee and $22.50 in Portland to $175 in Los Angeles and $219 in New York. Those three-figure seats are the ones right on the court where customers like Jack Nicholson sit. Nobody hates those more than the press, because in places like Los Angeles, Chicago, and Philadelphia they have displaced press rows and moved the media behind the baseline.

Philadelphia went even further. It put the Fourth Estate in kiddie chairs at the end of the court behind low tables, so that the people behind could see the action. The management marked the kindergarten arrangment by passing out milk and cookies to the disgruntled reporters.

Five of the 23 NBA teams offered tickets costing $100 or more, and 9 others had prices of $50 or over. You can still buy a cheap seat in some pro basketball venues, but they're getting rare. The lowest regular price in the league is a two-dollar seat at the Lakers' Fabulous Forum, while eight teams still have tickets priced at five bucks or less.

One of those is Atlanta, which paradoxically doubled the tab on its highest ticket in 1987, going to $50. But there's nothing special about that. Seventeen NBA teams boosted their top prices in 1987.

Baseball appears to be the best bet for bargain-hunting sports fans. Fans could still see the Braves, Expos, Phillies, and Yankees for a buck in 1988 if they weren't too picky about where they sat. The top price anywhere was $15 at Toronto where the cheapest seat was $4. Second was Boston for $14 and then Montreal for $12. The most expensive minimum seat was the $6 charged by the Mets.

Of course none of these figures include ego seats, nor do they take into account season ticket packages. Season tickets are cheaper, and they were selling better than ever in 1988.

If you're really looking for a deal, go to Arizona for a Cactus League game. Nobody charged more than $6 for one of those.

Better yet, go last year. That's right, ticket prices were lower for 14 of the 26 major-league teams in 1987 than they were in 1988, and they kept right on climbing in 1989.

It could be worse. You could develop an itch to attend the Super Bowl. Bring lots of scratch. When that regal event was first contested in 1967, it was possible to purchase a ticket for $8. Top price was $12. Three years later, the NFL took a one-size-fits-all approach to Super Bowl tickets and sold the lot for $15.

That's how it stayed for four years. Then in 1975, the price jumped to $20 and since then it's gone up 500% to the current level of $100. Not that it matters what the face of the ticket says. You can't get your hands on one anyway.

SPORT$BIZ STATS

Super Bowl Ticket Prices

Super Bowl (playing season)	Site	Teams (score)	Price ($)
I (1966)	Los Angeles	Green Bay/Kansas City (35/10)	12
II (1967)	Miami	Green Bay/Oakland (33/14)	12
III (1968)	Miami	New York Jets/Baltimore (16/7)	12
IV (1969)	New Orleans	Kansas City/Minnesota (23/7)	15
V (1970)	Miami	Baltimore/Dallas (16/13)	15
VI (1971)	New Orleans	Dallas/Miami (24/3)	15
VII (1972)	Los Angeles	Miami/Washington (14/7)	15
VIII (1973)	Houston	Miami/Minnesota (24/7)	15
IX (1974)	New Orleans	Pittsburgh/Minnesota (16/6)	20
X (1975)	Miami	Pittsburgh/Dallas (21/17)	20
XI (1976)	Pasadena	Oakland/Minnesota (32/14)	20
XII (1977)	New Orleans	Dallas/Denver (27/10)	30
XIII (1978)	Miami	Pittsburgh/Dallas (35/31)	30
XIV (1979)	Pasadena	Pittsburgh/Los Angeles Rams (31/19)	30
XV (1980)	New Orleans	Oakland/Philadelphia (27/10)	40
XVI (1981)	Pontiac	San Francisco/Cincinnati (26/21)	40
XVII (1982)	Pasadena	Washington/Miami (27/17)	40
XVIII (1983)	Tampa	Los Angeles Raiders/Washington (38/9)	60
XIX (1984)	Stanford	San Francisco/Miami (38/16)	60
XX (1985)	New Orleans	Chicago/New England (46/10)	75
XXI (1986)	Pasadena	New York Giants/Denver (39/20)	75
XXII (1987)	San Diego	Washington/Denver (42/10)	100

Note. Information compiled from *Sports inc. The Sports Business Weekly*, January 25, 1988, and *Saints 1988 Official Media Guide*, p. 143.

Settle for a regular-season game. You might get into one of those for as little as $6 if you live near Pontiac, Michigan, where the Lions play, or for $8 in Atlanta, where the Falcons performed for thousands of empty seats in 1987.

Those minimums are pretty hard to come by. In fact, in some cities any kind of ticket at all is pretty hard to come by.

The Green Bay Packers are an extreme example of that. They have been sold out through season tickets for decades. There are long waiting lists in both Green Bay and Milwaukee, where some Packers' home games are played, and ownership of Packers' season tickets has been a hotly contested item in more than one divorce settlement.

That's in a city that hasn't been within a first down of the Super Bowl for 20 years. It doesn't seem to matter. The law of supply and demand is regularly violated in the NFL.

The Dallas Cowboys, who have been on a four-year attendance losing streak, nevertheless charge $32 for their top tickets, which is just a dollar short of the league-leading price commanded by the New England Patriots. And the Cowboys boosted prices across the board again in 1988.

"I don't have any regrets at all about it," said Cowboys owner Bum Bright when he was questioned about the raise in December of 1987. "Even with the decline in attendance, our ticket revenue is ahead of last year. We get about $10 million in ticket revenue, and you've got to pay one-tenth of that to Herschel Walker."

That last statement is significant, and we'll look at it more closely in just a little while. For now, it's enough to say that Bright is not at all out of step with his NFL colleagues.

Despite the '87 strike and all the grumbling that caused, 17 of the NFL's 28 teams hiked ticket prices in 1988. Six clubs—New England, Dallas, the Jets, San Diego, Seattle, and Washington—have a top price of $30 or more, and 10 others are over $25 for their choicest regular seats.

"This is normal," said Pittsburgh spokesman Dan Edwards after the Steelers bumped the cost of most of their tickets by $3. "If you look back, about every two years we've raised prices. This is really a move to stay competitive."

Well, it does cost money to put on a football game. It runs more in some places than others, but the example of the Packers is probably pretty typical. Bill Hanrahan, the manager at Milwaukee's County Stadium, figured a Packer game to be about a $40,000 proposition. It goes like this:

Scoreboard costs $1,100; ground crew $6,300; sound system $750; ushers $14,500; security $7,000; cleaning $7,000; parking attendants $1,200. The Packers pay a flat rent of $39,000, making one of their games a $1,000 blob of red ink on the county books, except . . .

The county makes $70,000 from concessions and $33,000 from parking. The Packers? They pay for hotels and accommodations and get to keep all the ticket money.

None of this takes into account the most costly element of all in putting on an NFL game—paying the players. That's done directly by the teams.

But indirectly, it's done mostly by television. And that brings us to the third and in many ways most important sports revenue source of all.

Radio and TV Revenues

It all started so modestly. On May 17, 1939, the Columbia baseball team faced Princeton in a crucial battle for fourth place in the Ivy League. It was the first sports event ever televised in America, and the announcer approached it praying that every batter would strike out. That was the only play he was sure his camera could record.

When the telecast was over a *New York Times* reporter remarked, "Seeing baseball by television is too confining. To see the fresh green of the field as the Mighty Casey advances to the bat and the dust fly as he defiantly digs in is a thrill to the eye that cannot be electrified and flashed through space."

Confining or not, the electronic media has spread throughout the major sporting world and dominated it. Forget the fresh green of the field. It's another kind of green that makes the difference.

One of the concepts football union leaders could never seem to get across to football fans was that salaries had absolutely nothing to do with the price of tickets. Television revenues more than covered the payroll of every team, and anything that came through the gate was gravy.

There were a lot of concepts that union leaders couldn't get across, but this was a particularly hard sell. They never really made it. And now it's not true anymore.

For the first time since the solemn wedding of Pete Rozelle and the American television networks, TV doesn't cover salary costs in the NFL. So when Bum Bright interprets Herschel Walker's salary as a percentage of the Cowboys' gate, there is some relationship between the two.

According to Dick Berthelsen, the general counsel for the NFLPA when the average NFL salary was $126,000 in 1983 and teams were making around $16 million apiece from their network TV contract, they were paying $10.7 million in player costs. In other words, teams could have added more than $5 million to their payrolls and still covered them before dipping into gate receipts.

At the time, player costs were only 46% of a team's gross revenues and 57% of their total costs. However, the short-lived but pesky USFL came along, and by 1986 it had helped drive the average salary up to $205,000.

Player costs were 63% of a team's total costs at that point. And the average payroll of $17.25 million barely made it under the $17.7 million each team was pulling in from the networks. When the USFL folded, salaries dipped, but they never did get under 60% of a team's total costs.

They're not likely to do so in the foreseeable future either. Berthelsen's projections show the average salary growing to $226,000 in 1988, and if player costs grow at 2.5% a year they'll be $18.1 million.

Suddenly, NFL teams have to find some other way than TV to keep up with salaries. The tube used to handle their payrolls with plenty left over for profit. That's no longer true.

Why not? Two reasons. Players are making more money, and networks are paying the NFL less. That requires a bigger adjustment on the part of NFL owners than owners in other sports, because the football people depended far more heavily on broadcast revenue. They still do.

The long-standing NFL equation was that for every dollar a team made from fans coming to the stadium, it made two from the networks. Baseball and basketball, on the other hand, have always derived more of their revenue from flesh-and-blood people than from electronic gadgets. Baseball figures network contracts account for a little more than half of its total revenues.

In the NFL, the only television is national television. Proceeds from network and cable contracts are divided into 28 equal shares. Baseball and basketball also have national TV deals that they share equally, but they're not nearly as lush as football's. And each team in those sports keeps its own local broadcast revenue.

Football has found other ways to make money. But it will have to get even more creative, according to Berthelsen's figures. While gross revenues increased 100% from 1981 through 1986, average salaries soared 127%.

Could it be that the long and torrid romance between pro football and network television has finally cooled? Well, not really.

It's just been severely tested. Ratings had been slipping for some time, and when the NFL played through the 1987 strike with its so-called replacement teams, the networks gagged before swallowing.

They swallowed anyway, because they had nothing better to put before the cameras. They also got some of their money back from the league.

Meanwhile, a new suitor had appeared on the scene. Cable television came courting the NFL in 1987, which was all right with the networks as long as it didn't get too pushy.

The result was a combination deal that forced the owners to get along on less, while at the same time proving that Commissioner Rozelle hadn't lost his electronic touch. Here's how it went:

A new contract was signed with the three networks running through 1989 and calling for them to pay the NFL $476 million a year or $16 million per club. Teams were making more than $17 million a year under the old deal, and they weren't thrilled with the cut.

So ESPN helped take the sting out of it by chipping in with another $153 million for eight regular season games, four play-off games, and the Pro Bowl each year. Why? Because pro football ratings are still pretty good and because ESPN wanted to add a big league product to its image. Nothing does that like the NFL.

CBS picked up the biggest share of the NFL tab with $494 million in rights fees, followed by NBC at $404 million and ABC at $377 million.

Football is still the unchallenged leader of the sports ratings world with 60.5 million viewers in 1987. But that represented a drop of 4.3% from 1986. And when you're dealing in tens of millions of viewers, a 4.3% drop represents a lot of potential customers for sports advertisers.

Sports in general lost ground in the ratings race, sinking from 608.4 million viewers in 1986 to 574.1 million in 1987, according to a survey by Simmons Market Research Bureau. The A.C. Nielsen Company did a similar study and came up with even gloomier results, a 7.6% sag.

Americans apparently don't have an inexhaustible TV appetite for sports, and now the networks know it. There was approximately 4% less network sports programming in 1987 than there was in 1986.

Baseball was sinking even faster than football, according to the Simmons study. It showed 57.7 million viewers for the national pastime in 1987, an 8.3% dropoff from 1986. College basketball, college football, boxing, everything was going down. And tennis tumbled worse than any of the others, showing a 17.1% loss.

The one exception to the trend was pro basketball, which continued an uptick that had begun in 1979. The Simmons study gave hoops 35.2 million viewers or a 1.4% gain. The NBA had even more dramatic figures in mind.

The league quotes Nielsen numbers that show its ratings rising 46% from '79 through '86, while pro football dropped 1% in that time and baseball plummeted 15%.

Armed with that data, the NBA struck a highly profitable deal with both the network and the cable people. The latest pro basketball contract is with CBS and TBS, Ted Turner's cable outfit. CBS is paying the league $175 million a year for the play-offs and 15 regular-season games.

Getting the network to take that many regular-season games represented a minor triumph all by itself. CBS loves play-off basketball, but it's not big on the day-to-day stuff. It carried only 11 regular-season games in the previous contract. And it was almost a sure bet that one of the teams on the tube would be the Celtics or the Lakers.

If viewers wanted to see somebody else on national TV, they almost had to have cable. TBS's new two-year deal with the NBA signed in November of 1987 gave it the rights to 50 regular-season games and 25 play-off games as well as the All-Star Game and the draft. Ted Turner paid $23 million in the first year and $27 million in the second for that package, double the amount that the previous contract cost.

And still, Turner apparently would have been happy to put out even more. He was believed to be interested in grabbing the whole NBA package for his Turner Network Television channel.

Maybe later. In the meantime the TBS package, combined with the CBS contract, left the 23 NBA teams dividing around $200 million a year or $8.7 million apiece.

Major-league baseball signed a four-year contract with CBS in January of 1989 that was worth a total of $1.1 billion. It takes in 12 regular-season games, plus the play-offs and World Series.

On top of that came a separate cable deal with ESPN that covered roughly 175 regular-season games to be carried over four years. The schedule called for telecasts on Sunday, Tuesday, Wednesday, and Friday nights, with double-headers on Tuesdays and Fridays.

The negotiations were pretty intense. ABC sports chief Dennis Swanson has indicated publicly that he wasn't overjoyed by his network's share of the national baseball deal in a time of declining ratings. ABC's baseball ratings slipped 7% in 1987, and NBC's were down 9%.

Ueberroth was saying the networks' next contract offer could be as low as $5 million a year or as high as $15 million. He figured the game might have to consider expansion, realignment, and/or interleague play to make it more attractive to television. It's about that tail and the wagging dog again.

The outgoing commissioner was also kicking around the idea of a 24-hour cable baseball network. Viewers could watch live games from noon Eastern time until the last West Coast match blinked out somewhere around 2 o'clock in the morning.

When there wasn't a game going on, the network could show tapes of yesterday's games or minor-league games or highlight films or tobacco chewing contests or Lord knows what else.

The idea was still on the drawing board in the spring of 1988, and the timing depended on whether NBC or ABC decided to exercise their options to extend the network contracts through 1991. They didn't. CBS got the whole package starting in 1990.

Ueberroth said baseball could either operate the all-day network itself or sell it to an existing cable network. Either way, it would face the same problems that all televised sporting ventures do. Somebody would have to pay for it.

Even in an age when networks are taking a closer look at the returns on their sporting investments, they are paying mountainous amounts to the leagues. And when they pass along that much cash to the leagues, somebody has to be passing even more along to the networks.

That somebody of course is the advertiser, who is putting out more on sports programming every year. *Sports Marketing News* estimated in its Jan. 18, 1988, issue that advertisers would spend $2.5 billion on sports shows in 1988, breaking the record of $2.087 billion in 1987, which of course broke the 1986 record, and so on.

The Olympics account for some of that jump, and the emergence of cable accounts for some more. Sports has been a boon to cable TV, or vice versa. It's hard to tell which. But stations like TBS and ESPN thrive on it. The cable outfits also help explain the slippage in network sports ratings. More competition.

TBS reported that $50 million of its $185 million in advertising revenue in 1987 came from sports. ESPN, which of course doesn't do anything but sports, had record ad revenues of $120 million.

The big money is still being paid to the networks because that's where the biggest events are. Network sports spending zoomed from $1.44 billion in 1986 to $1.59 billion in 1987.

The $650,000 that advertisers paid for a 30-second spot on the 1988 Super Bowl telecasts tops the list of sports outlays by a wide margin, but it has plenty of six-figure company.

Half a minute of the viewers' time at the NCAA basketball championships runs $350,000, which is only $50,000 more than ABC charged for an Olympic spot. The World Series ad carried a $267,000 price tag, while the Orange Bowl game for the national collegiate football championship was commanding between $200,000 to $225,000 for 30 seconds.

Who's buying the time? It's usually the same people every year. Car people, beer people, computer companies, department stores, and brokers are always up there. And the Army. The Armed Forces ranks an impressive fourth in sports advertising.

The Television Bureau of Advertisers in New York puts out an annual list of who spends the most advertising on TV sports. The top 10 in 1987 were:

General Motors, Anheuser-Busch, Phillip Morris, U.S. Armed Forces, Chrysler Corporation, AT&T, Tandy, IBM, Sears Roebuck, and Ford. GM weighed in at an impressive $111 million in 1987, while tenth-place Ford was at $26 million.

Those are the companies who are paying the leagues, who are paying the teams, who are paying the players. Oh, there's one other group that gets paid, and very substantially at that. The golden throats who describe the action.

Remember the time television tried to do an NFL game without a play-by-play man or even a color commentator? All they did was train the camera on the field and pick up the sound from the public address system.

It must not have been a very good idea, because it never caught on. And anything that saves that much money for the networks and doesn't catch on can't be a very good idea.

How much would CBS save if it faced life without Brent Musberger? Try $1.9 million. That's the current estimate of his salary, according to sports media experts.

Trailing after Musberger in estimated earnings were Al Michaels, $1.5 million; Pat Summerall, $1.2 million; Vin Scully, $1 million; Dan Dierdorf, $900,000; John Madden, $800,000; Bob Costas, $600,000-$800,000; Dick Stockton, $600,000; Al McGuire, $400,000-$500,000; Keith Jackson, $400,000; and Gary Bender, $300,000.

Jimmy the Greek, incidentally, booted away an estimated $450,000 a year when he stuck his foot in his mouth with his controversial remarks on the subject of race.

You do have to remember that all of these fellows are national celebrities. The rights fees and advertising rates we have been talking about are national, too. Local sports television is a different world and a very important one to every major sport except pro football.

Baseball and basketball have a myriad of local arrangements, and the important thing to keep in mind about them is that not a penny of the revenues is shared among the teams in the league. The result is a vast financial disparity between the haves and have-nots in baseball and basketball. Sometimes, but not always, that translates into a disparity in their performance on the field.

A team in a relatively small market like Kansas City has all the same costs as one in a broadcast paradise like New York. The players don't come at discount rates just because there aren't as many television sets in town.

The New York Yankees made an estimated $16.5 million in local television, radio, and cable rights fees in 1988, compared to $3 million for the Cleveland Indians. Same sport, same division—different universe as far as broadcast revenues are concerned.

The Yanks in fact were raking in more than twice as much from this source as anyone in the AL East. Toronto was a distant second with $7.7 million. So is George Steinbrenner going to share his millions with less fortunate teams whom he just happens to be battling for a pennant? Not in this century anyway.

The only major-league teams with television exposure that rivals the Yankees' and Mets' in New York are the Chicago Cubs and Atlanta Braves. They're on all the time and all over the place because of superstations WGN in Chicago and TBS in Atlanta.

Almost 300 Braves and Cubs games are shown every year across the country, making them kind of the orphan home team for cities that don't have their own franchises. There is some argument about whether they're contributing to an overexposure problem for baseball. About 1,500 games are shown every season on network, superstation, and regional cable TV, and that doesn't even count the local over-the-air stations.

Ueberroth's 24-hour network might push out the superstations eventually, but while we're waiting for that, the Cubs and Braves don't seem too worried about being overexposed.

Nobody would have to worry about that if the nation wasn't getting wired at such a frantic clip. In 1980, 19.8 million U.S. households had cable TV. In 1989, ESPN alone reached 50.1 million homes.

Baseball and basketball owners see cable as a most promising source of new revenue. That's the good part. The bad part is that cable will just widen the gap between the haves and their less fortunate rivals. If Kansas City can pick up a few extra million in cable money, how much more can New York make from it?

Every major-league baseball team has some kind of over-the-air television coverage, with the number of games ranging from 30 in Seattle to 85 in

SPORT$BIZ STATS

Major League Baseball TV Markets

Market*	Rank	Teams	Local television	
			Cable	Over-the-air
New York	1	Mets	Sports Channel	WWOR-TV
		Yankees	Sports Channel	WPIX
Los Angeles	2	Dodgers	Dodgervision	KTTV
		Angels		KTLA
Chicago	3	Cubs	WGN	WGN
		White Sox	SportsVision	WFLD
Philadelphia	4	Phillies	PRISM	WTAF
San Francisco/Oakland	5	Giants	Giantsvision	KTVU
		Oakland		KPIX
Boston	6	Red Sox	NESN	WSBK
Detroit	7	Tigers	PASS	WDIV
Washington, DC	8	Orioles	Home Team Sports	WMAR
Dallas/Ft. Worth	9	Rangers	Home Sports Entertainment	KTVT
Cleveland	10	Indians		WUAB
Houston	11	Astros	Home Sports Entertainment	KTXH
Pittsburgh	12	Pirates	TCI	KDKA
Atlanta	13	Braves	WTBS	WTBS
Seattle	14	Mariners		KTZZ
Minneapolis	17	Twins	Twinsvision	KMSP
St. Louis	18	Cardinals	St. Louis Cardinal Network	KSDK
Baltimore	21	See Orioles (#8)		WMAR
Cincinnati	28	Reds	Home Team Sports	WLW-TV
Kansas City	29	Royals		12-station network
Milwaukee	30	Brewers		WVTV

* Two MLB teams are based in Canada, so U.S. television market ranks are not applicable.

Note. From *QV Publishing, Inc.*, 1987. Adapted by permission.

Philadelphia. But six American League clubs and one National League team had no cable agreement as of 1988. And the ones that didn't were usually the ones in the smaller markets.

It's not that they didn't try. Pittsburgh, Seattle, Minneapolis, and Milwaukee all launched regional sports channels on cable TV, and all of their attempts failed.

Some might not have had enough programming to fill up a whole sports channel. Some, like Milwaukee, didn't have enough sets wired in the area at the time they tried. All of them have had to rely instead on their over-the-air deals with local television stations.

Basketball is in the same unbalanced boat as baseball. It shares the national revenues, but not the local. It also shares the international ones, by the way.

The NBA has taken its product overseas, showing a game of the week to 42 different countries. It's not a big money-maker, with fees ranging from $1,000 to $15,000 and the total coming to what Commissioner David Stern calls "the low seven figures," but it is opening a lot of new markets that the NBA thinks it can expand greatly in the future.

Back at home, seven NBA teams don't have any pay TV deals at all. Once again they're the small markets of Cleveland, Denver, Indiana, Milwaukee, Sacramento, Seattle, and Los Angeles. Los Angeles?

Well, the Clippers don't have anything. The Lakers, of course, show 23 games on a regional network. Talk about haves and have-nots.

Everybody in the league has an over-the-air deal of some kind, and the teams that don't have a cable arrangement are likely to try to get one soon. Nobody knows better than the NBA how it pays to maximize your TV revenue. That had a lot to do with reviving the league in the early '80s.

It might even have had something to do with who got into the league when expansion franchises were awarded in 1987. The winners and their

SPORT$BIZ STATS

NBA Television Contracts (1982-1990)

Network	Contract years	Number of games	Total value ($ millions)
CBS	1982-83/1985-86	12	88
CBS	1986-87/1989-90	15	175
USA, ESPN, TBS	1983-84	150[a]	10
TBS	1984-85/1985-86	75	20
TBS	1986-87/1987-88	75	25

[a]ESPN and USA each carried 50 games; TBS aired 50 Atlanta Hawks games.

Note. From QV Publishing, Inc., 1987. Adapted by permission.

national rank in television market were Miami, No. 16; Minneapolis, No. 17; Orlando, No. 27; and Charlotte, No. 32.

Strange as it sounds, there may be such a thing as too much television. National overexposure is one possible problem. Another is local exposure at the expense of ticket revenues.

Owners in all three sports do a delicate little balancing act, trying to get all the broadcast revenues they can without losing anything from their live gate.

If a fan can see the game in his living room where the seats are soft and the weather is warm, why should he put up with the crowds, traffic, and expense involved in going to the game? Owners ask themselves that question, too, and when the answer comes up wrong, they switch off the signal.

Basketball teams generally refrain from televising local home games, although they make occasional exceptions for things like play-off games when they're sold out. There are no provisions in the NBA to black out national network games.

Cable telecasts on the other hand can't be shown within a 75-mile radius of the arena where the game is being played.

Baseball usually stays away from local telecasts of home games, too. Fans with cable TV can always pick up the Braves and Cubs if their service includes the superstations, and it used to be that fans with satellite dishes could do even better than that.

But in January of 1988, the major leagues contracted with a company in San Diego to scramble the team's TV signals. Now if you want to watch a game with the help of a dish, you have to buy a decoder. And to get one of those you have to apply to the commissioner's office.

Teams have to be careful, though. If the fans think they're getting arrogant in their blackout policies, they know how to make the appropriate noises. That's what happened to the NFL.

The NFL used to routinely black out a 75-mile area around the city where any game was being played. But then in 1972, the Redskins made the play-offs and played a couple of postseason home games with Green Bay and Dallas. Both were blacked out as usual, despite the fact that they were sold out.

The Redskins happen to play in Washington, D.C., where Congress lives, and many Congressmen happen to enjoy watching football games on TV. The result was something called Public Law 93-107, enacted as an amendment to the Communications Act of 1934. It said that blackouts had to be lifted on all games that were sold out 72 hours before kickoff.

The law officially expired after the 1975 season, and the NFL managed to persuade Congress not to make it permanent by promising to abide by the spirit of the statute. That's led to some interesting business arrangements, with TV stations buying up remaining tickets so they can carry local games.

Getting the fans to abide by the spirit of the statute can be a little tougher. It was in Houston when the Oilers played the Cleveland Browns in November of 1987. The game eventually sold out, but not 72 hours before kickoff. So it was blacked out in the Houston area.

A few Houston sports bars showed it to their patrons anyway, buying the signal from the NBC station in Atlanta and risking the possibility of being sued by the NFL. The bars didn't mind the league's blackout rule for games that weren't sold out, but they did object to the 72-hour policy.

A statement signed by about 1,000 fans said in part: "Once the tickets are all gone, why should the NFL be so greedy as to deny the fans a chance to see the game? We help build stadiums with our tax dollars, and we support advertisers who in turn pay the networks and the teams millions of dollars."

That pretty well sums up the economic arrangement of every major sport in the land. Whether teams' revenues come from luxury boxes, concessions, ticket sales, or radio and TV, one thing hasn't changed. It's the fan who's paying the bills.

Appendix

A

Sample
Contract Clauses

Examples of Typical Contract Clauses
for Professional Athletes

Prohibited Activities Clause (NBA)

The Player and the Club acknowledge and agree that the Player's participation in other sports may impair or destroy his ability and skill as a basketball player. The Player and the Club recognize and agree that the Player's participation in basketball out of season may result in injury to him. Accordingly, the Player agrees that he will not engage in sports endangering his health or safety (including, but not limited to, professional boxing or wrestling, motorcycling, moped-riding, auto racing, sky-diving and hang-gliding); and that, except with the written consent of the Club, he will not engage in any game or exhibition of basketball, football, baseball, hockey, lacrosse, or other athletic sport, under penalty of such fine and suspension as may be imposed by the Club and/or the Commissioner of the Association. Nothing contained herein shall be intended to require the Player to obtain the written consent of the Club in order to enable the Player to participate in, as an amateur, the sport of golf, tennis, handball, swimming, hiking, softball or volleyball.

Integrity of Game Clause (NFL)

The Player recognizes the detriment to the League and professional football that would result from impairment of public confidence in the honest and orderly conduct of NFL games or the integrity and good character of NFL players. The Player therefore acknowledges his awareness that if he accepts a bribe or agrees to throw or fix an NFL game; fails to promptly report a bribe offer or an attempt to throw or fix an NFL game; bets on an NFL game; knowingly associates with gamblers or gambling activity; uses or provides other players with stimulants or other drugs for the purposes of attempting to enhance on-field performance; or is guilty of any other form of conduct reasonably judged by the League Commissioner to be detrimental to the League or professional football, the Commissioner will have the right, but only after giving the Player the opportunity for a hearing at which he may be represented by counsel of his choice, to fine the Player in a reasonable amount; to suspend the Player for a period certain or indefinite; and/or to terminate this contract.

Promotions Clause (NBA)

The Player agrees to allow the Club or the Association to take pictures of the Player, alone or together with others, for still photographs, motion pictures or television, at such time as the Club or the Association may designate, and that no matter by whom taken may be used in any manner desired by either of them for publicity or promotional purposes. The rights in any such pictures taken by the Club or by the Association shall belong to the Club or to the Association, as their interests may appear. The Player agrees that during each playing season he will not make public appearances, participate in radio or television programs or permit his picture to be taken or write or sponsor newspaper or magazine articles or sponsor commercial products without the written consent of the Club, which shall not be withheld except in the reasonable interests of the Club or professional basketball. Upon request, the Player shall consent to and make himself available for interviews by representatives of the media conducted at reasonable times. In addition to the foregoing, the Player agrees to participate, upon request, in all other reasonable promotional activities of the Club and the Association.

Trade or Assignment Clause

(NFL) Unless this contract specifically provides otherwise, the Club may assign this contract and Player's services under this contract to any successor to Club's franchise or to any other club in the League. Player will report to the assignee club promptly upon being informed of the assignment of his contract and will faithfully perform his services under this contract. The assignee club will pay Player's necessary traveling expenses in reporting to it and will faithfully perform this contract with Player.

(NBA) The Club shall have the right to sell, exchange, assign or transfer this contract to any other professional basketball club, and the Player agrees to accept such sale, exchange, assignment or transfer and to faithfully perform and carry out this contract with the same force and effect as if it had been entered into by the Player with the assignee club instead of with this Club. The Player further agrees that, should the Club contemplate the sale, exchange, assignment or transfer of this contract to another professional basketball club or clubs, the Club's physician may furnish to the physicians and officials of such other club or clubs all relevant medical information relating to the Player.

Trade Payment.   Notwithstanding provisions of paragraph 10 of the Uniform Player contract, the Club shall not have the right to sell, exchange, assign or transfer this Agreement without the Player's consent except upon the payment to Player of the sum of One Hundred Thousand Dollars ($100,000.00) by the assignee or transferee club. The foregoing shall not, however, preclude the sale, exchange, assignment or transfer of this Agreement without the Player's consent and without any payment to the Player in the event such sale, exchange, assignment or transfer is in connection with the transfer of all or substantially all of the assets of the Club.

Partial or Conditional Guarantee Clause, 1989-90 Contract Year

In the event the Player is, in the opinion of the Neutral Physician, in good physical condition so as to render the Player fit to play skilled basketball for the 1989-90 National Basketball Association playing season, which determination shall be made by the Neutral Physician prior to the expiration of twenty-one (21) days of the end of the 1988-89 National Basketball Association playing season, including playoffs, then, in that event, the termination of this Agreement by the Club:

(1) on account of the Player's failure to exhibit sufficient skill or competitive ability; or

(2) on account of the Player's failure to render services hereunder, if such failure has been caused by the Player's death (provided that, at the time of such failure, the Company is not in material breach of this Agreement); or

(3) on account of the Player's failure to provide services hereunder, if such failure has been caused by the Player's becoming disabled and/or unfit to play skilled basketball as a direct result of any injury sustained while participating in any basketball practice or game played for the Club; or

(4) on account of Player's failure to provide services hereunder, if such failure has been caused by the Player's becoming disabled and/or unfit to play skilled basketball as a direct result of illness or injury (provided that, at the time of such failure, the Player is not in material breach of this Agreement, and provided that such illness or injury does not result from the Player's participation in activities prohibited by paragraph 17 of the Uniform Player

Contract), shall in no way affect the Player's right to receive the compensation payable pursuant to paragraph 2(B)(1) of this Addendum for the 1989-90 Contract Year, in the amounts and at the times called for by said paragraph, unless said termination occurs within twenty-one (21) days of the end of the 1988-89 National Basketball Association season, including playoffs, in which event Club shall pay Player Two Hundred Thousand Dollars ($200,000.00) of the compensation payable pursuant to paragraph 2(B)(1) as the total compensation protected for the 1989-90 Contract Year.

The foregoing paragraphs 7(A) and 7(B) shall not require the Club to continue the Player as a member of the Club's Team, Active List or Roster; nor shall it afford the Player any right to continue or to be deemed as having continued as such member for any purpose.

Injury or Disability Clause (NBA)

Injury and Disability

(a) The Club agrees that in the event the Player shall die or suffer or sustain from any cause whatsoever any illness, injury or disability, whether permanent or temporary, at any time during the first five (5) Contract Years of this contract, the Club shall continue to make the payments to the Player's estate, to the Player's designated beneficiary or to the Player, as the case may be, under the terms of this contract, except that this paragraph shall not apply with respect to such illnesses, injury or disability suffered or sustained as a result of the activities specified in Paragraph 17 of the Uniform Player Contract.

(b) If the Player is injured as a direct result of participating in any basketball practice or game played for the Club, the Club shall pay the Player's hospitalization until he is discharged from the hospital and also his medical expenses and doctor's bills, provided said hospital and doctor are selected or approved by the Club.

(c) The obligations of the Club to make payments to the Player hereunder shall be reduced by any workmen's compensation benefits as well as by any amounts actually paid to the Player pursuant to policies of disability insurance or life insurance obtained by the Club, as the case may be, and the Club shall pay the Player only the event of such obligations as it may have which are in excess of the amounts of any such workmen's compensation or insurance benefits actually paid to the Player pursuant to policies obtained and paid for by the Club.

(d) The Player shall have the right to purchase, at his option, a sufficient amount of disability insurance to cover the total amount of compensation due to the Player in the Fifth Contract Year, under the payment schedule for such compensation set forth in the Addendum ($260,000.00), in the event the Player suffers accidental death, dismemberment, loss of sight, or other physical disability during said Fifth Contract Year only, which disability directly causes the Player to be unable to perform his basketball services for the Club under this Contract during said Fifth Contract Year. The Player further agrees that the Club shall be designated as the beneficiary of said disability insurance policy.

Signing Bonus Clause

In consideration for the Player's executing this contract, the Club agrees to pay the Player a bonus of One Hundred Fifty Thousand Dollars ($150,000.00), which bonus shall be payable in accordance with the following schedule:

a. Twenty-five Thousand Dollars ($25,000.00) upon the execution of this contract

b. Ten Thousand Dollars ($10,000.00) on April 1, 1987

c. Ten Thousand Dollars ($10,000.00) on April 1, 1988

d. Ten Thousand Dollars ($10,000.00) on April 1, 1989

e. Ten Thousand Dollars ($10,000.00) on April 1, 1990

f. Ten Thousand Dollars ($10,000.00) on April 1, 1991

g. Twenty-Five Thousand Dollars ($25,000.00) on April 1, 1992

h. Twenty-Five Thousand Dollars ($25,000.00) on April 1, 1993

i. Twenty-Five Thousand Dollars ($25,000.00) on April 1, 1994

Club agrees that if the Player is not on the Club's active roster on the first day of the 1986 NBA playing season, payment of each of the bonuses set forth in subparagraphs b through i above (''deferred bonuses'') shall be accelerated one (1) year, to commence April 1, 1986. The Club further agrees that there shall be no withholding from any of the above bonus payments for federal, state or local taxes or for any other purposes whatsoever.

Interest-Free Loan Clause

Loan. Upon the execution of this Contract, the Club agrees to loan to the Player the principal sum of Three Hundred Thousand Dollars ($300,000.00) at no interest to be repaid in seventy-two (72) equal installments of Four Thousand One Hundred Sixty-Six Dollars and Sixty-Seven Cents ($4,166.67), payable on the 1st and 15th day of each month commencing November 1, 1989. Such loan shall be evidenced by a Promissory Note in the form attached hereto as Exhibit A. The Player agrees that the Club shall have all rights of set-off provided by applicable law, and in addition thereto the Company agrees that if at any time any payment or other amount owing by the Player under the Note is then due to the Club, the Club may apply to the payment or other amount any and all payments due from the Club to the Player under this contract.

Individual Incentive Compensation Clause

In addition to the annual salaries to be paid to the Player as set forth above, during each year of this contract the Club agrees to pay the Player as additional compensation ("Bonus") the amounts hereinafter set forth upon the following terms and conditions:

(a) If the Club wins the Conference Title for any of the seasons covered by this contract, the Player shall receive, in addition to his share of the Playoff Pool, an additional sum from the Club equal to such share each Contract Year the Club wins said Title.

(b) If the Club wins the National Basketball Association League Championship Title during any of the playing seasons covered by this contract, the Player shall receive, in addition to his share from the Player Playoff Pool, an additional sum from the Club equal to such share each Contract Year the Club wins said Title.

(c) If the Player is selected the Most Valuable Player (MVP) in the National Basketball Association as voted by the Association's players in the Association's administered election, the Player shall receive, in each Contract Year so selected, a sum of Fifty Thousand Dollars ($50,000.00).

(d) If the Player is selected to the Association's postseason All-League First Team, as selected by the broadcasters' and writers' poll conducted by the Association, the Player shall receive, in each Contract Year so selected, a sum of Twenty Thousand Dollars ($20,000.00).

(e) If the Player leads the league among Forwards in any of the following:

1. Field Goal Percentage
2. Free Throw Percentage
3. Assist Average
4. Offensive or Defensive Rebounds
5. Steals

then the Player shall receive additional sums of each of the following categories attained in each Contract Year in which the Player leads the league as indicated above.

First Place: $10,000.00
Second Place: 7,500.00
Third Place: 5,000.00

Fourth Place: 2,500.00

Fifth Place: 1,500.00

Any Bonus earned pursuant to this Contract shall be payable, less applicable withholding tax (if any), other normal payroll deductions and any amounts required by law to be withheld, within thirty (30) days after the Player's attainment of such Bonus.

Current and Deferred Compensation Clause

Annual Compensation.   The Club agrees to compensate the Player for the Player's services described in the Agreement in accordance with the following schedule:

Contract Year	Compensation
1985-86	$_____
1986-87	$_____
1987-88	$_____
1988-89	$_____
1989-90	$_____
1990-91	$_____
1991-92	$_____

Payment of Compensation.   The Compensation to be paid during the Contract Year is referred to as "Current Compensation" as set forth below and for each Contract Year the Current Compensation shall be paid in twenty-four (24) equal semimonthly installments, the first installment payable on October 1 of each Contract Year and continuing with such payments on the 1st and 15th day of each month until the current compensation for the Contract Year is paid in full.

The Player acknowledges that with respect to payments for the 1985-86 Contract Year, the October, November, and December, 1985, and the January and February 1, 1986, payments have previously been paid in full to Player pursuant to the terms of a Prior Agreement between Player and Club dated October 2, 1982.

Compensation for the 1986-87 Contract Year is entirely Current Compensation and as such will be paid as indicated above commencing October 1, 1986, and terminating September 30, 1987.

The 1987-88, 1988-89, 1989-90, 1990-91 and 1991-92 Contract Years are payable as Current Compensation and as Deferred Compensation as follows:

Current Year	Current Compensation	Current Compensation
1985-86	$_____	$_____
1986-87	$_____	$_____
1987-88	$_____	$_____
1988-89	$_____	$_____
1989-90	$_____	$_____
1990-91	$_____	$_____
1991-92	$_____	$_____

The Current Compensation for each Contract Year will be paid to Player as indicated above.

The Deferred Compensation shall be paid to Player as follows: On June 1, 1993, a payment of $_____; on June 1, 1994, $_____; on June 1, 1995, $_____; and on the first day of each month thereafter through May 1, 2009, a payment of $_____.

Termination

(a) The Club may terminate this contract upon written notice to the Player (but only after complying with the waiver procedure provided for in subparagraph [f] of this paragraph [20]) if the Player shall do any of the following:

(1) at any time fail, refuse or neglect to conform his personal conduct to standards of good citizenship, good moral character and good sportsmanship, to keep himself in first class physical condition or to obey the Club's training rules; or

(2) at any time fail, in the sole opinion of the Club's management, to exhibit sufficient skill or competitive ability to qualify to continue as a member of the Club's team (provided, however, that if this contract is terminated by the Club, in accordance with the provisions of this subparagraph, during the period from the 56th day after the first game of any schedule season of the Association through the end of such schedule season, the Player shall be entitled to receive his full salary for said season); or

(3) at any time fail, refuse or neglect to render his services hereunder or in any other manner materially breach this contract.

(b) If this contract is terminated by the Club by reason of the Player's failure to render his services hereunder due to disability caused by an injury to the Player resulting directly from his playing for the Club and rendering him unfit to play skilled basketball, and notice of such injury is given by the Player as provided herein, the Player shall be entitled to receive his full salary for the season in which the injury was sustained, less all workmen's compensation benefits (which, to the extent permitted by law, the Player hereby assigns to the Club) and any insurance provided for by the Club paid or payable to the Player by reason of said injury.

(c) If this contract is terminated by the Club during the period designated by the Club for attendance at training camp, payment by the Club of the Player's board, lodging and expense allowance during such period and of the reasonable traveling expenses of the Player to his home city and the expert training and coaching provided by the Club to the Player during the training season shall be full payment to the Player.

(d) If this contract is terminated by the Club during any playing season, except in the case provided for in subparagraph (c) of this paragraph 20, the Player shall be entitled to receive as full payment hereunder a sum of money which, when added to the salary which he has already received during such season, will represent the same proportionate amount of the annual sum set forth in paragraph 2 hereof as the number of days of such season then past bears to the total number of days of such schedule season plus the reasonable traveling expenses of the Player to his home.

Typical Addendum to a 1988 NFL Player Contract

Special Provisions

Roster Bonus.   Player will receive $12,500 if he is a member of the club's Active List for a minimum of two (2) games during the 1988 regular season.

Playing Time.   Player will receive $2,000 if he plays 30% of the offensive plays; AND $2,500 if he plays 35% of the offensive plays; AND $2,500 if he plays 40% of the offensive plays; AND $4,000 if he plays 45% of the offensive plays; AND $4,000 if he plays 50% of the offensive plays; AND $5,000 if he plays 55% of the offensive plays; AND $5,000 if he plays 60% of the offensive plays; AND $5,000 if he plays 65% of the plays, excluding special teams, during the entire 1988 regular season as compiled by Club. The maximum the Player can earn under this clause is $30,000.

Incentives

1. Player will receive $10,000 if he leads the team in pass receptions; OR $5,000 if he is second on the team in number of pass receptions during the 1988 regular season.

2. Player will receive $10,000 if he leads the team in average yards per reception; OR $5,000 if he is second on the team in average yards per reception (minimum of 30 receptions) during the 1988 regular season.

3. Player will receive $10,000 if he leads the team in touchdown passes; OR $5,000 if he is second in touchdown passes during the 1988 regular season.

4. Player will receive $5,000 if he leads the team in punt return average (minimum of 20 returns); AND $5,000 if he leads the team in kickoff return average (minimum of 20 returns) during the 1988 regular season.

Honors

1. Player will receive $5,000 if he is selected first or second team All-Rookie by the *Professional Football Writers Association* (PFWA) or *United Press International* (UPI).

2. Player will receive $10,000 if he is selected NFL Rookie-of-the-Year by *Associated Press* (AP), the *Professional Football Writers Association* (PFWA) or *Sporting News* (SN).

3. Player will receive $5,000 if he is selected second team All-Conference; OR $7,500 if he is selected first team All-Conference by *United Press International* (UPI). The maximum the Player can earn under this clause is $7,500.

4. Player will receive $7,500 if he is selected second team All-NFL; OR $10,000 if he is selected first team All-NFL by *Associated Press* (AP), *Sporting News* (SN), or the *Professional Football Writers Association* (PFWA). The maximum the Player can earn under this clause is $10,000.

Appendix

B

Season Ticket Price Comparison for Three Professional Sports

American League Ticket Prices (1988 and 1987)

Franchise, Venue, and Capacity	1988	1987
Baltimore Orioles, Memorial Stadium, 53,198	$9.50, $8.50, $7, $6.50, & $4.75	Same
Boston Red Sox, Fenway Park, 33,583	$14, $12, $11, $9, & $5	Same
California Angels, Anaheim Stadium, 64,593	$8, $7, $6, $5, & $3	$8, $7, $5, & $3
Chicago White Sox, Comiskey Park, 43,931	$10.50, $9.50, $8.50, $6.50, $5.50, & $4	Same
Cleveland Indians, Cleveland Stadium, 74,000	$9.50, $8, $4.50, $4, & $3	$9, $7, $4, & $3
Detroit Tigers, Tiger Stadium, 52,000	$10.50, $8.50, & $4	Same
Kansas City Royals, Royals Stadium, 40,625	$10, $9, $7, $6, & $3	Same
Milwaukee Brewers, Milwaukee County Stadium, 53,192	$11, $10.50, $10, $9, $6.50, & $4	$10, $9.50, $9 $8, $6, & $3.50
Minnesota Twins, Metrodome, Minneapolis, 55,122	$10, $8, $5, & $3	$9, $7, $5, & $3
New York Yankees, Yankee Stadium, 57,545	$11, $9.50, $7.50, $4.50, $2.25, & $1	$10, $8.50, $4.50, $3, $1.50, & $1
Oakland A's, Oakland-Alameda County Coliseum, 48,219	$9, $8, $6, & $3	Same
Seattle Mariners, Kingdome, 59,438	$9.50, $8.50, $6.50, $5.50, & $3.50	$9, $8, $6, $5, & $3
Texas Rangers, Arlington Stadium, 43,508	$10, $9, $8, $5, $4, & $2	$9, $8, $7, $5, $3.75, & $2.25
Toronto Blue Jays, Exhibition Stadium, 43,737	$15, $13, $10, $7, & $4 (Canadian)	$13, $11, $9, $6, & $4

Note. From *Amusement Business: The International Newsweekly for Sports and Mass Entertainment,* February 13, 1988, p. 13. Adapted by permission.

National League Ticket Prices (1988 and 1987)

Franchise, Venue, and Capacity	1988	1987
Atlanta Braves, Atlanta-Fulton County Stadium, 52,934	$9.50, $8, $6, $4, & $1	$8.50, $7, $5, $3, & $1
Chicago Cubs, Wrigley Field, 37,272	$10.50, $9, $8, $4, & $3.50	Same
Cincinnati Reds, Riverfront Stadium, 52,392	$8.50, $8, $7, $6, $5.50, & $3.50	Same
Houston Astros, Astrodome, 45,000	$10, $8, $7, $6, $5, & $4	$8.50-$4
Los Angeles Dodgers, Dodger Stadium, 56,000	$7, $6, & $4	Same
Montreal Expos, Olympic Stadium, 58,838	$12, $10.50, $7.50, $6.75, $4, & $1 (Canadian)	Same
New York Mets, Shea Stadium, 55,300	$11, $9, & $6	Same
Philadelphia Phillies, Veterans Stadium, 64,000	$9, $8, $6.50, $5, $4, & $1	Same
Pittsburgh Pirates, Three Rivers Stadium, 54,598	$9.50-$3.50	$8.50-$3.50
St. Louis Cardinals, Busch Memorial Stadium, 53,112	$10.50, $8, $5, & $4	$9.50, $7, $4, & $3
San Diego Padres, Jack Murphy Stadium, 51,319	$8.50, $7.50, & $3.50	Same
San Francisco Giants, Candlestick Park, 58,000	$10, $9, $8, $7, & $2.50	$9, $8, $7, $6, & $1.50

Note. From *Amusement Business: The International Newsweekly for Sports and Mass Entertainment*, February 13, 1988, p. 13. Adapted by permission.

NBA Ticket Prices (1987-88 and 1988-89)

Franchise	Venue/capacity	Prices & Packages*
Atlanta Hawks	The Omni/16,400	$3,223-$215 for 43 games; $1,875-$125 for 25, including two pre-season
Boston Celtics	Boston Garden/14,890	$1,170-$390 for 39 games; $750-$250 for 25
Charlotte Hornets	Charlotte Coliseum/23,000	$2,050-$287 for 41 games
Chicago Bulls	Chicago Stadium/17,458	$5,670-$399 for 42 games (one pre-season); $1,260-$199 for 21
Cleveland Cavaliers	Richfield Coliseum/20,900	$738-$246 for 41 games; $360-$120 for 20; $234-$78 for 14
Dallas Mavericks	Reunion Arena/17,007	$1,254-$430 for 43 games; $642-$220 for 22; $612-$210 for 21
Denver Nuggets	McNichols Arena/17,022	$2,100-$336 for 42 games; $357-$168 for 21; $187-$88 for 11
Detroit Pistons	Palace of Auburn Hills/21,000	$699-$599 for 41 games plus five other events; $320 for 20 games; $160 for 10
Golden State Warriors	Oakland-Alameda County Coliseum Arena/15,025	$1,435-$246 for 41 games; $385-$66 for 11-game mini-plan
Houston Rockets	The Summit/16,288	$2,860-$286 for 44 games; $352-$143 for 22 (share-a-seat plan)
Indiana Pacers	Market Square Arena/16,600	$756-$252 for 42 games; $294-$126 for 21
Los Angeles Clippers	Los Angeles Memorial Sports Arena/15,178	$1,050-$378 for 42 games; $400-$96 for 16
Los Angeles Lakers	The Forum/17,505	$10,500-$357 for 42 games
Miami Heat	Miami Arena/15,200	$1,050-$252 for 42 games

Milwaukee Bucks	Bradley Center/17,700	$919-$229 for 42 games; $143-$89 for 10-Packs
New Jersey Nets	Meadowlands Arena/19,975	$2,050-$246 for 41 games; $378-$126 for 21; $180-$60 for Pick 10
New York Knickerbockers	Madison Square Garden/19,591	$1,475-$516 for 43 games
Philadelphia 76ers	The Spectrum/17,900	$2,932-$349 for 41 games; $185-$85 for 10
Phoenix Suns	Arizona Veterans Memorial Coliseum/12,666	$924-$294 for 42 games; $285-$133 for 20
Portland Trail Blazers	Portland Veterans Memorial Coliseum/12,666	$2,580-$323 for 43 games; $187-$113 for 15
Sacramento Kings	ARCO Arena/16,500	$1,245-$315 for 42 games
San Antonio Spurs	HemisFair Arena/15,700	$1,290-$215 for 43 games; $374-$176 for 22; $132-$88 for 11
Seattle SuperSonics	Seattle Center Coliseum/14,301	$1,025-$205 for 41 games; $378-$189 for 21; $234-$117 for 13
Utah Jazz	Salt Palace/12,716	$1,134-$315 for 42 games; $315-$225 for 20
Washington Bullets	Capital Centre/19,125	$4,200-$735 for 42 games; $428-$238 for 19; $210-$150 for 13

*Specific playing season not indicated; prices rounded to nearest dollar.

Note. From *Amusement Business: The International Newsweekly for Sports and Mass Entertainment,* September 10, 1988, p. 15. Adapted by permission.

NFL Ticket Prices (1988 and 1987)

Franchise, Venue, and Capacity	1988	1987
Atlanta Falcons, Atlanta-Fulton County Stadium, 59,709	$25, $17, $13, & $8	Same
Buffalo Bills, Rich Stadium, 80,290	$24, $18, & $12	Same
Chicago Bears, Soldier Field, 65,793	$25 & $22	$20, $17, & $10
Cincinnati Bengals, Riverfront Stadium, 59,754	$22.50, $20, $18.50, & $17.50	Same
Cleveland Browns, Cleveland Stadium, 80,098	$27, $23.50, $21.50, $17.50, & $15.50	$23, $19.50, $17.50, & $11.50
Dallas Cowboys, Texas Stadium, Irving, 65,010	$32 & $23, plus 8% sales tax	$32 & $23, plus 7.25% sales tax
Denver Broncos, Mile High Stadium, 76,274	$25, $20, & $17	$22, $17, & $15
Detroit Lions, Pontiac Silverdome, 80,638	$15.50 & $6	Same
Green Bay Packers, Lambeau Field, 57,041, & Milwaukee County Stadium, 56,051	$17 & $14 at Lambeau; $19, $16, $14, & $12 at Milwaukee	Same
Houston Oilers, Astrodome, 50,495 after baseball, 47,695 during	$25, $19, & $16, plus 8% state entertainment tax	$23, $17, & $12, including tax
Indianapolis Colts, Hoosier Dome, 60,127	$24, $19, & $12	$21, $17, & $10
Kansas City Chiefs, Arrowhead Stadium, 78,063	$20, $17, $15, $14, $12, & $7	Same
Los Angeles Raiders, Los Angeles Memorial Coliseum, 92,488	$28, $20, & $13	Same
Los Angeles Rams, Anaheim Stadium, 69,008	$25, $19, & $13	$21, $15, & $10
Miami Dolphins, Joe Robbie Stadium, 75,000	$26	Same

Minnesota Vikings, Metrodome, 63,939	$20	$18
New England Patriots, Sullivan Stadium, Foxboro, MA., 60,794	$33, $27, $23, & $15	$30, $24, $21, & $13
New Orleans Saints, Louisiana Superdome, 69,548	$23, $20, $16, & $12	$19, $16, & $12
New York Giants, Giants Stadium, East Rutherford, NJ, 76,891	$21 & $18	Same
New York Jets, Giants Stadium, East Rutherford, NJ, 76,891	$32.50 & $20	Same
Philadelphia Eagles, Veterans Stadium, 65,356	$25, $22, & $12	$20 & $10
Phoenix Cardinals*, Sun Devil Stadium	$40, $30, & $25	$22 (St. Louis)
Pittsburgh Steelers, Three Rivers Stadium, 59,000	$27, $24, $22, & $20	$21, $19, & $17
San Diego Chargers, Jack Murphy Stadium, 60,766	$30, $23, $21, & $15	$25, $20, $18, & $14
San Francisco 49ers, Candlestick Park, 64,252	$25 & $19	$21 & $13
Seattle Seahawks, Kingdome, 64,757	$30, $25, $21, $15, & $10	$25, $20, $16, $13, & $8
Tampa Bay Buccaneers, Tampa Stadium, 74,314	$21, $18, $14, & $9	$15, $11, & $6
Washington Redskins, RFK Memorial Stadium, 55,642	$30, $23, $20, & $15	Same

*1988 price figures from club office; capacity figures not available.

Note. From *Amusement Business: The International Newsweekly for Sports and Mass Entertainment*, March 18, 1988. Adapted by permission.

Appendix

C

Two-Season Attendance Comparison for Four Professional Sports

Major Leagues

Franchise	1988*	1987
Baltimore Orioles	1,660,738	1,835,692
Boston Red Sox	2,464,851	2,231,551
California Angels	2,340,865	2,696,299
Chicago White Sox	1,115,525	1,208,060
Cleveland Indians	1,411,610	1,077,898
Detroit Tigers	2,081,162	2,061,830
Kansas City Royals	2,350,181	2,392,471
Milwaukee Brewers	1,923,238	1,909,244
Minnesota Twins	3,030,672	2,081,976
New York Yankees	2,633,703	2,427,672
Oakland Athletics	2,287,335	1,678,921
Seattle Mariners	1,020,354	1,134,255
Texas Rangers	1,581,901	1,763,053
Toronto Blue Jays	2,595,175	2,778,429
American League Total	28,497,310	27,277,351
Atlanta Braves	848,089	1,217,402
Chicago Cubs	2,089,034	2,035,130
Cincinnati Reds	2,072,528	2,185,205
Houston Astros	1,933,505	1,909,902
Los Angeles Dodgers	2,949,142	2,797,409
Montreal Expos	1,478,659	1,850,324
New York Mets	3,047,724	3,034,129
Philadelphia Phillies	1,990,041	2,100,110
Pittsburgh Pirates	1,865,713	1,161,193
St. Louis Cardinals	2,892,629	3,072,122
San Diego Padres	1,506,896	1,454,061
San Francisco Giants	1,786,482	1,917,168
National League Total	24,460,442	24,734,155

*Unofficial attendance through October 2, 1988.

Note. From the offices of Major League Baseball.

NBA

Franchise	1987-88	1986-87
Atlanta Hawks	583,061	549,652
Boston Celtics	611,228	622,622
Chicago Bulls	740,501	650,718
Cleveland Cavaliers	504,833	447,125
Dallas Mavericks	695,606	696,333
Denver Nuggets	520,864	494,943
Detroit Pistons	1,066,505	908,240
Golden State Warriors	465,350	423,997
Houston Rockets	681,051	660,175
Indiana Pacers	502,332	520,007
Los Angeles Clippers	359,693	316,140
Los Angeles Lakers	714,466	681,707
Milwaukee Bucks	452,066	450,987
New Jersey Nets	476,051	452,704
New York Knickerbockers	586,751	538,058
Philadelphia 76ers	513,115	587,748
Phoenix Suns	461,291	471,172
Portland Trail Blazers	519,306	519,306
Sacramento Kings	423,653	423,653
San Antonio Spurs	347,024	328,368
Seattle SuperSonics	492,328	356,362
Utah Jazz	503,972	491,382
Washington Bullets	433,370	485,352
Totals	12,654,387	12,065,351

Note. From *Sports Marketing News*, May 1, 1987 and May 13, 1988. Adapted by permission.

NFL

Franchise	1987*	1986
Atlanta Falcons	533,239	825,056
Buffalo Bills	808,119	881,034
Chicago Bears	1,172,914[a]	495,484[b]
Cincinnati Bengals	889,828[c]	1,004,227[c]
Cleveland Browns	534,604[b]	800,742[b]
Dallas Cowboys	959,874[c]	1,287,567[c]
Denver Broncos[d]	--	--
Detroit Lions	581,625	854,294
Green Bay Packers	696,811	865,341
Houston Oilers	866,430[c]	871,829[c]
Indianapolis Colts[d]	--	--
Kansas City Chiefs	856,469[c]	1,004,233[c]
Los Angeles Raiders	1,079,831[c]	1,294,721[c]
Los Angeles Rams[d]	--	--
Miami Dolphins	786,790	996,891
Minnesota Vikings	1,068,150[e]	1,081,480[c]
New England Patriots	806,041	1,088,574[f]
New Orleans Saints	842,424[f]	874,303
New York Giants	778,853	1,066,268
New York Jets[d]	--	--
Philadelphia Eagles	733,832	905,388
Phoenix Cardinals	523,284	719,143
Pittsburgh Steelers	933,903[c]	1,106,666[c]
San Diego Chargers	371,676[b]	414,611[b]
San Francisco 49ers	821,764[f]	1,007,270[f]
Seattle Seahawks	1,003,272[a]	1,173,040[c]
Tampa Bay Buccaneers	888,936[c]	821,728[c]
Washington Redskins	939,782[g]	1,106,312[h]

*Strike season.

Note. Information compiled from 1988 team media guides.

[a]Includes four preseason and one postseason game. [b]Home games only.
[c]Includes preseason games. [d]Information not available. [e]Includes three of four
preseason and three postseasonf games. [f]Includes one postseason game.
[g]Includes two postseason games and Super Bowl. [h]Includes three postseason
games.

NHL

Franchise	1987-88	1986-87
Boston Bruins	548,301	485,159
Buffalo Sabres	571,088	527,241
Calgary Flames	756,615	671,920
Chicago Blackhawks	672,515	672,100
Detroit Red Wings	785,532	750,225
Edmonton Oilers	678,270	691,889
Hartford Whalers	582,969	569,219
Los Angeles Kings	452,248	425,769
Minnesota North Stars	457,617	540,460
Montreal Canadiens	690,399	689,609
New Jersey Devils	572,558	503,160
New York Islanders	582,871	594,382
New York Rangers	686,972	686,396
Philadelphia Flyers	696,180	688,497
Pittsburgh Penguins	598,534	598,614
Quebec Nordiques	597,691	568,519
St. Louis Blues	580,212	529,613
Toronto Mapleleafs	654,310	646,643
Vancouver Commanches	440,095	436,070
Washington Capitals	638,212	611,606
Winnipeg Jets	507,237	543,703
Totals	12,750,426	12,430,794

Note. From *Sports Industry News*, April 22, 1988, Game Point Publishing, (207) 236-8346. Adapted by permission.

Index